Northwest Vista College
Learning Resource Center
3535 North Ellison Drive
San Antonio, Texas 78251

D1558924

# MARRIAGE, VIOLENCE, AND THE NATION IN THE AMERICAN LITERARY WEST

In *Marriage, Violence, and the Nation in the American Literary West*, William R. Handley examines literary interpretations of the western American past. Handley argues that although recent scholarship provides a narrative of western history that counters the optimistic story of frontier individualism by focusing on the victims of conquest, twentieth-century American fiction tells a different story of intra-ethnic violence, surrounding marriages and families. He examines works of historiography, as well as writing by Zane Grey, Willa Cather, Wallace Stegner, and Joan Didion among others, to argue that these works highlight white Americans' anxiety about what happens to American "character" when domestic enemies such as Indians and Mormon polygamists, against whom the nation had defined itself in the nineteenth century, no longer threaten its homes. Handley explains that once its enemies are gone, imperialism brings violence home in retrospective narratives that allegorize national pasts and futures through intimate relationships.

WILLIAM R. HANDLEY is Assistant Professor of English at the University of Southern California. His articles have appeared in *Arizona Quarterly*, *Contemporary Literature*, and *Twentieth Century Literature*.

# MARRIAGE, VIOLENCE, AND THE NATION IN THE AMERICAN LITERARY WEST

WILLIAM R. HANDLEY

*University of Southern California*

CAMBRIDGE
UNIVERSITY PRESS

PUBLISHED BY THE PRESS SYNDICATE OF THE UNIVERSITY OF CAMBRIDGE
The Pitt Building, Trumpington Street, Cambridge, United Kingdom

CAMBRIDGE UNIVERSITY PRESS
The Edinburgh Building, Cambridge CB2 2RU, UK
40 West 20th Street, New York, NY 10011-4211, USA
477 Williamstown Road, Port Melbourne, VIC 3207, Australia
Ruiz de Alarcón 13, 28014 Madrid, Spain
Dock House, The Waterfront, Cape Town 8001, South Africa

http://www.cambridge.org

First published 2002

Printed in the United Kingdom at the University Press, Cambridge

*Typeface* Baskerville Monotype 11/12.5 pt      *System* LᴬTᴇX 2ε   [TB]

*A catalogue record for this book is available from the British Library*

*Library of Congress Cataloguing in Publication data*
Handley, William R.
Marriage, violence, and the nation in the American literary West / William R. Handley.
p.    cm.    (Cambridge studies in American literature and culture; 132)
Includes bibliographical references and index.
ISBN 0 521 81667 x (hardback)
1. American literature – West (US) – History and criticism.    2. Domestic fiction, American –
History and criticism.    3. National characteristics, American, in literautre.    4. Western stories –
History and criticism.    5. Frontier and pioneer life in literature.    6. Family violence in literature.
7. Women pioneers in literature.    8. West (US) – In literature.    9. Marriage in literature.
10. Violence in literature.    I. Title.    II. Series.
PS271.H29 2002
810.9′3278 – dc21        2002016593

ISBN 0 521 81667 x hardback

*For my parents*

# Contents

# Illustrations

# Acknowledgments

The support of family, friends, and colleagues over the years has sustained me in ways too numerous to recount in this limited space. At the least I would like to acknowledge those who have made this book possible and, I hope, worth reading. My study of western American literature began at the University of California, Los Angeles under the inspiring guidance of Martha Banta and Eric Sundquist. Not only their remarkable personal and intellectual gifts but often their smallest gestures had a powerful effect on me, as when Martha Banta, who knew how much I loved Virginia Woolf, gave me a Western by Zane Grey. In ways not as different as Woolf is from Grey, these two accomplished scholars fed my mind, showed me new ways of reading and thinking, and continue to be living proofs of why this profession matters and what great things can be accomplished in it. The good fortune of working with them is one I owe in the first instance to the late Daniel Calder, whose influence on so many careers has been enduringly positive. At UCLA, I also benefited from working with Blake Allmendinger. He shared his knowledge generously and with humor and wore his affection for things western on his red, leather-fringed sleeve.

To others who have supported me in the writing of this book, generously read portions of the manuscript, and offered criticisms and suggestions, I am very grateful. Chief among them are Nancy Bentley, Sacvan Bercovitch, Charles Berryman, Joseph Boone, Lawrence Buell, Philip Fisher, Kris Fresonke, Marjorie Garber, Keith Gessen, Melody Graulich, Tim Gustafson, Gregory Jackson, Barbara Johnson, Carla Kaplan, Nathaniel Lewis, Carol Muske-Dukes, Sharon O'Brien, Susan Rosowski, Hilary Schor, Werner Sollors, Stephen Tatum, and Lynn Wardley. I am also grateful to the anonymous readers for Cambridge University Press for their insights and suggestions, and to my editor, Ray Ryan, and the editor of the series in which this book appears, Ross Posnock, for their support.

Reading groups at Harvard and at the University of Southern
California with colleagues whose fields are different from my own have
helped to shape the book, to sharpen its prose, and to provide me moral
support: to Jed Esty, Judith Jackson Fossett, Barbara Freeman, Shannon
Jackson, Jeffrey Masten, Tara McPherson, Wendy Motooka, Viet
Nguyen, and Jonah Siegel, I owe thanks. For helpful research assistance
I am also indebted to Andrew Cooper, William Arce, and Elizabeth
Callaghan. The collegiality I have found in the Western Literature
Association, whose conferences have provided a stimulating forum for
developing the ideas in this book, is a model of intellectual exchange –
and the WLA knows how to dance.

I have been fortunate to have an unbroken chain of other extraor-
dinary teachers in my life whom it is my pleasure also to thank:
Gerald Kuroghlian, Kathryn Blumhardt, the late Frank Wiener, Gita van
Heerden, George Dekker, Anne Mellor, Diane Middlebrook, Ronald
Rebholz, and Lucio Ruotolo.

For financial support and leave time I am grateful to Harvard
University, the Harvard English Department's Robinson and Rollins
Funds, and the University of Southern California. A semester at the
Huntington Library, with the assistance of a fellowship provided by the
Keck and Mayers Foundations, gave me access to the Turner papers
and other invaluable resources. By permission of the Houghton Library
at Harvard University, I have paraphrased letters from Willa Cather to
Houghton Mifflin. Chapter 4 is reprinted from *Arizona Quarterly* 57: 1
(2001), by permission of the Regents of the University of Arizona.

In addition to many of those above, there are others whose support
and friendship over the years have made life both in and outside of this
profession a lasting pleasure. I am very grateful to Tom Augst, Frank
Geraci, Jay Grossman, Rachel Jacoff, Del Kolve, Leslie Lacin, Dwight
McBride, Jocelyn Medawar, Ann Pellegrini, Cristina Ruotolo, and Adam
Weisman. My brother, George B. Handley, has been my best friend in
academia since we were in graduate school. His scholarship in comparative literatures of the Americas has also served as a stimulus for
thinking about how genealogies and national legacies intertwine in the
literary imagination. My work is better for his having read it and for
my having read his. By unfailingly sharing her vitality and her passion
for reading and teaching literature, my aunt, Helen Houghton, has had
a profound and positive influence on me. She is a woman of many letters.
Adam Christian has made the completion of this book possible in numerous ways. His humor, his wisdom, his patience, and his keen editorial

eye (with which he would tell me to curtail this list and spare the reader) have kept me more than once from falling through the cracks in my prose. Finally, this book is dedicated to my parents, Kate and Ken Handley, without whom, of course, I would be nothing, but more significantly, who have blessed me with their support, love of reading, open and inquisitive minds, and the friendship they share with each other. It is a sign of the sometimes happy incompatibility between what one wants from literature and what one wants from life that I am grateful both as a reader and as a son that there is so little resemblance between their marriage and the fictional ones in this book.

# Introduction

Clashing stories haunt the physical and cultural landscapes of the American West, stories that led or kept people there, and that Europeans and Americans used to drive indigenous people away. Inasmuch as people believed them, stories are historical forces that demand interpretation and that, to a significant degree, explain the settlement and conquest of this vast and complex region. Books of fiction and religious faith; oral stories passed through generations; exaggerated travel accounts and the tall tales of boosterism; feverish fantasies of speculation and geographic mastery; and persistent Old World myths and allegories have all directly affected western migration and development. The West has, in other words, inextricably wedded what we conventionally refer to as the historical and the literary, the experiential and the imaginative.

The literature of the American West tells and retells the fictions and histories that have been born of this union and that in turn shape our perception and experience of the West. So intertwined are the facts of imagination and the facts of historical experience "out West" that their nominal difference can seem a mere disciplinary effect or convenience. Historians who give attention to the "imagined" West effectively demarcate it from the "real" West and so reinforce a disciplinary divide even as they cross it.[1] One of my aims in this book is to demonstrate why literary and historical imaginations should not be thought about separately, and to employ an intertextual methodology that insists on bringing the two together by locating the historical in the literary and *vice versa*, rather than by treating one as the "background" of the other. American literary studies of the West have often been as resistant to theoretical matters, even to formal aesthetics, as the field of western history has been resistant to literary concerns, which makes the aim of this book all the more pressing.[2] Western American literature is ripe for bringing together formal and historical analysis because it has long been burdened by readers' nostalgic desire for historical authenticity, as Nathaniel Lewis argues about the rise of the western author in the nineteenth century.[3] Yet Westerns are works of imaginative art, despite the historical content that seems especially to mark them. To treat literature simply as content (ideological or otherwise) and not as verbal art is, to paraphrase Michael Kowalewski, to put it on trial rather than to give it a *hearing*.[4] Critics' neglect of western writing's aesthetic dimension has only served to reinforce the sense that the value and significance of western literature lie in the regional and historical "reality" it mimetically (and naively) represents. This neglect perpetuates the presumption, in some particular cases merited, that western fiction is aesthetically less imaginative and complex than other American literary genres.

An important aspect of the aesthetic complexity of western literature, however, derives precisely from writers' anxiety about historical content, especially insofar as historians and novelists alike have wrestled with the supposed divide between the so-called frontier and post-frontier Wests. Retrospection has been a hallmark of western writing even before Frederick Jackson Turner sought to formulate the significance of the frontier in American history. This study's starting point would seem to mark an ending, the final transformation of western "foreign" lands into national territory in the 1890s. But most of the fiction and the essays I examine (with the exception of Turner's and Owen Wister's work), stress continuity over disjunction between frontier and post-frontier, past and present, western settings in an ongoing literary history. Twentieth-century avatars of the literary West reveal the persistence and influence of the frontier as both setting and theme – up through the "revisionist" 1960s, when many new stories about the West's literary legacies emerge.

Yet, even more than with the frontier, much of the literary West's recurring preoccupation is with marriage, the unexpected but inescapable lens through which writers in this book focus on the West's ongoing national significance. That literary focus has served its own revisionist imagination of history. Literary concerns with western marriage, in settings both before and after the "end" of the frontier and in both formula Westerns and more "high brow" western fiction, counter the prevailing cultural myth that the frontier chiefly produced the masculine individual, that national figure celebrated in much formula Western fiction and film. In contrast, the nation we find epitomized in so much literature of the West resembles what we might call (to put it mildly) a dysfunctional family. As Wallace Stegner writes, "the exacerbated individualism of the frontier has left us with . . . a set of assumptions and beliefs that are often comically at odds with the facts of life."[5] Marriage is not a past and finalized historical process but an ongoing social fact through which the fiction in this study revises nineteenth-century allegorical readings of the West as America's progressive destiny. Like their literal counterparts in the nineteenth century, twentieth-century literary marriages in the American West are burdened by the clash between belief and experience. They also carry in themselves a nation's anxious wish – and because of the violence that surrounds them, ultimately a futile one – to perpetuate a "civilized" genealogy in a region not known for American civility during western conquest and settlement.

Historically, the analogy between marriage and the nation has had profound effects. The founders of the Republic, as Nancy Cott demonstrates in *Public Vows: A History of Marriage and the Nation*, "learned to think of marriage and the form of government as mirroring each other," as two forms of consensual union. The similarity was thought to be more than analogical: "actual marriages of the proper sort were presumed to create the kind of citizen needed to make the new republic succeed" and, later, to perpetuate "the race" and civilization. During the latter half of the nineteenth century, "the thematic equivalency between polygamy, despotism, and coercion on the one side and between monogamy, political liberty, and consent on the other resonated through the political culture of the United States." If monogamy "founded the social and political order," Cott writes, "then groups practicing other marital systems on American soil might threaten the polity's soundness." Marital nonconformists, such as Indians and Mormons, were most commonly defined as racially different from the white majority, even when, in the case of the Mormons, they were white.[6] Yet some government officials in the early nineteenth century, reinforcing the analogy between marriage and nation, had thought of interracial marriage as a means toward civilization-building and national unity. In 1816, Secretary of War William Crawford recommended that the US government should encourage intermarriage between Native Americans and Americans if other attempts at harmony failed.[7] French and American explorers also thought intermarriage would help solidify political alliances, and in a critical respect, the marriage between Toussaint Charbonneau and Sacagawea during the Lewis and Clark expedition ensured the survival of that national expedition. Especially after the Civil War, in which the non-consensual nature of slavery was seen to violate the necessary consent within both domestic and national life, the institution of laws in many western states prohibiting interracial marriage, which aligned racial with religious and national forms of identity, disguised the ways in which such consensual unions were once thought to help the nation. The Mormons, as this book explores in the work of Zane Grey, were an important transitional group against which the nation defined itself based on marital practice and the question of consent. For decades much of the nation perceived them as domestic aliens whose "unChristian" practice of polygamy its opponents compared to slavery and who were often seen to be nonwhite, in conspiracy with Indians, and a threat to the nation. With their adoption of monogamy, the Mormons became nationally assimilable, "white," and eventually of little interest to western fiction, which turned instead toward images of alienated domesticity once marital and racial "others," against whom the nation constructed its identity out West, were thought of in the past tense.

In the present moment, with court and electoral battles being waged against resurgent polygamy and the possibility of same-sex marriage, marriage has remained pivotal in many Americans' self-understanding and identity as a purportedly unified citizenry that freely consents to representative government. Yet beliefs in consent, like the conventional love plot in fiction, obscure the ways in which marriage laws and conventions – and not the consenting parties – have prescribed gender roles, circumscribed racial identity, and delineated the parameters of citizenship. It has never been simply a private institution, and literary representations of it have always, self-consciously or not, engaged social questions, traditionally by domesticating women.

While a happy marriage has rarely been the sustaining subject of good fiction (as opposed to its culmination in the marriage plot), marriage and the novel have had a long affair.[8] In literature of the American West, the preoccupation with marriage is especially fraught with questions about the identity of American whiteness and the meaning of western history. As the literal and figurative bearer of personal hopes and national legacies, marriage throws open a previously sealed window onto the relation between western literature and western history. There are three main reasons for this. First, the stories told in these fictions often abjure the romance with individualism upon which popular western myth and some past western historiography so relies – and on this thematic level they share with the New Western History an important revision of the optimistic story of frontier individualism. Second, and more significantly, because the often violent conflicts surrounding marriage usually occur between family members and whites, the fiction in this study represents a shift away from the historical and the literary preoccupation in pre-twentieth-century western writing with white/Indian ethnic difference and conflict. Violence between familiars, in the West's allegorically burdened context, suggests that the terms of a dominant culture such as masculinity and the racial and national identity of the American are unsettled once "civilization," in the name of which the West was settled, no longer defines itself against the "vanishing" and "savage" Other. While violence is the traditional preserve of masculinity in formula Westerns, the pervasive theme of female domesticity versus male lawless freedom breaks down in other twentieth-century western texts, in which marriage does not serve to civilize the savage male violence of the frontier but rather serves to bring that violence home. Third, the relationship between marriage and nation demonstrates how allegory operates in literary and historiographical retrospection, by putting one set of narrative terms ("this story about these two people") into a metaphorical relationship with another, often "larger," set of terms ("this story about the West"), transforming the personal into the political, the literary into the historiographical, and *vice versa*. Allegory structures the relationship between marital particulars and national universals, but also structures the present's reading of the past, whether in historiography or literature. As Doris Sommer shows in the context of Latin American romances, and as stories of the American West demonstrate in their own way, the allegorizing of nation through intimate relationships has consequences, both literary and historical, that need to be considered in tandem in order adequately to assess how readers imagine themselves as citizens.[9]

I share in the revisionist spirit of feminist scholars who have moved the focus away from masculine genres to literature by women, yet I have chosen to focus on both genders in relation to each other – to see women and men in texts by women and men – and to look at Westerns in relation to other western fiction. Early twentieth-century Westerns, I argue, have important literary relations outside of the genre that they influenced. This collective focus attempts to trouble both the identity politics of race, gender, or genre, and the binaries that critics of western literature too often rely upon in revising the Western's dominance – as if, to paraphrase Sommer in her study, one's discourse were grounded in the allegedly stable discourse that is other to it. Such binary structures of myth and counter-myth, masterplots and subversive plots, dominant and marginal, masculine dominance and feminine resistance, "old" and "new" (a western binary that is getting old) – and indeed the binary of history and literature – put things into relief politically, but they do not always relieve us of the contradictions of literary history.

While I favor these progressive politics and admire many aspects of the criticism they inspire, I also want to be circumspect about the tendency to romanticize the figure of the author that can ensue, often in an attempt to salvage what is redemptive in the troubled West. The opposite tendency – to reject reading an author for political reasons – is one I have more sympathy with, but see as structurally related to the romanticizing tendency. (I am thinking, for example, of the title of Elizabeth Cook-Lynn's *Why I Can't Read Wallace Stegner and Other Essays*, and of how some critics have celebrated that title in studies about neither Stegner nor Cook-Lynn.) These concomitant tendencies – to romanticize the good folks and divide them from the demonized bad folks – are a legacy of the Western itself (if not the Western world). It is that dualistic tendency I want to resist and rethink in this book. To see such binaries in structural relation to each other is neither to neutralize their moral or political differences nor to ignore the historical legacies that shape canons. In the culture and politics of identity, it is difficult not to take authors and texts personally and politically, and yet the ethics of reading involve a necessary displacement of the reader's self in order properly to read the alterity within literary ambiguity, and to respect the otherness within the self. This is not a matter of "eating one's spinach," but of appreciating what the particular act of reading involves, and by so doing, of increasing its pleasures and surprises. As critics we should be as open to confronting literary history as we are open to confronting history itself, with revisionist eyes. When we shy away from the challenge to reread books we think we already know, books that seem to justify our political disdain of them, we have started to give up the critical battle, though we may win the political fight.

I confess that I am not a fan of Westerns. I don't like the social categories they often celebrate, let alone the effect they have had on so much American culture and politics. But the literary effects of demonization fascinate me: what gets left out; how the text reveals its blindnesses; whether the ethical failure of a novel like Wister's *The Virginian*, for example, is related to its aesthetic form or narrative methods. I am also fascinated by how our own critical retrospect blinds us to what a book's first readers immediately recognized. The chief villain of Zane Grey's most popular Western is a Mormon cleric, not a cattle rustler or Indian – and the historical specificity of the Mormon polygamist, who holds relatively little interest for most readers and critics today, enthralled the novel's first readers. As with people, the books that we think we know best can surprise us when we suspend our assumptions. There is, for example, more *overt* male homoeroticism and female homosocial desire in Owen Wister and Wallace Stegner, respectively, than in Willa Cather, and there is more violence, if one merely counts literary corpses, in Willa Cather and Joan Didion than in Owen Wister's and Zane Grey's influential Westerns. Most significant of all, in bringing together Westerns and other major western writers from the turn of the century through the 1960s, this study reveals that women as a civilizing force are no longer what the American Adam, like Huck Finn, lights out for the territory to escape. Indeed, there are no American Adams from the classic mold here. Neither are there particular, Turnerian individuals – even in Turner's historiography. Instead, there are complicated, often very unromantic and at times exceedingly violent relationships that carry the burden of the western past, rendered for us through the distortions of retrospection and the perspective of lonely narrators. It is as if the American Adam has grown up and realized that his youth has passed him by. He looks back into someone else's relationship or domestic situation, searching for but not finding that which no American has ever found: a perpetually happy home on the range.

In chapter 1 I lay out the interrelated thematic, formal, and historical reasons that marriages in the literary West represent allegories of national consolidation and conflict. Violence between familiars in these novels compels us to rethink the binary of savagery and civilization upon which Manifest Destiny and Turner's historiography relied in order to justify western conquest. Retrospective readings of the West's national significance in the twentieth century, I argue, continue to allegorize the American nation, but with far less confidence as to what masculinity, whiteness, and American character mean after the end of so-called "frontier democracy." Chapters 2 to 7 form two parts: chapters 2–4 concern writers who would seem to serve the designs of American empire (after the era of conquest) and chapters 5–7 concern writers who call imperial designs into question by self-consciously distinguishing between narrative and experience and by figuring marriage in ways that revise the Western's traditional allegories of male conquest and female submission, of male freedom and female civilizing constraint. In both parts, however, I explore the persistence of forms of violence surrounding marriages that are resistant to assimilation within (white) nationalist ideology. Self-consciously or not, all of the writers in this study read the West in ways that undermine popular American faith in individual freedom and the promise of Progress. Yet the writers in this study are by no means an exhaustive list of the western writers, from Jack London to Marilynne Robinson, who have imagined the western past and future through marriage and family. Nor are they universally representative: this book does not, for example, attempt to represent what literary marriages might mean in relation to national identity for Native American, Chicano/a, and other writers of color. My hope is that my readings will provide a way of thinking through such issues in other texts as well as the comparative functions of nostalgic retrospection; that it will offer a way of contrasting relations between the personal and the public, between historical legacies and the literary imagination, or between violence and romance among any number of literary canons that make up the cultural complexity of a region we can only ethnocentrically call "the West."

I examine Turner's poetic historiography in chapter 2 as a fusion of secularized Christian allegory and Emersonian organicism and argue that the frontier thesis represses historical agency and violence in order to create a unified national meaning by means of its literary debts. In chapter 3, I explore how Owen Wister's influential Western *The Virginian* drives toward the altar of marriage in order to perpetuate the author's racial ideology, which figures "democracy" in quite different ways from Turner's. What Wister omits – chiefly, the challenge posed to the heterosexual imperative by same-sex desire – produces a narrative of affective disjunctions that mirror the divorce between first-person narrative and forms of omniscience throughout the novel. In chapter 4, I argue that although Mormon polygamy has largely been neglected in readings of Zane Grey's immensely popular Western *Riders of the Purple Sage*, it in fact impels the imperialistically loaded plot to rescue the heroine Jane Withersteen, especially in the context of the racially "not-quite-Other" figure of the Mormon polygamist who seeks to claim her. A magazine crusade against resurgent polygamy, which Grey was aware of when he began writing his novel, aroused both paranoia and nostalgia in American readers – who would make Grey's novel a bestseller.

Chapter 5 turns to the divided world of Willa Cather, who writes against the sort of western marriage plot found in Owen Wister in order to create an anti-masculinist form of western heroism and a "country" resistant to the call of Americanization, especially through her decoupling of marriage from prevalent notions of civilization. In *O Pioneers!*, *My Ántonia*, and *A Lost Lady*, Cather's nostalgia draws on the desire for western romance yet ironically and self-consciously reveals the nationalist and blinding effects of such nostalgic retrospection. I trace the development of this critique of the West's function in US national symbolic culture through a writer Cather influenced, F. Scott Fitzgerald, in chapter 6. *The Great Gatsby* is also a response to the Turnerian ideals that had become popular in American culture by the time Turner republished his essays on the frontier in 1920. Writing against a Turnerian paradigm, Fitzgerald portrays the self-reflexive and destructive allure of "the West" through the marriage and violence of Tom and Daisy Buchanan and through the longing and retrospection of Jay Gatsby and Nick Carraway, all of whom Nick calls "westerners." In his unfinished novel *The Love of the Last Tycoon: A Western*, Fitzgerald extends the idea of the West into a form of the Hollywood imaginary in order to offer a critique of American Enlightenment ideas and to demonstrate how retrospection and indeed the sign of "the West" itself allow one to imagine causality where there are accidents and to erase agency where there is responsibility for violence. In chapter 7, I turn to Wallace Stegner and Joan Didion, whose literary debts to Cather and Fitzgerald, respectively, emerge in their shared concerns for how belief and historical experience collide in shattered western marriages. For both Stegner and Didion, the troubled western past is irresolvably present in marriages that draw upon both historical and literary sources and that represent the causal effects of romantic hopes on western American experience. In the Afterword, I revisit debates about the relationship between western literary and historical study in order to argue that the literary West and western literary criticism not only provide a thematic revision of some "old" western history, as recent critics have argued, but also challenge us to recognize why the literary and the historical are inseparable whenever we read the West. And there is another challenge for western literary critics: to locate, in the literary object of our study rather than in the disciplinary disagreements between ourselves and western historians, the value of our own critical enterprise.

CHAPTER ONE

# Western unions

The United States is unique in the extent to which the individual has been given an open field.

Frederick Jackson Turner, "The Problem of the West" (1896)

The nomadic, bachelor West is over, the housed, married West is established.

Owen Wister, preface to *Members of the Family* (1911)

Is the Marlboro Man lonely? Answering this question demonstrates the social truth behind this icon of the antisocial western individual. If we answer yes, we imply that his solitude is neither desirable nor sustainable. If we answer no, we have yet kept company with him by believing in his contentment and admiring him for it. Whether we answer yes or no, we have put ourselves in the picture, animated him. Of course, we can also refuse to pose the question and consider it meaningless, in which case we kill him off. Indeed, he cannot live without us. His continuing life, manifest in a dying advertising campaign, attests to a deep contradiction in American beliefs and experience. Many Americans celebrate an individual in the landscape of the American West who never settled the West by himself or even much lived there in his grand isolation. He does not refer to himself in his individuality so much as to some need in those who believe in him; he is a social creation who embodies a profoundly asocial ideal. To the extent that he ever existed, he always had a family, if only one he left behind; he probably had a best friend, some admirers and enemies, occasionally a wife and children – and a federal government that backed him up. He resembles his admirers more than they may want to believe, and perhaps for this reason he is left alone without having questions put to him about his feelings.

In her analysis of a more fleshed-out cousin of the Marlboro Man, Joan Didion argues that in making a hero of Howard Hughes, Americans exhibit their instinctive love of "absolute personal freedom, mobility, privacy ... the instinct which drove America to the Pacific, all through the nineteenth century." Of course, she adds, "we do not admit that. The instinct is socially suicidal." As a result, there is an apparently bottomless gulf between "what we officially admire and secretly desire, between, in the largest sense, the people we marry and the people we love."[1] In the twentieth-century American literary West, Didion's analogy is aptly played out in some of Americans' most valued books, but with an important twist: the characters that readers love both marry and fight over marriage – and with fictive results that are often murderous and suicidal. Even if many Americans ward off social suicide, in Didion's sense, by not marrying the Marlboro man and by loving him from a distance, threats of violence, if not murder and suicide themselves, surround representations of marriage in the literary West, including in the fiction of Joan Didion.

The Marlboro Man and Howard Hughes are figural descendants of the American Adam, that orphan who set out for the territory and encountered the Indian in the nineteenth century, in tales by James Fenimore Cooper and others after him. The American frontier has come to be imagined throughout the world predominantly through that unself-conscious emissary of empire after the fact of conquest, the "nomadic, bachelor" cowboy, a representative individual who had an open field for the exercise of his freedom in the American West. Yet western history tells a more complicated story, one of families shaping and being shaped by the frontier long before the ascendance of the cowboy and his collateral folklore. Even Frederick Jackson Turner, who argued in his famous hypothesis that "the frontier was productive of individualism," nevertheless saw that this individualism arose when the wilderness transformed "complex society ... into a kind of primitive organization based on the family." Where Turner suggests a direct correlation between the family and individualism, with "anti-social" results, so many narratives of the West – including some renderings of Turner's frontier thesis – have seen them as distinct, if not contradictory, as in Didion's distinction between the people we love and the people we marry.[2] While often seen as incompatible with each other in respect to the exercise of freedom, the individual and familial versions of the western past reveal not only a contradiction about American beliefs, as Didion describes it, but a history of a different sequence and significance from the one often ascribed to Turner. Whereas Turner's thesis about social evolution on the frontier made it seem that the family "culminated rather than coordinated settlement," as Kathleen Neils Conzen describes it in her discussion of western families in the nineteenth century, families were there early on.

But in Turner's time American reformers "had come to doubt the ability of the family to withstand the pressures of the new urban environment. What role, then, could such a feeble institution hope to play in the face of the even greater savagery of the wild?"[3] Quite a large one, in fact. Entitlement to land – whether for whites to claim it or, later, for Indians to reclaim it – was primarily granted through heads of households. As an 1846 observer misleadingly put it by removing the paternal role, "All we had to do was to let our women and children go [to the Oregon region] and, without assistance from any one, they would take possession of the country."[4] In his groundbreaking study of the American family in 1917, Arthur W. Calhoun recognized that "the family was the one substantial social institution" on the frontier and was profoundly influenced by it. Indeed, the most important influence on the American family in the decades after the Revolution, he argued in Turnerian fashion, was pioneering and the frontier.[5] It was not until the 1960s that historians returned to the role of marriage and families in western settlement, because Turnerian approaches had up until then become "so thoroughly discredited that the question of a specific western or frontier influence on the American family was barely raised."[6]

Contemporary western historians have tackled this question. In her study of western marriages and families, Glenda Riley explores why the American West, in the nineteenth and early twentieth century, had the highest divorce rate in the world. A major contributing factor was "western values and beliefs themselves," the very ideology of free individualism that Turner championed and that for a time in the nineteenth century, as Riley also demonstrates, encouraged flexibility and experimentation in marital and familial relationships.[7] Those beliefs also had a damaging effect on western marriages in large part because of the high expectations for personal happiness that they raised. Hence Turner's figural individual, as unrelated as he has come to seem to the familial version of the western past and as comparatively less corporeal, is intimately tied up with western marriages and families, like the figure of Shane in Jack Shaefer's 1949 novel of that name, who becomes for a time part of the family, but who is, in the end, loved from a distance. At the end of the 1953 film version of *Shane*, as he is about to ride off and leave the family forever after having disposed of his enemies who threatened the homestead, Shane asks the boy who longs to be him to tell his mother that, with his departure, "there aren't any more guns in the family." As if satisfying a Cold War need to externalize threats of violence away from the homeland, the film effectively demarcates violent masculine

individualism from family life. At once a threat to marriage and its pro-
tector, the lone gunman leaves the domestic scene. But in much twentieth-
century western fiction, he does indeed, as the boy in *Shane* vainly calls
out for him to do, "come back." Violence comes home, but without the
clearly defined enemies with whom Shane and others like him have so
often battled: bad white men, savage Indians.

The literary works in this study consistently play out the consequences of frontier settlement through scenes of marital conflict in which
"domestic aliens," such as Indians and Mormon polygamists who threatened domestic virtues, are replaced with scenes of alienated domesticity
that carry, as so many battles with Indians and others had seemed to carry
for whites, the burden of civilization's fate. This substitution, historically,
is not an accident: the cult of domesticity as women's "separate sphere"
arose in the US in the 1840s and 1850s along with the rhetoric of Manifest
Destiny, and it served American expansion by imagining the borders of
home against the foreign.[8] In the twentieth century, after the settling of
the West, once conventional figures of foreignness, especially Indians, are
often missing from even the most popular and nostalgic forms of western
American literature. Scenes of domestic discord and violence represent,
in effect, a white dominant culture turning inward, after its conquest
of native peoples and cultures, against its most cherished myths about
how American character was formed and about the individual's and
nation's seemingly manifest destinies. The popularity of these texts suggests an historical and cultural shift in how majority white Americans
imagine the meaning and consequences of western conquest and settlement. Where once the American fought racial others, often violent
conflict occurs in much twentieth-century western fiction between
familiars close at home. Without serviceable binaries of otherness provided by the "civilized" and the "savage," markers of identity such as
whiteness, masculinity, and "American character" find themselves in violent conflict with each other. Figuratively speaking, whereas domesticity
and imperialism in the nineteenth century pretended to dance apart in
their separate spheres while courting each other, in the twentieth century
they have settled down together, have become estranged, and are often
at each other's throats, once "frontier democracy" – the supposed source
of American character which they collectively gave birth to – and its attendant enemies are thought to be gone. Having conquered its domestic
enemies, imperialism brings its guns home.

The popular idea about the nineteenth-century American West in
Turner's rendition is that it made Americans American: self-reliant,

idealistic, egalitarian. Especially as handed down to us through formula
Westerns in literature and film, that American individualism is decidedly
masculine and often violent. Although Turner de-emphasized violence
in his notion of the frontier's significance, it is nonetheless conquest's
most persistent legacy. Where Turner left an obvious gap, Westerns have
rushed to fill it in: violence in the name of a man's or nation's honor is
immediately apparent in just about all of them. Revision of the western
hero in historiography as well as fiction and film has flourished in the last
thirty years; studies by Christine Bold, Lee Clark Mitchell, and Richard
Slotkin, to name a few critics, have enriched our understanding of this
iconic figure.[9] Krista Comer and Susan Rosowski have recently studied
alternative, female-centered western traditions that constitute divergent
regionalisms and nationalisms and that suggest new ways of reading
the relationship between region and nation.[10] Collectively, these studies
present a dialogue between genders and genres in the West that ranges
across literary history. Individually, and with justification, they take the
boundaries between the genders and types of artistry seriously, given the
cultural power of the male western myth and the critical desire to read
against it or to read it against itself.

 This study, however, originated from a desire to read across, rather
than within, genders and genres – to read books in relation to other
writers regardless of whether they are men or women or writers of mid-
dlebrow or highbrow Westerns. I want here to challenge our sense of
the genealogy and generic context of Owen Wister's and Zane Grey's
transitional and influential Westerns – books that often seem to bear
only a passing family resemblance to their progeny – by placing them
in a new context: not within the succeeding formula in fiction and film
that they influenced, but, as I have begun to suggest in the Introduction,
within the context of other, related works of fiction and historiography
about the American West by women and men. In the early stages of this
project, what I saw were writers who found competing allegories of national identity in the West's regional materials, who treated the West as a
stage upon which they interpreted the meaning of democracy, especially
in a "post-frontier" world, and the value of the nation's westering past.
Writers in this study see quite different nations when they look West, and
the Westerns of Owen Wister and Zane Grey, following the nationalist
readings of the West by Turner and Theodore Roosevelt, serve more
narrowly racialized and masculinist goals than the ethically ambiguous
texts by the other writers in this study, Cather, Fitzgerald, Didion, and
Stegner. If, for a time, these more highly literary and canonical writers

did seem to me to stand apart in their literary methods and ideological impulses from the writers of Westerns I examined alongside them, now I see them in another, more provocative, relation to their popularizing contemporaries.

Given that preoccupations about gender, violence, and the myth of the frontier exist in the work of Cather, albeit revisionistically, it is curious that she is nowhere mentioned, for instance, in Richard Slotkin's otherwise encyclopedic study of the twentieth-century frontier myth, *Gunfighter Nation*. Is that because, despite the number of gunshots in Cather's work, there is no shoot-out between hero and villain? Why, in other words, has the formula Western come to dominate critical discussions of western literature with regard to the relationship between gender and violence on the frontier, an issue that, as Cather's work illustrates, is hardly unique to it? One reason is of course the formula Western's international popularity and powerful cultural influence on film; as such, it merits scrutiny within and by virtue of its conventional generic boundaries. And the Western, to be sure, more explicitly forges a relationship between violence and masculinity than other western genres. Many Westerns, from James Fenimore Cooper's novels to Hollywood movies, are also concerned with white/Indian ethnic difference. Yet while Leslie A. Fiedler has argued that "tales set in the West seem to us not quite Westerns, unfulfilled occasions for myth rather than myth itself, when no Indian ... appears in them," no Indians appear as represented characters in *The Virginian* or *Riders of the Purple Sage*, two of the most popular Westerns of all time.[11] The early twentieth-century Westerns included in this study, in fact, begin to look less and less like Westerns, as critics have conceived them, and more like the literature that Westerns, according to Jane Tompkins, react against: they are deeply concerned with marriage and domesticity – and in the case of Zane Grey, religious issues that are not just included for their own sake, but for their significance for the nation and its western myths.[12]

Odd family resemblances emerged between Westerns and other western texts as I followed an unconventional trail of literary history. Whereas formula Westerns often reject a religious frame of reference, religion frames questions of cultural identity and marital fate out West in fiction by progenitors of the formula Western, Wister and Grey, and by Cather, Stegner, and Didion. Where there were once always Indians in Westerns to occupy the place of the Other, according to Fiedler, in the twentieth-century literary West heterosexuality becomes the structure of difference, and often men are "other" to women who are imagining their own destiny.[13] In place of the ethnic differences against which the early nation constructed its identity and that the popular western myth promoted, the texts canvassed here reveal instead, to borrow René Girard's term, "crises of distinctions" between familiars that produce a form of violence resistant to easy assimilation by nationalist ideology.[14] With the exception of Turner, whose notions about frontier individualism and American (masculine) character in the nineteenth century are located in that "nomadic, bachelor West" that Wister describes in the epigraph with which I began this chapter, other twentieth-century writers consistently and surprisingly see the West and its significance in relation to marriage and family, even when they are writing about the period before the supposed end of the frontier and its masculine individualism. Questions of masculinity and violence do not fade from view with these new considerations in mind; they simply do not stand alone. Yet the individual, of course, has never stood alone, except in the cultural and ideological imagination. While it may hold true that, as Tompkins argues, many subsequent formula Westerns reject everything domestic from their worldview, other important western texts, including the Westerns of Wister and Grey, find in marriage and family the very struggles and issues – concerning democracy and empire, promises kept and betrayed, greed and possession, optimism and pessimism, romance and violence – that are played out in the West with a sense of national stakes. It is as important to read, say, Wister with Cather or Fitzgerald as to read him with Zane Grey because such new pairings allow us to reconsider the nature and meaning of the early Western's violence, too often circumscribed by its resemblance to a later (and often filmic) formula, and also to recognize the literary canon's debt to popular western fiction. It was *Hopalong Cassidy*, after all, that James Gatz, before he became Jay Gatsby, loved to read.

Violence between familiars is perhaps the most unexpected thing we find at home in the West, since the formula Western's violence is most often portrayed between whites and Indians or between good and bad white men. But even in the case of Wister and Grey, such categorical descriptions of the individuals or groups at odds with each other become difficult to defend: though the Virginian is attacked by Indians, for example, the scene is never represented, and though he kills two "bad" white men, one of them is his best friend Steve, who left a note for the Virginian explaining that he would not say goodbye before being hanged because he did not want to cry like a baby. In the case of Zane Grey, the ethnic and religious differences that seem to structure his novels increasingly blur, to the point that enemies and families, strangers and lovers become diffi-cult to distinguish meaningfully according to group identity. In the work of Willa Cather, violence is always around the corner, often unaccount-able in its causes and effects, committed by types almost unprecedented in western literary history: the suicide by gunshot of a heroine's father, the fatal shooting of a young wife and her lover by a jealous husband, a marital murder-suicide driven by greed and jealousy, and a suicide of a tramp in a threshing machine are among other disturbing moments that involve only whites. Fitzgerald's *The Great Gatsby*, which is a response to western motifs and Turnerian ideals, is famous as much for its chain of murder and suicide as for its romance. Myrtle Wilson is killed by a car, her husband kills the man he thinks was at the wheel, and then he kills himself. With Wallace Stegner and Joan Didion, the scope of violence and betrayal in marriage widens as the nation's western myths loom larger with passing time and fall under the scrutiny of skeptical, revisionist eyes. Murder and suicide in the context of marriage – to mark only the most violent moments in Stegner and Didion – serve explicitly to call into question the hope of the West itself.

Why should the setting of the West, with its "open field" for the in-dividual – one that, according to Turner, made America exceptional in the nineteenth century – be so occupied by marital and familial con-flict in the twentieth, even when novels are retrospectively set in the nineteenth? How and why does a culture shift from romanticizing the Turnerian individual with his great western opportunities and dreams to representing almost obsessively domestic discord and failure? The very ideals of individualism that Turner claimed the frontier produced not only created expectations that could not be met in western contexts, but could not sustain social life in the West where kinship was key to communal survival. The idea of the masculine individual who thrives out West has had a longer cultural life than his actual, brief history. Romanticizations of this figure in the last third of the nineteenth century, including the more misogynistic ones in the context of mining towns, are often conjoined with a bemused longing for women and children. Mark Twain sang praises to the ephemeral culture of young men mining in California in *Roughing It* (1871): "It was a splendid population . . . a wild, free, disorderly, grotesque society! *Men* – washed their own shirts! . . . only swarming hosts of stalwart *men* – nothing juvenile, nothing feminine visi-ble anywhere!" But when a woman appears, the men demand to "FETCH HER OUT!" to see her; on another occasion, a miner offers a hundred and fifty dollars in gold dust to kiss a child.[15] In Bret Harte's most famous story, "The Luck of Roaring Camp" (1868), the orphaned baby of the camp prostitute brings out domestic virtues of clean living in the men of the camp who try to raise him. Owen Wister, following the lead of historian Theodor Mommsen, thought the cowboys a "queer episode" in the nation's history, a cycle through which all nations passed: "Purely nomadic, and leaving no posterity, for they [the cowboys] don't marry."[16] But the romantic nostalgia for this episode collapses with the arrival of civilization and the bride. In his story "The Bride Comes to Yellow Sky" (1898), Stephen Crane parodies this abrupt transition: once the former gunslinger brings a bride to the western town, his gun-toting foe is defanged and flummoxed by this transformed, civilized apparition, who calls up the ghosts of a life that "civilization" has transformed. In Wister's *The Virginian* (1902), marriage again marks the end of the hero's (necessary) violence – most dramatically, his lynching of his best friend Steve, who has taken individual freedom too far by stealing cattle – and the beginning of his domestication, happily ever after. But that is the last we see, among the influential texts in this study, of a happy marriage marking the end of an historical era. From this point on, marriage only betokens trouble. For Wister, who would go on to write one of the most famous happy endings in Westerns, the trouble begins with the West's loosening of marital norms through interracial marriage in settings where men and even women have few choices of mate. In his first western story, "Hank's Woman" (1892), the new Austrian bride, recently fired as a lady's maid and thus desperate to marry, smashes in her black husband's skull with an axe and, in an attempt to throw his body into a bottomless ravine, falls to her own death.

If in the nineteenth century, as Amy Kaplan argues, "domesticity not only monitors the borders between the civilized and the savage but also regulates traces of the savage within itself," in the twentieth century "civilized" violence comes home in all senses of the word – among family members, best friends, and members of the same race.[17] The Westerns of Zane Grey and Owen Wister continue, in part, to align domesticity with the imperial project of civilizing, but even these Westerns represent conflicts between familiars as well. In this regard, western literature carries the traces of historical violence on a local, identifiable scale – yet not always for discernibly political ends. Whereas the sentimental novel, especially *Uncle Tom's Cabin*, sought to achieve a sympathetic identification by its white readers with fictional black slaves in a domestic space, the novels in this study were probably unnerving for white readers in that the social or national cause which their sympathetic identification was meant to serve is unclear. Hence the violence in the text has no unambiguously compensatory value. When Wister's Virginian hangs his best friend; when Cather's Frank Shabata murders his wife and her lover Emil and Emil's sister forgives him; when Cather's Bohemian immigrant Mr. Shimerda commits suicide; or when Grey's heroine gains her freedom at the price of her land and her people: what is lost usually exceeds whatever might be gained. Are such instances allegories of the difficulty of justifying American conquest and the process of "Americanization," in contrast to the ease of justifying the Civil War and the abolition of slavery? Turner's frontier thesis attempts to treat slavery as a "mere incident" in American history, a suppression which can be read as an allegory of *not* reading the national significance of slavery's domestic and civil violence. In this regard, it is worth noting that so many early twenti-eth-century Westerns are set retrospectively in the decades after the Civil War and before the "end" of the frontier, in border regions of transition in which antagonistic religious, territorial, ethnic, and legal interests have yet, historically, to be resolved in favor of American federal control and "Americanization." Their suspense-value was a form of nostalgia, since at the time of the novels' publications, the resolution of conflict in favor of American national interests had already been determined.

There are at least three important ways in which we can understand the shift in the literature of the American West from the alternately romanticized and violent encounter with Indians-as-Other to the ro-manticized but often violent encounter with familiar-as-Other. From an anthropological standpoint, to borrow René Girard's model of pure and impure violence, nineteenth-century western American culture lacked any of the rites of "sacrificial" violence of so-called "primitive" societies, the "purifying" sort that serves to put an end to cycles of revenge by selecting a victim who is not an explicit enemy. With the loss of these traditional sacrificial rites, a culture loses the difference between impure and purifying violence. "When this difference has been effaced," Girard writes in terms that might describe the cycles of violence in the work of Cormac McCarthy or in unredemptive Westerns like Clint Eastwood's *Unforgiven* (1992), "purification is no longer possible and impure, conta-gious, reciprocal violence spreads throughout the community."[18] Western conquest has all the hallmarks of a kind of frenzied insanity. The destruc-tion of native peoples served not nearly so much to bind whites as a com-munity, since there was nothing purifying or sacrificial in the violence committed against Native Americans, as it served to spread aggression throughout the nation in the name not just of insatiable greed but of bloodlust. How else do we understand, for example, the slaughter of sixty million buffalo, especially passengers shooting buffalo from speeding trains for amusement? For native peoples, in contrast, hunting buffalo often bore the characteristics of ritual sacrifice. If, as Girard argues, once the sacrificial distinction is obliterated in categories of violence, all other distinctions upon which a culture is based are obliterated as well, we might hypothesize that violence against Indians and against nature proves uncontainable: it spreads into the nation's homes and across the nation's borders.[19] Terms such as "white," "American," and "masculine" undergo a resulting crisis that produces struggles within these categories for distinction and supremacy.

A second way in which we can understand this shift from inter-ethnic to intra-ethnic scenes of western violence is through the question of consent, which is key to the American analogy between marital and national union. One man's or woman's consent was often another's captivity, often depending not so much on ethnicity as on which side of the nation one stood. Mutual consent was intrinsic to the American model of marriage derived from the Christian religion and English common law, a model that political and legal authorities "endorsed and aimed to perpetuate nationally," as Nancy Cott argues. Because of the intrinsic matter of consent, "this form of marriage was especially congruent with American political ideals: consent of the parties was also the hallmark of representative government. Consent was basic to both marriage and government, the question of its authenticity not meant to be reopened nor its depth plumbed once consent was given."[20] The federal government's conquest of others, including marital nonconformists within whose practices the monogamous Christian majority presumed there could be no consent on the part of women, did not depend upon or presume the consent of the conquered. Neither is a woman's consent always assumed in marriages in this study – consent is forced, if only by a woman's limited options. Marital choice and romantic conflict often share the logic of the forced choice of American domination in western territories, as we see in the dilemma of Zane Grey's heroine Jane Withersteen, torn between the claims of Mormon empire and American imperial imperatives: give up your Mormon father's land and keep your virtue and freedom to marry, or keep your land and lose both your virtue and your consent to Mormon polygamy. Either way, her choice is forced.

Related to consent is a third question of legitimacy and law. Today most would agree that conquest is illegitimate according to a higher ethical standard than that of a racist sense of "natural right" or of physical force.

The establishment of federal law and control in western settlements retroactively gave legitimacy-by-law to that which "civilization" and "right" had claimed. Likewise, marriage, seen as the very "cornerstone of civilization," is the legitimating contract *par excellence* that justifies the romantic conquest. As Tony Tanner describes it, "For bourgeois society marriage is the all-subsuming, all-organizing, all-containing contract. It is the structure that maintains the Structure."[21] At least in theory: long before the revisionism and sexual revolution of the 1960s, marital contract and legitimacy are challenged in the literary West. In Willa Cather's *O Pioneers!*, for example, Alexandra Bergson's heroism in stewarding the land is purchased without the benefit of a marital contract. When she finally does marry, it feels anti-climactic by the standards of the conventional marriage plot. In contrast, in Cather's *My Ántonia*, Jim Burden, as a lawyer for one of the railway companies that consolidated the West, gains his expedient marriage to a woman with her own fortune at the expense of feeling love or romance. Meanwhile, Ántonia, whom he romanticizes in his memory and who "seemed to mean the country" of his youth, bears a child outside of marriage at the age of twenty-four and suffers many hardships. Cather's Niel Herbert in *A Lost Lady* alternately invests in Marian Forrester his vision of western romance and his disillusionment with a changing West – explicitly *as* her marital status changes – while Marian Forrester's experience is one of endurance, survival, and ultimate happiness regardless of marriage and the allegorical burden she bears.

The romance of the West and the romance of marriage share the same bed and hearth and meet similar fates in much of the literary West. Civilization's "cornerstone" does not so much secure civilization as question its very meaning and future. F. Scott Fitzgerald's depiction of Myrtle Wilson's torn breast along the side of the road – a murder and mutilation born of marital misery, betrayal, and the carelessness of the wealthy – is an unmistakable figure for and revision of the "fresh green breast of the new world" that the Dutch mercantilists saw before the founding of the American nation. Fitzgerald's alignment of domestic misery and national destiny is only the most famous of fictional moments in this study in which marriage and nation intersect. The literary West imagines American pasts and futures not simply through the masculine individual but through the nexus of ethical relations and responsibilities – the hopes, promises, dreams, and betrayals – that presume there are always at least two people testing the romance of the West against its often brutal reality. In these imagined relationships, women figure often, unsurprisingly, as both the repository of ideals and the sacrificial victims.

That this romance is persistently heterosexualized is in part because of the long history of feminizing the land that the masculine conqueror possesses; divine, feminized nature both legitimates American conquest and falls as corruptible victim to it.[22] Self-conscious about gendered rhetorical figures, the historically persistent need to locate (or dislocate) the nation in familial relationships, and particularly the fate of romantic heroines, Cather and Didion revise that heterosexual logic, in which women and land are subjugated by male desire in acts of courtship (in Wister's case) or conquest (in Turner's gendered metaphors), or in which romance sanctions that subjugation and violence.

I have been speaking thus far, necessarily but somewhat misleadingly, about violence "in" fiction, as plot device and theme. Not only is there of course no literal violence in verbal art, but scenes of violence in much western fiction of the first half of the twentieth century either occur, as it were, "off-stage" or are represented obliquely. Lee Mitchell has observed that the crucial, plot-turning "acts" of violence in Owen Wister's *The Virginian* are undescribed. As a result, Mitchell argues, this and other early Westerns influence the genre when its readers "fill in" what they expect is already there.[23] While the thematic effect of violence in fiction is undeniably important to readers, it is nevertheless critical not to dissociate it from the verbal occasion in which it exists. As Michael Kowalewski cautions, violence in fiction needs to be approached not as a represented fact, but as a fact of representation.[24] Violence is never just ideologically or thematically functional; it also stands as a limit and expressive challenge to the force of verbal representation. Whether it is occasioned in realist or romantic prose, whether it is rendered directly or obliquely, violence "in" fiction is of a piece with its verbal means of expression.

When violence is "there" in a text without being represented – when Jay Gatsby is shot, when the Virginian hangs his best friend – we have an altogether different kind of verbal occasion than the sort Willa Cather mercilessly presents to the reader, for example, in *A Lost Lady*, when Ivy Peters catches a woodpecker.

He held the woodpecker's head in a visc made of his thumb and forefinger, enclosing its panting body with his palm. Quick as a flash, as if it were a practised trick, with one of those tiny blades he slit both the eyes that glared in the bird's stupid little head, and instantly released it.

The woodpecker rose in the air with a whirling, corkscrew motion, darted to the right, struck a tree-trunk, – to the left, and struck another. Up and down, backward and forward among the tangle of branches it flew, raking its feathers, falling and recovering itself.

The assonance of "quick...trick...slit" is as excruciating as any graphic image could be. The bird's corkscrew flight is a horrifying minia- ture of mutilated nature, both sensate and helpless – and a chilling hint of Ivy's approach to it as an adult. The Blum boys, who can only watch and "who lived by killing things.... wouldn't have believed they could be so upset by a hurt woodpecker."[25] And neither might a reader, habituated to graphic and repeated violence in contemporary cinema and televi- sion, believe how upsetting such a moment can be – or how disturbing the hanging of the Virginian's friend is in Wister's novel precisely *because* the narrator cannot bear to look.

The means of representing violence are inseparable from the im- plications of such scenes, especially if we consider more generally the relationship between pervasive western nostalgia and actual historical violence. In fiction, violence so often seems to *have* happened, to be the unviewable moment toward which, or away from which, retrospective narratives move; it both threatens and organizes narrative coherence. To an important extent this is true of historiography, which has either blocked violence from view, in the case of Turner's optimistic view of frontier history, or brought it to the fore, in the case of the tragic view of New Western historians. Debates among western historians about the significance of the western past hinge not only upon the causes and im- portance of violence, but as a result, on the narrative means by which it is made to matter. One can read some histories of war without feeling the kind of visceral recoiling that Cather's image of the blind woodpecker provokes. The turn to literary models among some western historians is a means of bringing questions of subjectivity more fully to bear on "objective" analysis, as a way of making once subordinated histories communicate with a human voice and feeling. Yet in doing so we also risk making the past seem more familiar than it really is, as it was lived; this is often the trade-off in imagining history from our unavoidably subjective standpoints.

There is no consensus about the United States' western past, nor has there ever been. Historians of the American West have debated, es- pecially over the last forty years, whether the West is best understood, following Turner, within a single paradigm – as a succession of frontiers or a legacy of conquest, for example – or as multiple stories, and whether the western past predominantly records the best or the worst about the American nation, as if the nation is either redeemed or put on trial in its western past. Revisionism about the West has been a constant: the West is a setting upon which American ideology gets figured and refigured,

upon which debates of national consequence are allegorized in competing ways, for different ethnic groups, business interests, religious beliefs,
and political agendas. Most pervasively, the West – as setting and even
as a word – has served as both a point of national consolidation and
a place from which to question empire and American faith in individual freedom and providential destiny. Against expectation, the popularly
embraced fiction examined in this study is filled not with examples of free
individualism but with forced choices and constraints, tragic marriages,
environmental hardships, group conflict and identity confusion, murder, failure, and accidents. These examples resemble the New Western
History but they are an old story, the story of a retrospective American
romance at odds with, and complicit in, ongoing American reality.

   In the three sections of this chapter that follow, I will explore the
West as a literary allegory in order to understand how and why it gets
narrated in relation to the American nation, both as historiography, in
the case of Turner, and in the novel. It is in part with the legacy of that
nationalism that New Western historians have had to do battle, who
have a hard enough time just defining the West in its reality. The cultural
legacy of western violence has endured through the life of that allegory.
It is also because of the West's function as national allegory and because
marriage has served culturally and historically as an analogue to national
union, that this study is justified in reading the troubled particulars of
romance and marriage in relation to American nationalism. The writers
of fiction in this study enact those allegories with varying degrees of self-
consciousness about their fictionality and about the limits and distortions
of retrospection. In the last section of this chapter, I will show why the
thematic and formal considerations in this book, and indeed in any
consideration of the literary West, need to be thought about together.

## ALLEGORIZING NATION

Writing in 1921 for Yale University Press's series the Chronicles of
America, the sometime western novelist Emerson Hough began *The
Passing of the Frontier: A Chronicle of the Old West* with a claim as large as his
subject's national significance: "The frontier! There is no word in the
English language more stirring, more intimate, or more beloved . . . It
means all that America ever meant . . . To a genuine American it is the
dearest word in all of the world." Since the frontier in history has had
"many a local habitation and many a name," he argued, "it lies somewhat
indefinite under the blue haze of the years, all the more alluring for its lack

of definition."[26] With its confident sense of an affective consensus among undefined and nominally "genuine" Americans about a word that is yet indefinite and hazy, Hough's rhetoric dates itself, at least in the context of current academic writing about the West. Yet today, what many western historians consider the ethnocentric "f-word" is nevertheless alive and well in American culture, shared by most Americans as a kind of "cultural glue" that holds them together, as Patricia Limerick has argued.[27] It is by virtue of their elusiveness that the words "frontier" and "West" have not only come to frustrate historians but have come to be saturated with American nationalist meanings, to signify "America" in the cultural imagination. Hough describes, as Ronald Reagan later would, some of those commonly held, retrospectively imagined reasons that made the word so dear to those who loved the American nation: "There lies our comfort and our pride. There we never have failed.... The frontier was the place and the time of the strong man, of the self-sufficient but restless individual... There, for a time at least, we were Americans."[28] The cultural work of a single word is clear: preserved beyond its history yet embedded in the past, the frontier made Americans American and that American was the strong white man, the restless individual, both self-reliant and unsatisfied. Born of no family and producing no progeny, the American was "made" out West, both satisfying a nation's sense of its exceptionalist difference from the inherited history of the Old World and simultaneously generating anxiety about how this exceptionalism might be perpetuated through a continuing national genealogy.

If we substitute "the West" for "the frontier," Hough's description and set of connotations accurately represent an imaginary site that Americans can still automatically visualize, even if the connection or distinction be-tween "frontier" and "West" largely goes unarticulated in popular cul-ture and both are imagined more as past places frozen in time than as historical processes connected with present sites and regions. The word "frontier" and the phrase "Manifest Destiny" are both freighted with what happened to any people who obstructed America's sanctified mis-sion to spread natural freedom, those people Jefferson alluded to, looking ahead to the settlement of the continent, as a "blot or mixture on [the] surface" of empire.[29] But today the word "frontier" has a clearer relation to the concept of Manifest Destiny than it did before Frederick Jack-son Turner first delivered his address "The Significance of the Frontier in American History" in 1893. Turner did not make the relationship between frontier and the ideology of Manifest Destiny explicit in his thesis, though he used the latter phrase. As Theodore Roosevelt said, he

Figure 1 "American Progress," by John Gast. Lithograph in *Crofutt's New Overland Tourist and Pacific Coast Guide*, 1879.

"put into definite shape a great deal of thought that had been float-
ing around rather loosely."[30] In arguing that the process of settlement
along frontier lines of continuous recession *explains* the development of
the *entire* nation up to his time, Turner provided a historiographical way
of affirming retrospectively the presumptions of proponents of Manifest
Destiny, who, seeing the vastness of the continent, believed in equally
large measure in the rightness of taking it. In other words, whatever descriptive, particular reference the term "frontier" might have had before
Turner's hypothesis it had no more. It became imbued retrospectively
with the greatest national significance, just as prospectors and presidents
surveying the continent had imbued the landscape with the American
mission. As Anders Stephanson describes it, "[Manifest Destiny] was
more than an expression: it was a whole *matrix*, a manner of interpreting
the time and space of 'America.'"[31] Manifest Destiny conflated the
sacred and the secular and turned time into space and gave world-
historical importance to the idea of moving west, an idea that was already
a commonplace in the eighteenth century and extending back to the an-
cients as *translatio imperii* – the "heliotropic" idea that, as the mediaeval
abbot and mystic Hugh of St. Victor wrote in *De vanitate mundi* (*On the Vanity
of the World*), "everything that happened in the beginning of time took
place in the East when the world began, while in the progress of the ages
toward the end of time, which is the end of the world, all things come to an
end in the West."[32] In western American terms, all things in civilization
had come to their zenith. The Reverend Thomas Brockaway preached
in 1784, "Empire, learning and religion have in past ages, been traveling
from east to west, and this continent is their last western state . . . Here
then is God erecting a stage on which to exhibit the great things of his
kingdom."[33]

The most widely disseminated image of the West in the nineteenth
century is also one of the most fantastic: John Gast's 1872 lithograph
"American Progress" (see figure 1), which as a painting is elsewhere variously titled "The Spirit of Progress," "Manifest Destiny," and "The
Spirit of Manifest Destiny," a fact which demonstrates that an allegory
may have many aliases but much the same spirit. It was especially reproduced in George Crofutt's many editions of his tourist guide of the West
in the 1870s, which sold over half a million copies; the painted version
has also been reproduced on the cover of recent studies of Manifest
Destiny, American exceptionalism, and the myth of the West, and
given attention by Alan Trachtenberg.[34] This image visually depicts the
kind of grand stage the Mr. Brockaway described a century before, in

some ways more secularized but just as theatrically allegorical. In it, images of empire, learning, and technology – borne only by men – move from east to west across the entire continent, banishing the buffalo and the Indians in the Far West into a receding darkness. Above these Turnerian "stages of civilization" floats a giant white Lady – the Spirit herself – with schoolbook in one arm and telegraph cable in the other. Woman-as-allegory weds, in this image, the particulars of western settlement to national destiny. Crofutt's Guide claimed that the star on her forehead is the " 'Star of empire,' " as it guided its readers through an interpretation of the image by pointing out that the Indians "turn their despairing faces toward the setting sun, as they flee from the presence of the wondrous vision. The 'Star' is *too much for them*. What American man, woman or child, does not feel a heart-throb of exultation as they think of the glorious achievements of PROGRESS since the landing of the Pilgrim Fathers, on staunch old Plymouth Rock!"[35]

Like the enduring, optimistic myth of the West, the picture figures history as geography, or turns time into space, by means of the governing allegorical Spirit – one the whole family can enjoy. The allegorical structure is immediately apparent: as if along vertical and horizontal axes, the tall, metaphorical spirit of progress dominates and gives meaning to the ground beneath her, in which a metonymic chain of historical events, men, and objects are typologically represented across the continent, any of them as iconic as the other of the West. The particulars of the painting become allegorical because of the governing spirit of "Manifest Destiny," which is also the spirit of allegory-as-nation-building. The painting enacts, for the viewers, what Manifest Destiny assumed, that the continent was given to them. By subsuming the vast continent and its history of progress within its frames, the painting "gives" the viewer the continent and its rationalization for doing so. Significantly, the Indians and buffalo, though dim in the darkness in their fast retreat, are nevertheless present. These are not vacant lands, as much American rhetoric would have it, but lands in need of the spirit of progress. The vanishing Indians give structural significance to that need; they are an essential part of the allegory, an allegory more of transcendence than history. Indeed, the image suggests transcendence over history, individual experience, and particularity, all for the sake of a nation's image of itself. As if the viewer needed more instruction, Crofutt's guide stresses that the picture is "of purely national design."

While the lithograph lacks images of marriage and family, five decades earlier, in 1820, the Reverend Jedidiah Morse headed a governmental investigation among American Indian groups in part to gain information on their "moral condition." Morse concluded that " 'the marriage institution, in its purity,' would serve as a vehicle of civilization among the natives," arguing that polygamy, like the individual Indians in Gast's painting fifty years later, "ever yields and vanishes before the light of civilization and christianity." Offering property and citizenship to Native Americans who were heads of families would remain conditional upon the renunciation of tribal affiliation. Marriage to a white American became evidence that an Indian had joined "civilized life."[36] After decades of Indian removal and their perceived recalcitrance in joining that life, Gast's picture simplifies and distorts the ways in which a younger nation imagined the civilizing effects of monogamous and even interracial marriage. In this image, citizenship and property rights are given solely to individual white men, regardless of whether they are heads of households. Gone is the family, replaced by the emerging frontiersman of the popular imagination, who stands for the progress of the nation. And while all the men in Gast's image are racially distinguished as either white or Indian, the white woman-as-allegory marries white–Indian difference to the transcendent star of empire. In contrast, Crofutt's guide begins, opposite its title page, with a drawing of "Utah's Best Crop," dozens of babies (see figure 2). These two introductory images in this popular travel guide imply that families were to follow in the march of progress (and substitute a better crop for Utah's). But the whole impulse to civilize and conquer in the early nineteenth century was predicated upon monogamous Christian marriage and the family. In the twentieth century, many writers who reimagined the consequences of settlement would return the focus to marriage and family, away from the masculine individual, but without the structurally important role of the Indian in defining civilization.

The nationalist intent of Gast's painting is not surprising in the context of nineteenth-century culture, but in the context of contemporary American culture, what is surprising is that so much *narrative* is given to an image of the West, and that the narrative sweep should have to be so large and explicit to guide people into the West. Contemporary Americans are apparently drawn toward images of the West that are mute as nature is mute, or that at least do not make their meaning explicit, as in numerous car commercials set in rugged western landscapes, and in a recent magazine advertisement by the Wyoming Division of Tourism that depicts the old "nomadic bachelor" West of the past, by means of a lone man on a horse near a mesa. The advertisement says, "The West is not a myth.

Figure 2 "Utah's Best Crop." Frontispiece, *Crofutt's New Overland Tourist and Pacific Coast Guide*, 1879.

Not in this place of cowboys and horses and cattle drives. Not in this place of mountains, sunsets, millions of stars and handshakes that still mean something. The West is not a myth, not here." It then describes the particulars that you, the tourist, can see or do in Wyoming, after which "you'll understand why Wyoming is the West." Covering iconic images and reaching from professions to the cosmos, from dignified geography to human dignity (because a handshake "means something"), the advertisement attaches particulars to an abstraction, the West, and thereby metaphorizes Wyoming: it "is the West." While the advertisement wants to say that the West is real (hence one can go there and spend money), it does so only by negating its mythic status – and no fewer than five times. Does it protest too much? "Not a myth" also implies that the West might be thought to be a thing of the past. The advertisement equates or confuses not only real particulars with a non-mythic abstraction, but past and present, time and place, sign and signified. Its success as an advertisement depends upon a consensual, if vague, understanding *not* that "the West" is geographically limited to Wyoming but that it is semantically richer. It is beside the point that there are states geographically "more" west than Wyoming, since the West is directed at a national idea.

The very contingency of "the West" points to its allegorical function: it always points back to the individual, culture, or nation facing or moving west. We can only be speaking ethnocentrically or nationalistically (we can only be allegorizing an American story), if we say, for example, that Mexicans, "central" Americans, and Asians going to California have "gone West." Even the well-intended title of a conference of the Western Literature Association, "Many Wests, Many Traditions," tells us more about liberal American pluralism than about real difference: those "Wests" include *El Norte.*

One way in which "the West" as an idea has absorbed so much allegorically nationalist meaning and consequently erased so many histories is the role of visual culture in the work of national identification, as the previous examples attest. Given its disconnection from the complexity of this ill-defined region, the myth of the West is more readily visualized in an instant than narrated, which is why the Marlboro advertising campaign has been one of the most successful in history, with its silent, rugged cowboys and sunset-glowing landscapes. The dominant visual image of the West today is the land itself (if not just Monument Valley), not the native victims of American conquest, nor even the fact of conquest. In their sublimity, the West's physical landscapes absorb, simplify, and resolve for public consumption the complex human narratives enacted in them. In the fiction of Zane Grey, for example, the landscape's suggested spiritual force lends a sense of sacred meaning to human destiny. But though the body of the landscape can be a blank slate upon which human beings write what they will, it is not a personal and articulate witness to social history, such as an ex-slave or an American Indian is. Landscapes bear scars and signs, but they tell at best a cryptic story, such as the "Cliff City" Tom Outland seeks to understand in Willa Cather's *The Professor's House*, the visual impression of which tells little about the fate of its former human inhabitants. "But what had become of them?" Tom Outland thinks. "What catastrophe had overwhelmed them?" Outland's questions, like his name, are allegories of displacement, and they displace onto or mediate through the Anasazi the question of more recent American dispossessions of Indian peoples. In the place of answers to both the historical and rhetorical questions stands a mute witness to them, a city that has become figuratively, if not literally, absorbed into the natural landscape and removed from historical rhythms and contexts: "In sunlight it was the colour of winter oak-leaves. A fringe of cedars grew along the edge of the cavern, like a garden. They were the only living things. Such silence and stillness and repose – immortal repose. That village sat looking down into the canyon with the calmness of eternity . . . preserved in the dry air and almost perpetual sunlight like a fly in amber, guarded by the cliffs and the river and the desert."[37] Though personified witnesses to human history, the cliffs and the city they guard are removed from even natural history. Geologically speaking, of course, the ancient landscapes of the American West are visible records of time's effects, on a very large scale, while human beings are the only living things to *practice* recording time. To call landscapes timeless or eternal is to observe how they withhold witness to the human stories enacted so briefly in them; it is, counterintuitively, to personify them. As such, they are ideal backdrops for the dramatization of myth which, for those who project myth onto the land, also withholds historical witness and absorbs particular moments, agents, and causes. Whether Cather intended the Anasazi ruins' silence to be allegorical of the more immediate dispossession of Indian peoples in the American West is undecidable. But the silence is the signifier of the image; what is signified can only apply to the listener, whether Tom Outland or the novel's readers. The scene becomes an allegory both of Americans' distance from these ancient ruins and of the relative (written) silence of Indian witnesses to American conquest – relative, I would add, to the written witness of slavery.

The West has often served the function of diverting attention away from other aspects of American history, especially slavery, in order to claim a particular national story for itself. The texts in this study mark a transference between regional and national identifications in the ongoing effort to explore the meaning of a nation by looking West. Turner enacted this transference historiographically when he claimed that frontier settlement explains *all* of American development. The eastern-bred and Harvard-educated Owen Wister transferred regional to national identifications when he made his Western hero a Virginian. It was no accident that when the Virginia-born Willa Cather chose the Nebraska of her youth as her fictional subject, she became a writer of national importance. When F. Scott Fitzgerald had his narrator in *The Great Gatsby* claim that this now canonic story set in New York is a story "of the West, after all," he knew that this allegorically increased rather than diminished his novel's significance and complexity. The literary West – like *The Great Gatsby* – is a story of America, after all, one that is far more complex than Nick Carraway's casual regional distinctions and summation might suggest.

In its idea of the West, American culture has found an exemption from history while at the same time being condemned to repeat the past. The same observation is true of Turner's description of the frontier process. Though it created something new – the American – the Turnerian frontier did so through a repetitive recapitulation of the stages of civilization, in which Americans were repeatedly returning to an older stage as the frontier line advanced, continually coming to terms with what the western myth claimed they were escaping: civilization, the past, the claims of family. The character traits that Turner codified in his description of the rugged backwoodsman are consistently re-envisioned and re-imagined in novels of the West, and with high national stakes, for they represent imaginary frontiers or border regions where open questions about national identity, the meaning of American history and democracy, and the struggle over the nation's present and future are worked through or "represented" in both the artistic and political senses. Region and nation assign each other meaning to the same extent that the literal and figurative do within allegory. This is one reason why western "types" have had such a long life beyond their emergence in local color fiction and are continually ripe for refiguring in the context of contemporary culture.

Doris Sommer articulates the dilemma that confronts a critic who seeks, as I do, to interpret the way a culture reads intimate relationships and national questions through each other, without repeating the reductive allegorizing process in traditional "parallel" allegory. Yet inasmuch as writers and readers have assumed a translatability between romantic and republican desires, Sommer writes, they "have in fact been assuming what amounts to an allegorical relationship between personal and political narratives . . . Allegory is a vexed term, but unavoidable to describe how one discourse consistently represents the other and invites a double reading of narrative events."[38] This double reading does not have to involve a kind of strict metaphoric parallelism between terms, as in Christian allegory. It can instead rely upon a looser, or more metonymic, association of interdependence, Sommer argues, such that each term feeds off the other, as in Walter Benjamin's dialectical notion of allegory that describes historical process: each signifying strand is a trace of the other, writing the other line and being written by the other line simultaneously. In a not inaccurate sense, this is what marriages and national culture have always been doing, and what much of the literary West has done in figuring a mutually signifying relationship between region and nation.

The context of the American West, however, poses a quite different set of allegorizing problems from those of the Latin American romances that Sommer writes about, not only because two allegorical relationships occur simultaneously (between region and nation, between marriage and nation), but especially with regard to the West's violence. If marriage and nation have historically been writing each other, then the violent impasses of western fictional narratives signal an end to this process of mutual signification, which is particularly the case in the work of Didion and Stegner at a time, during the 1960s, when the states of both marital and national union became deeply unsettled. Marriages in the literary West so often separate, even as they participate in, the double helix between love and nation, becoming allegories of a failed national metaphor of unity in a region where many Americans hoped to locate a common identity.

Can we ever locate the West – disentangled, for instance, from the allegorical braids of marriage and nation – or is it just an allegory for anything? This unending source for the literary imagination is also an intractable historiographical problem. A point of consolidation and consensus for the audience of Gast's allegorical painting of American progress, as for Emerson Hough's readers and many after them, "the West" is for contemporary western historians a point of departure in historiographical debates, which collectively do not offer a common definition or singular significance. The historical significance of "the frontier" and "the West" is no more settled than their definitions are analytically clear. Whether defined by climate and terrain, culture and ethnicity, or proximity to either the Pacific Rim or Mexico, the West proves a contradictory and unstable place. "No large geographic area," writes Stephen Aron, "certainly not one stretching from the Great Plains to the Pacific Coast... is culturally or environmentally consistent. If homogeneity is the standard, then all regions are fictions"[39] – a point that I, as a literary critic, agree with in a sense different from the one he intends. Donald Worster writes that he cannot put his finger on the map "and say, 'There is the West,'" because studies "have attached too abstract a meaning to the word, so abstract in fact that it has become bewildering."[40] The recently published *Atlas of the New West* includes only eastern California in the West, a surprise to Los Angelenos and others who, like Walt Whitman, are "Facing West from California's Shores." When Walter Nugent conducted a survey of western historians, editors, and writers and asked simply "Where is the American West?", the consensus seemed to be that only four states in their geographic entirety could be said to be what he called "the unambiguous West": Idaho, Nevada, Utah, and Arizona.[41] By that consensus, the only texts in this study that are unambiguously western are Zane Grey's – and Wyoming, according to its Division of Tourism, is out of business.

While literature is made of what historians have often considered "soft" metaphorical materials – counterbalanced, as Kerwin Lee Klein has shown, in gendered ways against the "hard" facts of history – the very process of metaphorical substitution demonstrates a principle about historical memory and historical analysis: we are always selecting a whole (the West, for example) to stand in for a vast array of particulars.[42] Narrative, including historical narrative, erases even as it incorporates the particularities of human experience by means of the governing metaphors that give a story significance, by means of how we substitute value and meaning for event. It is therefore helpful – and not a way to cloud things – to approach the West as a literary site or process, as that which is in the process of being written and rewritten, in order to understand its cultural significance as a vast set of experiences that individuals and cultures alternately erase from or re-inscribe into that imaginary field called America. The literary West is an allegory of that process of imagining and reconstituting the past.

## RETROSPECTION AND FICTIONS OF IMMEDIACY

After the settling and consolidation of the West, Americans wanted increasingly to imagine what settlement had transformed, displaced, or destroyed. Imagining an older West was a phantom act of discovery.

Debates that the literary West engaged about the status of women, racial "threats" to white America, and the threat to democracy by capitalism made the West of the past seem vitally connected to the reader's present. The use of both omniscient and first-person narration allowed for a sense of immediacy and the overcoming of the retrospective distance involved in reading the western past. The narrative voice in *The Virginian* is alternately first-personally situated in the story's events and omniscient, both the eastern tenderfoot's voice and Wister's, offering an illusion of connection between the reader and a "vanished" life. Narrative omniscience often works in concert with a nostalgia for the exercise of imperial power on the domestic scene in both Wister and Zane Grey. Their novels make a struggle over the racial and religious suitability of western marriage consonant with a struggle over American democracy and empire before the close of the frontier. The sense of an all-knowing narrative power gives the heroine's consent the quality of a forced choice to conform to a national and imperial project to become the new American, as if a self-conscious recognition of epistemological limitations were necessarily resistant to imperial designs.

As Cather, Fitzgerald, Stegner, and Didion re-imagine western literary landscapes, they demonstrate with greater self-consciousness and ethical doubt, as well as success, what Wister and Grey had capitalized upon: the notion that the romance of the past is available to realism, or that, as Wister puts it in *The Virginian* in his address to the reader, "Any narrative which presents faithfully a day and a generation is of necessity historical."[43] The former cluster of authors' retrospective narratives question powers of omniscience (the kind represented visually in "American Progress," which situates the viewer nowhere in particular and everywhere in general) by incorporating gaps and by suggesting other, unnarrated histories, including the narrators' own. There is often a tenuous but critical distinction between retrospective writers in this study who explicitly dramatize their own values by setting them in the narrative western past, such as Turner, Wister, and Grey, and those who, in their fictional narratives, self-consciously dramatize the significance of doing so through the creation of first-person narrators distinctly different from the author. Authorial self-consciousness about the limits of narrating the reality and breadth of the human content of the past would seem to fail imaginatively where other writers succeed – yet for that reason such self-consciousness succeeds ethically where other writers who are blind to their imaginative limits too often fail.

The degree to which a writer is self-conscious about the limits of narrating the past from a particular vantage point, in other words, shapes the politics of a narrative and reveals the political and social assumptions of the writer about western significance. Whereas Turner argued that the pioneer's immediacy to his experience left him unconscious of its "spiritual" significance – the significance Turner can with hindsight read allegorically – later writers of fiction stage that retrospection and reveal self-consciously or unconsciously how retrospection leaves the narrator blind to the significance of his narrative. Willa Cather's narrator Jim Burden and F. Scott Fitzgerald's Nick Carraway are framed precisely *as* narrators with particular investments in their retrospectively told tales. The distance between them and their titular subjects is at once melancholic, nostalgic, romanticizing, and disdainful. Given the protagonist's alignment with the country itself or with an old national dream, the distance is also an allegory of the distance between western (and American) idealism and reality, between a frontier past and an increasingly urbanized present.

But while the degree of an author's self-consciousness about the limits of knowledge may differ among writers, all of the writers in this study depend upon romances, marriages, and relationships – often viewed from without by an unmarried narrator – in order to particularize, imagine, and situate a complex national history. Marriage and romance are wedded to allegories of nation that exceed the consciousness of the couple; that work is left to narrators like Wister's tenderfoot, to Cather's Niel Herbert, to Fitzgerald's Nick Carraway, or to Stegner's Lyman Ward. Thematic and formal concerns in stories of western marriage are especially inseparable when a novel is told from the point of view of a narrator or character who is a bachelor, is divorced, or is unhappily married. Their retrospective investments in the intimate lives of the characters they tell about not only determine the shape and meaning of the novels but are co-extensive with a larger romantic nostalgia for a past western life. Retrospection as both theme and narrative device can serve simultaneously as a polemic against the present *and* as a sign that what is wrong with the present is retrospect's ability to blind. Cather's Niel Herbert, for example, who "resolved to remain a bachelor," burdens Marian Forrester with the expectations for an old western life that her first husband, a railroad man, represents: "it was as Captain Forrester's wife that she most interested Niel, and it was in her relation to her husband that he most admired her. Given her other charming attributes, her comprehension of a man like the railroad-builder, her loyalty to him, stamped her more than anything else."[44] *A Lost Lady*'s nostalgia for this past West, however, is infused as much with Niel's critical disdain as it is with Marian Forrester's inexhaustible charm, once the meaning that Niel invests in her through her marital bond dissolves with her changing circumstances: "It was what he most held against Mrs. Forrester; that she was not willing to immolate herself, like the widow of all these great men, and die with the pioneer period to which she belonged; that she preferred life on any terms." Like Fitzgerald's Nick Carraway, whose characterization was inspired by this novel, Niel's romance sows the seeds of his own disappointment, and he leaves "without bidding her good-bye. He went away with weary contempt for her in his heart." The polarizing logic of romance and disappointment over the passing of the frontier points to the personal investments and perspectives that situate both individual characters and the Wests they figure – even Turner's mythic abstraction of the western "individual."

By virtue of the fact that fiction highlights the gap between narrative and experience that Turner's historiography wants to erase, it is in fiction that future debates among western historians are already spelled out: who is telling whose story, and with what investments? During the revisionism of the 1960s, Didion and Stegner explore this question by crossing and mixing the genres of journalism, fiction, and history, but especially by framing the limits of their narrators' voices, rendering the past as subjectively as they do the present in order to understand the conflicted present of failed marriages and failed national designs. Reading history becomes an allegory of the present – or, as Turner argued, expanding upon Emerson, "*each age writes the history of the past anew with reference to the conditions uppermost in its own time.*" The narrative structure of Stegner's *Angle of Repose* demonstrates this point, as Lyman Ward, the historian who battles with both the social changes of the sixties and his wife's abandonment of him, simultaneously invests in his grandparents' western marriage and experiences the personal and national hopes and disappointments he has yet to resolve for himself in his troubled present.

LITERARY NARRATIONS OF HISTORICAL CAUSALITY

Miserable, both of them, everything hopeful in them run down, everything joyous smothered under poverty and failure. (Wallace Stegner, *Angle of Repose* (1971))

Who could think that the building of the railroad could guarantee salvation, when there on the lawns of the men who built the railroad nothing is left but the shadows of migrainous women, and the pony carts waiting for the long-dead children? (Joan Didion, *Slouching Towards Bethlehem* (1968))

Indispensable to an exploration of marriage, violence, and the nation in the American literary West is a narratological concern. How and why do retrospective narratives, that often look back to the time before the "end of the frontier," produce these allegorical ramifications? And how do these narratives, by linking the fate of marriages to that of the nation, help both to construct and to undermine beliefs in progress and an American nationalism located in the West?

Hayden White and others have explored ways in which writers of history use traditional fictional plots to organize historical data. [45] Reading Turner alongside fictional texts about the West deepens our understanding of the immense and often still unconscious debt that the writing of history owes to fiction. Writers of fiction have resoundingly revised the Turnerian individual beyond the level of theme and have proposed more deeply historical models for understanding the western past – and for recognizing the limits of our understanding – than Turner's poetic historiography and even much revisionist history. By "historical" I do not mean to suggest a set of incontrovertible facts but a set of questions about what it means to narrate the past and about how we do it: do particulars take priority over even revisionist abstractions? Do representative individuals carry more historical weight than groups and communities? Do we emphasize romance or tragedy, the dreams that drove people or the brutal experiences that they met? To what extent do we ascribe importance to intentionality, belief, or ideology and are they effects or causes? Allegorical structures for understanding can distort or erase lines of causality and human agency and imaginarily locate moral evil and responsibility in some elsewhere. Such structures include presentist ones, which assume the past is worth reading only in terms of its relation to the present, and even the label "the West" itself in its ability to help us to read or give ground to the process of allegorizing. Causality and agency, like the location of moral evil, in other words, are equally historiographical and literary concerns inseparable from questions of narrative sequence in retrospection and from the metaphors that structure allegory and personify agency.

Turner's historiography depends for its effectiveness upon abstractions, such as "the United States," "the individual," and "an open field" in his claim that "the United States is unique in the extent to which the individual has been given an open field." In contrast, most fiction insists upon the imaginative, particularized embodiment of all human activity, even when those particulars participate in cultural typologies or serve culturally to erase other bodies. Joan Didion's rhetorical question "*Who* could think that the building of the railroad could guarantee salvation?" personalizes both the human agency and purpose of what seems otherwise to be, to borrow Frank Norris' description, a mechanical octopus. By rhetorically embodying one of the largest business enterprises in western development, Didion's question also serves to transform the most pervasive abstraction of that development – Progress (and "the men who built" it) – from a teleological phenomenon into a drama about the failure of human hopes and those "migrainous women" and "long-dead children" she proceeds to invoke, who are left out of the Turnerian story. American technological and individualistic triumph confronts the ghost town, finding no one at home. That most un-American and un-Western theme of failure is perhaps the most pervasive theme in nonformula fiction about the West, even though it is often conjoined with themes of endurance and persistence. Stegner's *Angle of Repose* not only thematizes the persistence of failure and collapsed aspirations in what he elsewhere and somewhat contradictorily liked to call "the geography of hope," but, by showing marital struggle as the foundation of his story, serves to point out a fallacy in Turner's reading of the West: there is no such thing as the individual. The smallest indivisible human unit is two people.

Turner's optimism, like the optimism of the myth of the West, depends upon a sense of exceptionalist significance in the presumption that "the individual" (disembodied, but almost certainly white and male) "has been given" (the passive voice suggests providential intention) "an open field" (because no one lives there). Because there are no embodied agents in his statement, it is ideological to the extent that Stegner's sentence above, describing Lyman and Susan Ward's misery, is historically conscious. Its historicity rests not in the fact that Stegner was inspired by an actual family history, but in its ability to enable us to imagine both the conditions in which particular people live and the possibility that intentions and hopes guarantee nothing. Whether a novelist's or a historian's, optimism and pessimism about the past or the future are states of imagination – of a literary imagination in which particulars are isolated, metaphorized, and narratively connected. Such narratives have far less to do with the totality of human experience in any given era than with the historically situated meaning of their own allegorical operations.

The allegory I have set up with the epigraphs at the beginning and end of this chapter concerns the West's function as a stage for debates about American nationalism. The gap between Turner's optimism and the sense of failure in Stegner and Didion is not meant to point to any resolution of this debate but rather to the gap between representation and historical experience, the self-conscious recognition of which can help us understand how literature conditions our sense of history, of temporal sequence and causality, and of the ultimately unknowable totality of western experience. The opening up of the American, and particularly the western American, literary canon in the last thirty years to include writers of all ethnicities has enlarged Americans' sense of human experience on this continent. Just as there can be no objective or totalizing history, neither can we escape the figural and allegorical structure of understanding itself. Revisionism is, in part, a way of substituting one grounding metaphor for another, as when Willa Cather makes "American" the sign of boyishness – or when Mexican-Americans rename themselves Chicanos. When western historians replace a Turnerian paradigm with another, or reject paradigms in favor of multiple stories or "zones of cultural interpenetration," they are rearranging the metaphorical grounding for understanding. This is not to argue that some narratives are no more or less true to historical experience than others. It is certainly the case that they have real historical impact. As just one example that had importance for the history of the Western, when religious converts adopted the allegorical narrative and identity of Mormonism, they crossed an ocean and walked vast distances to establish an empire in the Far West, one that would eventually be in conflict with another allegorizing empire surrounding it, a conflict that would have direct and immediate consequences on their marriages and families. The clash of American and Mormon competing notions of their respective manifest destinies resulted in a forced choice to renounce the key practice of the Mormon religion, plural marriage. If the West tells us anything, it is that stories have powerful consequences. As western historians discover in their often heated debates, narrative matters – not only its content, but also the teller's perspective and investments. And as Willa Cather demonstrates in *My Ántonia*, itself a narrative palimpsest, storied experience can claim or save lives, alter the landscape, rearrange space and time, and build a nation. In his claim, Turner was not inaccurate, even if we drain it of his moral inflections: "pioneers" were often idealists and dreamers, and their dreams shaped reality and changed history. But as Fitzgerald, Stegner, and Didion explore, dreams clash and become nightmares in the physical and social landscapes and in the imaginary field of "America." The interdependent relationships between western romantic nostalgia and violence within national and marital unions are played out in western fictions by means of their concomitant blindnesses and insights, the narrative results of looking back in order to dream ahead. From that angle of vision, the American literary West is still an unsettled and unsettling territory.

CHAPTER TWO

## *Turner's rhetorical frontier*

The poet turns the world to glass, and shows us all things in their
right series and procession . . . he stands one step nearer to things,
and sees the flowing or metamorphosis . . .
                    Ralph Waldo Emerson, "The Poet"

Stand at Cumberland Gap and watch the procession of civilization, marching single file – the buffalo following the trail to the salt
springs, the Indian, the fur-trader and hunter, the cattle-raiser, the
pioneer farmer – and the frontier has passed by. Stand at South
Pass in the Rockies a century later and see the same procession . . .
          Turner, "The Significance of the Frontier in American History"

No text has been more influential with regard to the writing and debat-
ing of western American significance than Frederick Jackson Turner's
1893 essay "The Significance of the Frontier in American History." The
elastic and contradictory terms of Turner's analysis are largely responsible for the chorus of debate in the last three decades about whether
the West is best understood as an idea, a place, or a historical process –
and what kind.[1] While Turner has had perhaps the greatest influence
on American historiography of any American historian, he is also the
most discredited. "Because Turner's frontier thesis necessarily ended in
1890," writes William Cronon, "it left historians few clues about what to
do with the West in the twentieth century: in an odd sense, Turnerian
western history almost literally ended at the very moment that Turner
created the field."[2] It also left Americans few clues about what to do with
democracy if its supposed source was gone. If Turner's thesis denied itself
historiographical usefulness by virtue of the frontier's finitude, then it is
in large part by means of Turner's literariness that we can discern why it
continues to have more significance and longevity than one might expect
from a superseded historiographical artifact.

Identifying not with Turner's particular blind spots but with the perils
of presentism more generally, Patricia Limerick has called contemporary

western historians "Turnerians All," part of the title of an essay in which she describes both the exhilaration and self-inflicted wounds that result from subscribing to Turner's claim that *"each age writes the history of the past anew with reference to conditions uppermost in its own time."*[3] Limerick's essay is a useful way to frame an examination of Turner's literary and rhetorical style because, as perhaps the major figure of the New Western History, Limerick describes the process of her own historiographical self-revisions through her rereadings of Turner while exhibiting his literary influence on her writing. The question of consequence, she writes, is no longer whether Turner was right about the frontier, but whether he was "right about the present-day value of historical understanding."[4] Consequential as that question is, another question Limerick only hints at, or rather enacts without drawing out its most radical implications, is whether we can ever understand the past, not so much without reference to the present, but without reference to literature and literary models in the broadest sense. Can we ever read the past or its relation to the present except as, or through, plots, stories, narratives, or poetic constructs that, as Hayden White argues, organize the chaos and indeterminacy of contingent events and possible outcomes? Turner is most famous for his frontier thesis in part because that is where he wrote his clearest and most compelling – if historically flawed – story. Limerick belatedly finds scattered throughout Turner's other writings his acknowledgment that the present is often not intelligible and that the past is not therefore readable through it, especially in his time, when industrialism and urbanization seemed unlikely outgrowths of frontier "forces." Such moments in his work demonstrate that Turner doubted the story he originated because he recognized how fractured history became if the frontier's finite force held the key to all of American development for four centuries. "In the first decades of the twentieth century," she writes, "the present was turning out to be *more* confusing than the past."[5] Or at least the frontier thesis made it seem so in its sense of a divided history. Arguably the past is never more intelligible than the present, but the past at least has the virtue that one can finish writing a story about the evidence one finds there. In this regard Limerick seems not fully to recognize her dependence on literary models and the paradox of using one to describe the flawed linearity in Turner's presentism. "Figuring out the present," she writes, "was an undertaking very much like reading the last pages of a novel; one checked to see how the plot one had been following in the earlier pages finally turned out . . . and when one had identified the outcome, or the past's product, one was in a much-improved position

to trace and understand the whole story." Yet the same can be said
of Limerick's reflective essay, which helps her to come to understand
the story of her own career in relation to Turner's. The "reflective essay," she writes, was Turner's favorite "literary form," one marked, as
is Limerick's, "by retrospect and reappraisal."[6] Rereading Turner becomes, in part, an allegory of the contemporary historian's self-revisions.

Limerick's rereading of Turner reveals how, to a significant degree,
the return to Turner is the (haunting) return of literary history within
western American historiography. With some bemusement about the
frontier thesis's "classic" status, Limerick observes that the more the
New Western History has declared the thesis irrelevant, the more they
have revitalized Turner's reputation and "restored his celebrity" (not to
mention established the new historians' own).[7] Drawing attention to the
intellectual fallacy of Turner's frontier "forces," which are not "real,"
she describes in literary fashion their ongoing "power to bruise," without examining in depth how Turner's literary style, even more so than
Limerick's, makes these forces so palpable and durable – indeed how his
literariness makes the frontier thesis possible. Among the most important
moments in Limerick's essay, for my purposes here, are ones that concern the unnamed but "controlling and predestining God" in Turner's
picture and the "metaphors that eliminated choice and decision" from it.
Though Limerick does not make the claim explicitly, one can infer from
her essay that Turner's chief historical blind spots were related as much
to his literary inheritance as to his race, both of which were of course
also related through his education. Just so, his historiographical legacy
endures because of his literary practices, especially since the reflective
essay endures in the writing of Patricia Limerick, who unwittingly drew
celebrity to the very man whose work she set out to debunk.

The figure of the historian-as-author is very much alive, whether the
historian is dead or alive, because in part that figure demonstrates the
"force" of the literary and literary ideas, for better and worse, over
the force of fact. For all the criticism his successors have directed
against his work, writes William Cronon, "no new synthetic paradigm
for western history has yet emerged to replace Turner's. We continue to
use the word 'frontier' as if it meant something."[8] In spite of the historical
flaws and ideological biases in the frontier thesis, Turner's construction
of American history continues to have a rhetorical power. Americans
still use one of Turner's two central terms (the other being "section")
precisely because "frontier" can have so many meanings, in Turner's
historiography but even more so in culture generally. As Turner used

the word, "frontier" worked poetically to bring together a constellation of meanings. Indeed, as Cronon writes, "Turner's vocabulary was
more that of a poet than a logician, and so his word 'frontier' could
mean almost anything: a line, a moving zone, a static region, a kind
of society, a process of character formation, an abundance of land. His
fuzzy language conferred . . . the illusion of great analytical power only
because his central terms – frontier, democracy, individualism, national
character – were so broad and ill-defined."[9]

While Donald Worster has argued that Turner started historians
"down a muddy, slippery road that ultimately leads to a swamp,"[10] others
have argued that Turner's thesis "expresses some of the deepest myths
and longings many Americans still feel about their national character"
and that the persuasive style in the thesis "had a profound rhetorical
impact upon our national psychology."[11] Whatever the merits or validity
of either set of views, the distinction between them is based on whether
Turner is seen as a historian or as a history-maker, as a person who
accurately writes about the past or as a person who influenced his present
and future – the latter being the aim and burden of the public intellectual
who wants to be of some usefulness. While many historians might enjoy
making history even as they write it, Turner would find the dual accomplishments especially meaningful and gratifying – the debunking of his
writings aside – since the roles of historian and prophet were to him not
distinct; neither were the roles of historian and poet. Invaluable as the historiographical criticism on Turner's thesis has been, to examine Turner
from the point of view of literary analysis can allow us to discern not only
his significance in American literary history but to discern why, since literary history is not progressive (Twain does not supplant Hawthorne,
for example), Turner's work continues to be read and his *literary* terms
continue to have currency to the extent that the "frontier" seems not at
all to be vanishing from American culture.[12] Moreover, by examining
Turner's literary strategies and tropes, which Henry Nash Smith first
drew attention to at the end of *Virgin Land*, we can better understand
their inseparability from the limitations and distortions of his historiography and how those very limitations enabled Turner's writing to shape
culture.[13] Far from being ornamental, Turner's literariness has a poetic
logic that makes his historiography both possible and powerful.

In order to illuminate the figural dream of Turnerian western historiography, both in its contradictions and in its ideologically useful economy,
I want first to examine two chief literary traditions that shaped Turner's
writing and ideas: Christian allegorical exegesis and Emersonian or

Romantic organicism, especially the Emersonian faith in the transcendence of poetry. Then I will show their stylistic emergence in the frontier thesis and in Turner's later essays on the West that Henry Holt and Company republished as *The Frontier in American History* in 1920, advertising it alongside titles by Bergson, Einstein, and Dewey, so great had his cultural influence become.[14] An examination of Turner as historian-poet can help us to understand why his hypothesis, with its "fuzzy language," has been difficult either to verify or entirely to discredit and hence why it continues to lend power to western myth.

The roles of historian and prophet may seem antithetical, yet antithesis, as Ronald Carpenter has observed in the only extended analysis of Turner's rhetoric, was one of his earliest and most lasting rhetorical devices. Turner's early writings "suggest that the young man was coming to view antitheses not as 'artificial' but as '*real*'. . . corresponding to a real opposition between ideas."[15] Whether such oppositions were between past and future or savagery and civilization, Turner's rhetorical staging of them in his thesis powerfully shapes the substance of his ideas there about the frontier. Indeed, the frontier itself, like Turner writing as historian-prophet, is the crux or site where conceptual oppositions such as man/wilderness fuse to create something new. That synthesis is the American and American history. It is by virtue of the historian-poet's language of opposition that this uniqueness is revealed as the reality beneath appearances. Antitheses as rhetorical devices were thus not "studied artifices, imposed *afterward* upon some statement," for the young Turner; rather, he seemed "to think antithetically."[16] Just as frontier oppositions forged a new man and a new society, poetic oppositions forge an aesthetic world in the Romantic sense.

Turner's thinking about the frontier is dialectic rather than dialogic. The other dominant subject in his life's work – sections – arguably resists dialectical thought in the manner in which "regionalism" often resists nationalist synthesis. While the frontier dialectic synthesizes the nation, sectional discourse entertains dialogue about internal national difference. Whether civilized (white) men versus savages (Indians) or the new versus the old world, the synthesizing term of Turner's frontier produces something new that escapes these oppositions: the American and the spiritual or world-historical significance of American development. Many contemporary western historians subscribe to a dialogic way of interpreting history, putting perspectives in conflict with each other and leaving that conflict unresolved, wary as they rightly are of the complicity of antithetical thought in nationalist one-making.

Oppositional or antithetical thought is an inheritance of Romantic thought and German idealism and it takes a peculiar form in Turner's thesis: in contrast to Hegelian thought, Turner's thesis necessarily does not end with an end to history but with an end to discernible historical significance. The meaning he finds in the forging of the frontier's oppositions is an optimistic one, but the frontier's closing puts that optimism in doubt for the future, which is a reason why one literary critic reads the thesis as an elegiac allegory of limited-resource capitalism.[17] Because he is writing from the vantage point of the frontier's hypothetical closing, of the end of those "free lands," the great source of American significance, Turner is not so much the prophet of an undetermined future as he is a Jeremiah mourning a lost past.[18] The frontier thesis is distinguished in this regard by its ending: "And now, four centuries from the discovery of America, at the end of a hundred years of life under the Constitution, the frontier has gone, and with its going has closed the first period of American history" (p. 60). The sense of the depletion of this fulness of times does give the thesis the tone of a secular Jeremiad, and it also returns America to temporality, to history, without any guarantee of transcendence. In this regard, Turner as prophet marks American exceptionalism within a broadly Christian allegorical structure while Turner the historian implicitly desacralizes the American mission by virtue of the frontier's geographic and temporal finitude. Without a divine guarantee of allegorical meaning, the meaning of the frontier is opened up rather than foreclosed at the historical moment when Turner argues the frontier no longer exists.

The frontier thesis's prophetic nostalgia is as old as America's Puritan self, yet the thesis records moments in which Turner does paradoxically see in the foreclosed frontier past seeds of optimism for a unique American future – even if only a hypothetical one. That antithesis within the frontier thesis – its pessimism versus its optimism – has divided its readers and critics. I will return to this undecidable aspect of Turner's thesis later, but here it is important to stress that Turner's optimism, as deconstructible as it has proven to be historiographically, is constructed upon and endures culturally because of its specifically *literary* qualities, which may be broadly described as Romantic not only because of the organicism and ironic opposition of Turner's thought but because there is much evidence to suggest that Turner viewed history not only literarily but *as* literary. In other words, Turner, following Emerson, finds in literature and literary language not simply a representation of experience but the highest, truest form and expression of that experience; for him,

literary language is not merely decorative artifice but the revelation itself
of real truths, meanings, or forces *behind* appearances. In the 1893 frontier
thesis he writes, "*Behind* institutions, *behind* constitutional forms and mod-
ifications, lie the *vital forces* that call these organs into life" (p. 31, emphasis
added). The United States "lies like a huge page in the history of society.
Line by line as we read this continental page from West to East we find
the record of social evolution" (p. 38). In his undergraduate commonplace book, Turner recorded a telling passage from Carlyle: following
Fichte, he writes, "all things . . . especially we ourselves . . . are as a kind
of vesture or sensuous Appearance – that under all lies, as the essence
of them . . . the Divine Idea of the World; this is the reality which lies
at the bottom of all Appearance." In the Cumberland Gap passage of
the frontier thesis, cited in the epigraph above, this idealist tendency is
apparent: despite the flow of particular actors, the "procession" is the
"same" from one century to the next, from one end of the continent to
the other. Turner's rhetoric imitates the Emersonian unity behind dif-
ferentiable appearance. The organicism in Turner's frontier hypothesis
finds its justification precisely in the language and metaphors that articulate it. Immersed in Emerson's essays, Turner copied long quotations
in his commonplace book that express this relation to poetic language:
"To true poetry we shall set down as the result and justification of the
age in which it appears, and think lightly of histories and statutes . . . Is
not poetry the little chamber in the brain where is generated the explo-
sive force which, by gentle shocks, sets in action the intellectual world?"
By this definition, Turner's thesis was itself a kind of poetry that, as he
wrote to Arthur Schlesinger, he had to "hammer pretty hard and pretty
steadily . . . to 'get it in.'"[19]

Turner's undergraduate orations exhibit this Emersonian view of poetic expression and shed light on his literary evolution as historian. Just
as the Emersonian Over-Soul's transcendence of historical contingency
and sequence is yet read through history in particular cases of (often literary) Genius, Christian allegory – Turner's other influence – reads the
transcendence of finite time and space through the Deity's act of becoming physical and historical. In Turner's orations, as Ronald Carpenter
and Allan G. Bogue have observed, there is evidence that the young
Turner was not simply developing and practicing a rhetorical style, but
was simultaneously testing and developing ideas through that style that
later appear in the frontier thesis.[20] In his 1878 prize-winning oration
"The Power of the Press," Turner writes of the significance of the printing press, beginning his oration, as he later ends his frontier thesis, by

allegorically describing an event that happened "about four centuries ago," though in this case it is not Columbus' discovery of America:

About four centuries ago was born in the brain of John Guttenberg [*sic*], an idea destined to be the propagator of learning, of Christianity, and of civilization, and thus to sway the future of the world . . . the art of letter press printing . . . Today that glorious sun, the Press, has reached its zenith, and we bless it for the present fulness of our civilization, and feel that it will never set . . .[21]

The impossibility of such a sun compares suggestively with the pervasive imagery of the American West's setting sun, as in Albert Bierstadt's painting "The Oregon Trail," which holds in locked tension – like the frontier thesis itself – both the West's promise of the future and the vanishing of the frontier past. As the pioneers in the foreground travel toward the radiant horizon, small Indian tepees in the background are made ephemeral by the intense light. As with Turner's image of the printing press, Bierstadt's painting erases the darkness of the past by shedding a fixed light on it. Bierstadt's suffused canvas suggests the 'fulness' of civilization Turner describes: the trajectory of civilization's advance, be it westering or printing, is retrospectively made visible by a sun that will not set.

Informing such allegories is a Christian teleology, in which the son of God is made historical in order for human beings to transcend temporality: the son dies in order to rise eternally and mark the significance of all future human history. Indeed, the significance of Christ in world history is as all-defining for Christians as the significance of the frontier in American history is for Turner, with the important exception that the frontier is finite. In a manner that resolves this contradiction between finite existence and infinite significance, Turner argues for the immortality of the press by means of the metaphor of baptism. With the advent of democratic access to all the world's finest books,

Today we may talk with all the great ones of the earth. We have only to go to our books, and poets of every age will sing their sweetest songs . . . historians show how empires have risen and decayed, orators persuade by their power and eloquence, and God Himself will point the path of rectitude in that first and greatest book ever published.

He who gives a truth or a grand conception to the world, knows that mankind will possess it forever . . . for the works which gained him honor have been baptized in the immortality of the Press.[22]

The young Turner transforms secular printing into the immortality of his sanctified age. Whereas the Christian medieval world viewed the world as God's text, Turner argues, like Emerson, that literature is the world, an immortal one. Turner's use of the allegory of "baptism" survives in his 1903 essay "Contributions of the West," in which he allegorically Christianizes American democracy by saying that "Thomas Jefferson was the John the Baptist of democracy, not its Moses" (p. 84).

The historical and immediate give way in his undergraduate oration to an absolute confidence in the transcendence of the literary. Images of Christian salvation and resurrection are displaced onto a secular, classical world:

Standing one day in a great library, I looked upon the army of books . . . It needed no incantation to call up the great ones of all ages and lands. From these books rose the "kings of Thought" as from a grave . . . Here the Ocean of Centuries was rolled away. The Past became the Present. Homer and Aristotle, Shakespeare and Bacon stood side by side, and by their genius ruled the minds of men. The "baptism of ink" has descended upon the past, and again Babylon is beautiful . . . [23]

Compact as a library, Turner's condensation of world history proceeds in the oration to sweep by the reader like a pageant, a technique he employs in the frontier thesis, especially in the Cumberland Gap passage: he crystallizes, suspends, and "immortalizes" the temporal. If we substitute "historian" for "Press," and "frontier" for "the printed page" in the following passage from this oration, we can see the sort of Hegelian or Whitmanian synthesis that marks the historian's stylized thought: "Thus the Press [historian] joined the Past and the Present and made them one . . . as we turn the leaves of *one* book, the Future is unveiled to our mortal gaze, and as the printed page [frontier] is read, the new Jerusalem rises in its divine beauty."[24]

In his 1883 prize-winning oration "The Poet of the Future," which marked the pinnacle of his undergraduate accomplishments at the University of Wisconsin, Turner argues that his own age "is magnificent: it is the poets who are lacking," as he sets the stage for his future role as historian-poet:

Democracy is waiting for its poet.
. . . The age will demand a mouthpiece, and at its bidding will arise the poet of the future . . . He will find beauty in the useful and the common . . . In his ear humanity will whisper deep, inspiring words, and bid him give them voice. He will unite the logic of the present and the dream of the past, and his words will ring in the ears of generations yet unborn . . . He will reflect all the past and prophesy the future.[25]

While no scholars would want their mature work to be judged by their undergraduate thought, Turner's description of the poet of the future is nevertheless a fair description of his future view of the historian – and it reveals his rhetorical fusion of Emersonian and Christian ideas. The common people are the purported text of Turner's interpretive projects and in his maturity Turner characterizes the historian as the people's prophet or poet; in his undergraduate commonplace book, Turner copied Emerson's line, "He is the true Orpheus who writes his ode not with syllables but with men."[26] Like Whitman, who asserts in "Democratic Vistas" that there is an incipient poetry in the people and who seeks to prophesy a fuller realization of the democratic spirit, Turner applied his vision to all of American history for the sake of fulfilling the dream of American exceptionalism.

Turner's essentially hermeneutic project has its roots in the Christian exegetical tradition. Seven of the titles in Turner's work contain the phrase "The Significance of . . ." The poet-historian's relationship to the present is like that of the Christian exegetes – and the Old Testament prophets they read – who bear witness to the fulfillment of the past for the sake of a destined future, but in Turner's terms for the sake of national unity. Cronon shares this view: "Like the prophets, he was drawn as an orator to exegesis and hermeneutics, to creating a web of verbal elaboration around a core set of ideas that never finally changed; like the prophets, he sought not to prove or disprove his vision, but to apply its sweep to all of American history."[27] Though he also stressed the need to reinterpret the past, Turner was caught between that revisionist impulse and his sense that history is the act of interpreting what is manifestly there behind particular events, which would, in effect, require no verification. His sense that history is literary, in other words, resists the need for empirical analysis. Literary critics do not seek to verify or disprove Whitman's democratic, idealist vision, since figural language resists empirical proof. The "spiritual" significance that Turner reads into the frontier is, as Emerson argues in "Experience," "*that which is its own evidence.*"[28]

Subsequent historians have left us with no doubt about what Turner failed to see, yet if Turner's vision is so limited, how did it then come to have such an impact on American historiography and on a wider readership? Or as Limerick has asked, how does a concept that historians have attacked as ethnocentric become "cultural common property"?[29] In part, this is because it so explicitly inserts itself into an American literary imagination. One of the chief signs of the thesis' literariness is the extent to which the thesis and Turner's later developments are laced with allusive quotations as opposed to historical documentation. In the thesis he quotes predominantly presidents and senators; in his later explanations, perhaps in order to give the thesis a lasting life, he quotes Henry Adams, Walt Whitman, James Russell Lowell, and Rudyard Kipling, among others. Turner's allusions are not ornamental, even though they have often been critically overlooked; they are the structural underpinnings of authority for his argument, the voices of past literary "prophets" who confirm his present view of the past. Other than the "blank page" of the continent, they are the texts upon which he performs his exegesis (p. 93). By bringing together past voices in one present, his quotations act as stays against the frontier's finitude, the significance of which he seeks to immortalize; and that significance, he notes in a 1910 essay after quoting from Kipling's "Foreloper," is "spiritual" (p. 102). Through these quotations Turner consigns his writing to an ongoing literary history now that frontier history, in his view, has certainly ended; although he seeks to close off interpretation of the frontier, his exegesis of other texts opens his own writing up to literary interpretation as opposed to historical verification. The spiritual significance of which he writes is once again produced by the hermeneutics of analogical and allegorized reading, as in his reading of Kipling: "Although Rudyard Kipling's 'Foreloper' deals with the English pioneer in lands beneath the southern Cross, yet the poem portrays American traits as well" (p. 103).

Although Turner wants to argue for American exceptionalism, paradoxically the literary means through which he performs his exegesis is by turning to an Old World text and by seeing sameness in the place of difference, which is the hallmark of the allegorizing tendency. Whereas the frontier is that sameness in his thesis, in his allusion to Kipling that sameness is "empire." It is, significantly, only when he alludes to another empire that Turner *names* the fact of American empire and thus invokes an allegory of imperialism: "For he must blaze a nation's way with hatchet and with brand, / Till on his last won wilderness an empire's bulwarks stand." Turner elaborates, "This quest after the unknown, this yearning 'beyond the sky line, where the strange roads go down,' is of the very essence of the backwoods pioneer, even though he was unconscious of its spiritual significance" (p. 103).

Questing after and yearning for significance is also "of the very essence" of allegory, as Joel Fineman has argued, if we also add that concomitant with that yearning and desire is mourning over the lack that is imagined to inaugurate it – in Turner's case, the lack of "free" lands, lands that were never free, except allegorically. If we think of the yearning implicit in the myth of the frontier for a lost and ever-receding Eden or truly original place of "perennial rebirth," as Turner puts it, then Fineman's structural description of allegory is particularly resonant with regard to Turner's interpretive project: "Distanced at the beginning from its source, allegory will set out on an increasingly futile search for a signifier with which to recuperate the fracture of and at its source, and with each successive signifier the fracture and the search begin again: a structure of continual yearning, the insatiable desire of allegory. Perhaps this is one reason why," as Angus Fletcher has remarked, "allegory seems by its nature to be incompletable, never quite fulfilling its grand design."[30] Stripped of divine authority, Turner's allegorizing reading of western significance both mourns a democratic past and desires its return, creating an interpretive gap between pessimism and optimism, between the fulness of times and the sense that time has run out, and finally, between historical experience and the literary imagination. In a later elaboration of his thesis, Turner quotes James Bryce, who describes in *The American Commonwealth* (1888) westerners, "driven to and fro by a fire in the heart. Time seems too short for what they have to do, and the result always to come short of their desire" (p. 67). Indicating the Western dream's temporality, Turner also writes that "even as he proclaimed the gospel of democracy the pioneer showed a vague apprehension lest the time be short – lest equality not endure – lest he might fall behind in the ascending movement of Western society. This led him on in feverish haste to acquire advantages as though he only half believed his dream. 'Before him lies a boundless continent,' wrote De Tocqueville, in the days when pioneer democracy was triumphant under Jackson, 'and he urges forward as if time pressed and he was afraid of finding no room for his exertions.'"[31]

While mourning and yearning can have vastly different objects, Renato Rosaldo has argued that imperialism knows a particular form of nostalgia in which "people mourn the passing of what they themselves have transformed." This imperialist nostalgia

occurs alongside a peculiar sense of mission, "the white man's burden," where civilized nations stand duty-bound to uplift so-called savage ones. In this ideologically constructed world of ongoing progressive change, putatively static savage societies become a stable reference point for defining (the felicitous progression of) civilized identity. "We" (who believe in progress) valorize innovation, and then yearn for more stable worlds, whether these reside in our own past, in other cultures, or in the conflation of the two. Such forms of longing thus appear

closely related to secular notions of progress. When the so-called civilizing process destabilizes forms of life, the agents of change experience transformations
of other cultures as if they were personal losses.[32]

Turner believed in progress, yet his frontier thesis is thoroughly nostalgic
for those progressive possibilities that no longer exist, now that the
"Western wilds," which "constituted the richest free gift that was ever
spread out before civilized man," are now taken: "Never again," he
writes, "can such an opportunity come to the sons of men. It was unique"
(p. 93). Given that Turner argues in the frontier thesis that ever since
Columbus, America "has been another name for opportunity" (p. 59)
and later in "The Problem of the West" that "the West was another name
for opportunity" (p. 68), and given that "now the frontier opportunities
are gone" (p. 74), there remains the implication that America and the
West have lost their names or their spiritual significance. This allegorical
search for names, the desire to see sameness in the place of difference –
Kipling's empire, America, or West – is bound to be nostalgic if, as
Rosaldo argues, those "static" savage societies that served as reference
points for civilized identity are thought to be vanishing. American Indians
are not entirely absent from Turner's thesis, nor are they mourned or
romanticized. Their peripheral presence is, rather, structural, as they
are in Gast's "American Progress." For Turner they are that stabiliz-
ing reference point which Rosaldo describes, the implicit condition and
even agency of progress. "The Indian trade *pioneered* the way for civilization," he writes, associating American pioneering with Indian agency;
"the effect of the Indian frontier as a consolidating *agent* in our history
is important." And again he writes that the "frontier stretched along the
western border like a cord of union. The Indian was a common danger,
demanding united action" (pp. 40–41, emphasis mine). Although it is ultimately the land itself upon which Turner grounds the frontier's alchemy,
it seems clear within his argument that without the Indian, progress, civilization, and American unity would have been thwarted or at the very
least altered in significance.

There are also no explicit American agents of violence in the frontier thesis. In spite of Turner's claim that the pioneer effected both
good and evil, the agency of American imperialism is put in the passive
voice, encouraging the sense of American innocence. After naming the
natural boundary lines of the frontiers with American – not Indian –
names, Turner writes, "Each was won by a series of Indian wars" (p. 33).
Nostalgia, writes Rosaldo, "is a particularly appropriate emotion to

invoke in attempting to establish one's innocence and at the same time talk about what one has destroyed."[33] The agents in American history that Turner names but does not speak about, such as the Indians, or that he speaks about, in the case of winning a series of Indian wars, but cannot name, are structurally related to that imaginary field – America and the West – that he can name as other names for opportunity but cannot confidently demonstrate that they exist any longer in their true spiritual forms. What the thesis produces is the literary structure of allegory that lacks the real presence of its grounding terms – free land, Indians, American agents – in order *not* to talk about the meaning of their real, historical absence or agency. "More historically," Joel Fineman observes, "allegory seems regularly to surface in critical or polemical atmospheres, when for political or metaphysical reasons there is something that cannot be said."[34]

The allegorizing and poetic transference of human, historical agency in Turner's thesis onto non-human agents or onto human non-agents is seen in the many passive constructions in the thesis and his casting of "savages" in their "important" role, but also in the personification of the wilderness when man meets it and it becomes frontier. In his 1903 essay "Contributions of the West," Turner also feminizes the wilderness (whereas women are almost entirely absent): "into this vast shaggy continent of ours," Turner writes, "poured the first feeble tide of European settlement. European men, institutions, and ideas were lodged in the American wilderness, and this great American West took them to her bosom, taught them a new way of looking upon the destiny of the common man" (p. 99). As in Gast's "Spirit of Progress," the figure of a woman appears in Turner's wilderness only as the very mother of empire, its grounding metaphor.

In one of his more metaphoric and blatantly feminized allusions, Turner quotes Henry Adams in his history of the United States, who has the American of 1800 exclaim to a foreign visitor, "Look at this continent of mine, fairest of created worlds, as she lies turning up to the sun's never failing caress her broad and exuberant breasts, overflowing with milk for her hundred million children." Turner then performs his exegesis on this poetic image: "The frontiersman's dream was prophetic. In spite of his rude, gross nature, this early Western man was an idealist withal. He dreamed dreams and beheld visions. He had . . . unbounded confidence in his ability to make his dreams come true" (p. 69). Unbounded confidence in America's destiny is not something Turner as Jeremiah or as historian can assert after 1890; instead, he can only go back in time in order to dream a future – but more specifically, he can only go back into literary history, make it present in his text, and thereby literarily immortalize an aesthetic image of America and the American. He continues his exegesis in "The Problem of the West" by quoting Harriet Martineau in 1834:

> I regard the American people as a great embryo poet . . . exulting that he has caught the true aspect of things past, and the depth of futurity which lies before him wherein to create something so magnificent as the world has scarcely begun to dream of. There is the strongest hope of a nation that is capable of being possessed with an idea. (p. 69)

One need only recall Turner's undergraduate oration "The Poet of the Future" in 1883 to confirm that Turner's idealism in his maturity was not only long-standing but was derived from poetic desire. Following Martineau's quotation, Turner adds, "It is important to bear this idealism of the West in mind . . . It has been, and is, preeminently a region of ideals, *mistaken or not*" (p. 69, emphasis added).

The elasticity and elusiveness of Turner's frontier that historians have attacked is not only the trope's strength, but is its very subject. Turner admits that the census definition based on density of population per square mile "is an elastic one, and for our purposes does not need sharp definition" (p. 33). In fact it cannot sustain such sharpness. By this definition, there is today plenty of frontier left.[35] Yet this contradiction in Turner's argument has a poetic logic to it: Once the "literal" frontier is seen to vanish or at the least not to refer to a stable object, the figural frontier is freed to achieve an endlessly suggestive significance in American history and culture. Just as Christian allegory claims to touch every corner of the world's text, Turner's frontier touches every corner and state name of what he calls "the fair, blank page" of the American continent or wilderness (p. 93). Turner's similes both naturalize and nationalize that process in a manner that sees nature as the Emersonian correlative of one American spirit: "Moving westward, the frontier became more and more American. As successive terminal moraines result from successive glaciations, so each frontier leaves its traces behind it" (p. 34). While the natural metaphor obscures the role of human agency, so does Turner's personification of the frontier. Like a giant pioneer striding across the continent, the frontier "has leaped over the Alleghenies . . . now it skipped the Great Plains and the Rocky Mountains" (p. 36). More pointedly for its erasure of human agency, Turner writes that the "gifts of free land *offer themselves*" (p. 59, emphasis added). As Limerick describes the

Cumberland Gap passage, "a historical procession led by a large herbi-
vore in search of salt was unlikely to provide the material for a celebration
of the human will and the power of individual choice."[36]

The most prominent metaphor Turner employs to create the sense
of a vital and natural force behind history – and that effectively unifies
American experience – is that of waves to describe both tides of emigrant
pioneers and the successive waves of the frontier process. The frontier
is "the outer edge of the wave – the meeting point between savagery
and civilization" (p. 32), he writes; railroads "sent an increasing tide of
immigrants into the far West" (p. 36). The farmer's advance also came
"in a distinct series of waves" (p. 44). Turner quotes what he calls a
suggestive passage from Peck's *New Guide to the West* in 1837, which describes classes of western settlements: "[T]hree classes, like the waves of
the ocean, have rolled on after the other. First comes the pioneer . . . The
next class of emigrants purchase the lands . . . Another wave rolls on. The
men of capital and enterprise come . . . Thus wave after wave is rolling
westward" (pp. 45–46). The passage in "The Problem of the West" in
which Turner quotes Henry Adams' hypothetical American of 1800 also
shares and reinforces this poetic image: "See my cornfields rustling and
waving in the summer breeze from ocean to ocean" (p. 69). Air, land,
and sea are fused in the image Turner quotes. For Europeans, he asserts,
the frontier extends across the Atlantic ocean to the Atlantic coast and
beyond. In a comparable passage that might suggest both where Turner's
deepest affinities as a writer lie and where Willa Cather might have found
inspiration, Cather's narrator Jim Burden in *My Ántonia* performs a similar poetic fusion of land and sea as agents of movement: "As I looked
about me I felt that the grass was the country, as the water is the sea.
The red of grass made all the great prairie the colour of wine-stains, of
certain seaweeds when they are first washed up. And there was so much
motion in it; the whole country seemed, somehow, to be running." What
the country is running to or away from is the historical question begged
by this compelling image, which has subtle epic overtones in Cather's
use of "wine-stains" that recalls Homer's "wine-dark sea." Turner makes
this epic connection explicit when he compares the significance of the
frontier for America to what the Mediterranean was for the Greeks.

The literary trope of frontier allows Turner to see American sameness
in place of regional difference. But waves are also a synecdoche for the
ocean itself; this trope suits the frontier because it is, like Whitman's
leaves of grass, both particular but also a unified plurality under the
universal and totalizing natural (and national) body. Although Turner

argues that "with all these similarities there are essential differences, due to the place element and the time element" and that "it would be a work of the historian's labors to mark these various frontiers and in detail compare one with another" (pp. 37, 38), this is a work his thesis not only does not perform but resists through its unifying and naturalizing imagery.

What makes Turner's language even more poetic as opposed to descriptive or merely rhetorical is that it imitates the imagery it employs, creating a poetic unity that imitates the frontier's unity. Turner's use of parallel repetitions creates a rhetorical wave effect and welds his rhetoric to his imagery. Carpenter has observed rhetorical parallelism in the following typical passages: "*to the changes* of an expanding people . . . *to the changes* involved in crossing a continent"; "*The exploitations of* the beasts . . . *the exploitations of* the grasses . . . *the exploitation of* the virgin soil"; "*It was western* New York . . . *it was western* Virginia."[37] Style fits content: the repetition of "western" and "exploitation" imitates waving grasses, ocean tides, and the waves of westering. In the Cumberland Gap passage, in which he invites the reader "to stand" and observe the waves of civilization, as if time were condensed or suspended by virtue of rhetorical repetition, Turner achieves a Whitmanian synthesis with his Emersonian eye: "Each passed in successive waves across the continent. *Stand at* Cumberland Gap and watch the procession of civilization . . . *Stand at* South Pass in the Rockies a century later and see the same procession . . ." (p. 39, emphasis added). Through the listing of particulars within parallel repetitions, Turner creates a sense of ultimate unity behind the particular spaces and times of American experience. Like the giant spirit hovering above the continent in "American Progress," Turner's reader is situated above ground and beyond the limitations of the senses and of time. "The influence of the senses," Emerson writes in "The Over-Soul," "has, in most men, overpowered the mind to that degree, that the walls of time and space have come to look real and insurmountable." Like the Emersonian soul, Turner's rhetorical frontier "circumscribes all things . . . contradicts all experience . . . [and] abolishes time and space."[38]

The unified symbol of the frontier's waves nevertheless cannot escape the temporality and difference that returns Turner's thesis to the literary realm of allegory, whose gap between the literal and the figurative – the nostalgic lack with which Turner begins his thesis – resists transcendence. While the imagery of waves suggests that the sea has a unity, like the frontier that is repeated but is always the same, those different particulars, to which Turner refers and that allegory wants to make the same, resist any symbolic totalization and reveal the inherently finite and temporal nature of Turner's interpretive project, as he announces at the close of his thesis. Turner's thesis lacks any self-consciously ironic sense of the distance between representation and experience; he does not call into question the intentionality of his rhetorical figures, since he believed, following Emerson, that those rhetorical figures were manifestations of something immanent and causal in history itself. Natural figures and symbols, according to Emerson, are the correlatives of the one universal mind. In his intention to promote a national self-consciousness that is spiritual, Turner demonstrates what Paul de Man describes as the (ultimately fallible) intentionality of the symbol: "The subjectivity of experience is preserved when it is translated into language; the world is then no longer seen as a configuration of entities that designate a plurality of distinct and isolated meanings, but as a configuration of symbols ultimately leading to a total, single, and universal meaning."[39] The sign of Turner's universal meaning is the frontier that nationalistically unites a configuration of entities, those geographic places and historical moments that are synecdoches designating a symbolic totality – America – of which they are a part. But temporality has crept into his symbolic configuration by virtue of the donnée of his thesis: the finitude of the frontier both as place and process. Turner's thesis wants to rely upon the infinitely suggestive and universalizable symbol of the frontier, but is actually caught in an allegorical rhetoric that is a sign of its own temporal origins, of the historical distance between the frontier and its articulated significance. The philosopher of hermeneutics Hans-Georg Gadamer writes that "Symbol and allegory are opposed as art is to non-art, in that the former seems endlessly suggestive in the indefiniteness of its meaning, whereas the latter, as soon as its meaning is reached, has run its full course."[40] Whereas Turner's historiographical frontier had run its full course once its allegorical meaning was able to be articulated, Turner's symbolic frontier – the vague but popular term that frustrates historians – is today still endlessly suggestive in its cultural meanings; in this sense, Turner prophetically and aesthetically dreamed a past.

The frontier thus becomes, by the end of Turner's argument, a synecdoche for America and its exceptionalism that subsumes all stages of history and creates something new, that synchronically unmoors America from the history of the Old World. Turner argues for American historical exceptionalism through hermeneutic tools that are historically old. This paradox is also revealed in the fact – for Turner a poignant one – that because the frontier is now closed, America has come to resemble the Old World: "We have so far won our national home," he writes in a later text, "wrested from it its first rich treasures and drawn to it the unfortunate of other lands, that we are already obliged to compare ourselves with settled states of the Old World."[41] Although he does not want to be a "rash prophet" in proclaiming American democracy doomed, now that the purported source of that democracy is no more, his thesis structurally suggests democracy more as past dream than as future reality.

For the historical period Turner is describing, of course, democracy was more a promise than a reality for most people in the US, a fact that Turner's insistent dream denies. It is important to keep in mind that Turner's thesis not only claims to read the significance of the frontier *in* American history, but its overriding and pre-eminent significance *for all* of American history. The lack that inaugurates his yearning for lasting significance may be not just the absence of "free" lands but the legal denial to many in American history of what Turner claims those free lands made possible: democracy. The fact that Turner argues explicitly against slavery as the defining feature of American history suggests the possibility that what Turner's thesis denies serves to fuel the democratic dream. Where slavery proves democracy's failure, in other words, the frontier provides for Turner another chance at its realization. In this sense, his thesis broadly regionalizes America in order to claim the western region as the greatest force in American history and the forger of American character. Only by incorporating what Turner wants to exclude from the frame of his thesis can we understand his poetics as not just a love of the literary and the sign of Emersonian idealism but as an ideological need, which history calls into being.

In the second paragraph of the thesis, Turner writes, "The *true point of view* in the history of this nation is not the Atlantic coast, it is the great West. Even the slavery struggle, which is made so exclusive an object of attention by writers like Prof. von Holst, occupies its important place in American history because of its relation to westward expansion" (p. 32, emphasis added). Later he argues that "the legislation which most developed the powers of the National Government, and played the largest part in its activity, was conditioned on the frontier. Writers have discussed the subjects of tariff, land, and internal improvement, as subsidiary to the slavery question. But when American history comes to be *rightly* viewed it will be seen that the slavery question is an *incident*" (p. 48, emphasis added). After his third and final reference to slavery, in which he claims that "slavery was a sectional trait that would not be put down, but in the West it could not remain sectional," he then claims Lincoln for the West: "It was the greatest of frontiersmen who declared: 'I believe this Government can not endure permanently half slave and half free. It will become all of one thing or all of the other' " (p. 53). The West's sectional difference, Turner implies, preserved national unity.

The history of American colonialism and imperialism that Turner represses in his thesis emerges in the imaginary forms he claims democracy achieved on the frontier and in the "safety-valve" theory of the frontier's socio-economic function. Even the diction in Turner's formulations – the idea that the frontier provided a "gate of escape from the bondage of the past" and that on the frontier "the bonds of custom" are temporarily broken (p. 59) – suggests an inverted or repressed allegory of the dominant strain in American history he argues against. Turner's trope of the frontier both subsumes and figuratively resolves social anxieties for Americans and thus "works to hold us together"[42] – or more precisely it holds Americans together by occluding what has torn them apart, especially the legacies of slavery and Indian conquest that Turner misrepresents, insistently downplays, or ignores. These historical repressions inaugurate the frontier's future as both richly pliable symbol and debunked history. The rhetorical frontier has itself operated culturally as Turner claimed the actual frontier had operated economically. It has remained a "gate of escape" from the bondage of racial and economic conflicts and anxieties that remain. The frontier continues to have a recapitulatory power in its culturally symbolic reincarnations.

The word frontier will continue to mean something as long as Americans want to give history a nationalist meaning, a very different enterprise from locating nationalism in history. Even when that national meaning shifts from Turner's ideologically conservative, white backwoodsman to the idea of multiculturalism – a concept arguably as vague and open-ended as Turner's frontier – historical experience is mediated through a rhetorical hermeneutic. It may be that Turner was more self-consciously aware of this fact, albeit with an uncritical faith in what it meant, than many revisionists are today, who nevertheless adopt literary models. Indeed, the "tragic" view of new western historians, a counterbalance to the frontier thesis that is therefore ineluctably shaped as a reaction to Turner's more optimistic story, equally relies upon narrative and rhetorical strategies to make its "historical" case. As Kerwin Lee Klein observes, "There is a Turnerian connection between Emerson's cry for a poem of America that could transpose our barbarous folk symbols into an allegory of democracy, and our current valorization

of our new histories as politically correct literary forms... these tales
have written us, as we have written them, and so we cannot simply will-
fully replace science with literature or irony with metaphor or comedy
with tragedy or democracy with holocaust," because they *collectively* explain how Americans have come to imagine themselves and the past.[43]
Yet Turner's poetic does not merely demonstrate the poetic structure
of all language and narrative, as Hayden White has argued – though
that is to demonstrate quite a lot. Within this structuralist view, all histories are then essentially poetic constructions of meaning with ideological
implications that are no more verifiably true or false than another.[44]
Western historians working in the last few decades to correct Turner
would vigorously assert the empirical, documented basis for their revi-
sions. In a paper entitled "Literary History and Historical Literature,"
Myra Jehlen takes Carlo Ginzburg, as opposed to Hayden White, "as a
guide in seeking historical truth while recognizing it is unattainable, as a
goal that assists our achieving as much of it as possible... I do maintain
that in accounts of the past, bringing slavery to the fore or the anni-
hilation of the Indians or the abuse of women, is a corrective."[45] As
much recent western historical writing demonstrates, historical particulars ought to condition how we read nationally universalist narratives,
rather than the reverse. Yet while recent paradigms such as "borders"
are more inclusive historically of the non-white, non-American experience Turner leaves out, their applicability can nevertheless be so broad
as to risk becoming analytically too abstract to be useful.[46] Indeed, if
one thinks about borders in American culture today, they seem to be
everywhere.

And so did the frontier seem to Turner. Turner's frontier thesis
persists culturally along with the search for national meaning. Turner
located this meaning in a spatio-temporal, moving site whose circum-
ference was nowhere but whose center was everywhere, to borrow
Augustine's description of God. Today the search for that site of revisionist meaning is as inescapably linguistic and cognitive as it was
for Turner, but we try to take more responsibility for our tropes and
figural language, acknowledging the recalcitrant particulars and the
historical Real around which we construct them. Our metaphors may
be more inclusive paradigmatically of actual historical experience, and
therefore in some sense more true or more accurate, but their explanatory power is always limited by what makes them possible: the desire,
through language, meaningfully and truthfully to incorporate the ultimately incalculable totality of past human experience – or in the case

of Frederick Jackson Turner's frontier thesis, to give significance to a frontier democracy that may never have been what Americans may dream.

It was left to subsequent writers to re-imagine the dream Turner figured. Fitzgerald's Nick Carraway in *The Great Gatsby* describes a man whose dream is, like Turner's, as elusive as it has proven enduring, and a future that "year by year recedes before us": "His dream must have seemed so close that he could hardly fail to grasp it. He did not know that it was already behind him, somewhere back in that vast obscurity beyond the city, where the dark fields of the republic rolled on under the night." By condensing its procession of civilization and rhetorically conflating time and space, Turner's frontier recedes year after revisionist year before us yet it remains, like literature itself, always open before us for the reading.

A Romantic rather than a realist, albeit one haunted by the sense of an ending his allegorical story inscribed, Turner participated in a common nostalgia for a story of American development that seemed unavailable in the early twentieth century to Americans who yearned for the putative "spirit" of the past as counterbalance both to the past's violent "letter" and to the quotidian letter of the present. In "Turnerians All," Limerick corrects the balance between the Turner of the Frontier Thesis and the Turner of what she calls the Frontier Antithesis – those numerous but scattered moments in Turner's work that resist the romance and synthesis of the frontier's past alchemy, moments in which Turner more realistically re-imagined the role of Indians, the frontier's non-exceptionalist nature and its comparative interest, the role of the federal government, and the problem of environmental degradation. As if acknowledging the very limits of the grand significance he assigned the frontier, Turner wrote, "Generalizations . . . upon the West as a whole are apt to be misleading."[47] Given especially Turner's "repeated declarations that our understanding of the past must adapt to changes in the present, it was . . . a deeply ironic choice" for Turner, according to Limerick, to withhold publicly his growing reconsiderations about the frontier.[48] And it is her own reconsiderations that she puts on display in "Turnerians All," while putting herself in the title's collective.

In her essay, Limerick quotes Turner in 1891 on historical dynamics and the relation between the past and present. I excerpt this passage and Limerick's succeeding interpretation in their entirety as a way of charting the dynamics of this book's literary history and of demonstrating what is at stake in thinking about literature and the writing of history in tandem, as this chapter has begun to do. After describing Turner's faith at the time in presentism, Limerick cites a passage in his essay "The Significance of History."

> The aim of history, then, is to know the elements of the present by understanding what came into the present from the past. For the present is simply the developing past, the past the undeveloped present . . . The antiquarian strives to bring back the past for the sake of the past; the historian strives to show the present to itself by revealing its origins from the past. The goal of the antiquarian is the dead past; the goal of the historian is the living present.[49]

Limerick then provides this reading:

> The true Turnerians, one could conclude from this memorable passage, were the historians who paid attention to, and put into practice, Turner's 1891 declaration of the need for writers of history to rethink and revise. The Turnerians who stayed loyal, instead, to the 1893 Frontier thesis observed the letter and defied the spirit of Turnerian history. But there was the puzzle again: by this categorization, Turner was both true Turnerian and so-called Turnerian, at once a person paying attention to his times and insisting that historical models must be constantly remodeled in response to changing conditions, and a person repeating old formulas that could no longer fit those changing times.[50]

Limerick uses the language of Christian allegory to describe her allegorical dualism: the "true" Turnerians followed the spirit, not the letter; the injunction to revise, not the thesis. In imitating the binaries that Turner establishes – historian/antiquarian, the living present/the dead past – Limerick's "exegesis" repeats the letter or the formula, but not the spirit, ironically, of Turner's 1891 declaration, in which his faith in the *immanent* allegorical relation between past and present (or indeed between historical events and the "spirit" of their overarching and contiguous significance) is clearly apparent, even as its "truth" may not be apparent to us. To hear the foreignness of Turner's rhetorical ideas, a historian would be wise to attend to how its rhetorical dualisms, parallelism, and chiasmi bespeak a dialectical sense of immanent historical forces, those very "forces" that Limerick insists are not real but can yet bruise us. Failing to attend to these rhetorical structures, and unselfconsciously repeating them in a way that marks the self's practice as "true" to the "spirit" of Turner, one can indeed get bruised, for the assignment of "the letter" to "the thesis" misses the spirit not only of the thesis, but of "spirit" and "significance" for Turner. Turner's revised significance becomes significance-for-us. Yet, paradoxically, as this chapter has aimed to demonstrate, we can productively approach the internal "life" of the frontier thesis from the vantage point of the so-called antiquarian, for whom the literary past is not a dead letter.

But the "puzzle" Limerick draws attention to – that Turner was both himself and not himself on Turnerian matters – is, as Mark Twain might put it, "a conundrum worth investigating." For it is precisely ambivalent stances, however resolved or left to stand in their glaring contradictions, that have an ongoing "life" in just about every book this study examines, especially with regard to formal narrative choices that are often divided in their aims – ambivalent stances toward the western past and the American present, toward Romanticism and realism, nostalgia, violence, and marriage. Indeed, as we will see, beginning with Owen Wister, marriage was often the literary vehicle by means of which writers, after Turner, not only re-imagined the West's significance but imagined the relation between (or divorced) the past and the present, the West and America – if only because the marital "union" can never synthesize two people. If the frontier's significance produced, in Turner's thesis, that historiographical fallacy called "American character," in western fiction that "character," like history itself, proves far more complex – and at least as contradictory as Limerick's description of Turner himself – than the historian could have imagined.

# CHAPTER THREE

# Marrying for race and nation: Wister's omniscience and omissions

> If men and women do not marry, and if there are not sufficient children to a marriage, the race will in a short time vanish – surely any one can see this... [T]here is no form of happiness on the earth, no form of success of any kind, that in any way approaches the happiness of the husband and wife who are married lovers and the father and mother of plenty of healthy children.[1]
>
> Theodore Roosevelt, 1911

> [N]othing would have induced me to unite him to the little Vermont person... I wouldn't have let him live & be happy; I should have made him perish in his flower & in some splendid and somber way.[2]
>
> Henry James to Owen Wister, responding to the ending of *The Virginian*

Owen Wister was not a very happy man. Yet his most famous novel, *The Virginian*, has a happy ending: the nomadic, bachelor cowboy known as the Virginian gets married to his sweetheart from Vermont, Molly. Wister wrote to his mother shortly after *The Virginian* appeared that the novel's " 'whole raison d'être' " was its " 'nationality.' "[3] With this sense of national consequence, the novel is plot-driven to the altar of marriage. Regionally identified with New England and the South, Molly Stark and the Virginian marry out West in Wyoming, and their union caps, among other things, the novel's extended polemic about the state of democracy in the American Union. It is specifically in the marriage plot of *The Virginian*, in which the hero must make difficult choices both to prove his character and ultimately to be made suitable and irresistible to Molly – with her implicit threat to traditional marriage as a single, New Woman trying to make it alone on the frontier – that Wister formulates, or rather reformulates, the meaning of democracy and American character.[4] In Wister's view, men are created unequally at birth and those of "quality" (among a restricted category of Anglo-Saxons) have a democratic opportunity to prove their superiority over those born without it, those he dismissively calls "the equality" or the masses clamoring for artificial rights. As Richard Slotkin has argued, "Wister's 'democracy' thus provides a biosocial rationale for class privilege." The Virginian's courtship of Molly "is played out as an ideological dialogue" in which the Virginian tries to persuade her to alter her belief in equality and to see democracy, like her classroom of unequally talented students, as "the means through which a naturally qualified ruling class can make its way to the top."[5] In a chapter that follows the Virginian's ventriloquizing the same views in his argument with Molly, Wister's narrator argues that with the Declaration of Independence, "we Americans acknowledged the *eternal inequality* of man . . . By this very decree we acknowledged and gave freedom to true aristocracy, saying, 'Let the best man win, whoever he is.' "[6] Wister omits his belief that only Anglo-Saxon men need sign up for the contest.

As was the case for Frederick Jackson Turner, for Owen Wister – in the 1890s, at least – the frontier had greater significance in American history with regard to the fate of democracy than slavery, the Civil War, and Emancipation. Yet there are significant differences between Wister and the historian whose frontier thesis has often been compared to *The Virginian*. Whereas Turner is not sure what guarantee there could be for democracy once the frontier, which was its engine, is gone, Wister implicitly finds democracy's perpetuation in the reproduction of a racial type. More significantly, whereas Turner's frontier thesis is an act of denial about the corruption of democracy by slavery and an act of hope that the frontier *made* democracy and enabled the North's victory, Wister nostalgically wants his imaginary frontier in *The Virginian* to undo the transforming effects of Emancipation upon the meaning of democracy and racial equality. *The Virginian* is Wister's response to the leveling implications of the Gettysburg address, his emancipation of the Anglo-Saxon from Lincoln's racially more inclusive sense of the equality of men.

It proved to be a difficult task. The depression and "neurasthenia" that this progenitor of the Western suffered much of his life, which prevented him from being "husband, father, or author with any persistence," arguably suggest the personal cost Wister paid for living with competing beliefs, desires, and responsibilities.[7] What prevented Wister from being father or husband with consistency was, in part, his extended periods of seclusion in order to recuperate: "I must have this sort of thing periodically as I suffer in some spiritual way," he wrote to his wife.[8] The deep resentment he bore against those social and economic groups that deprived his class of its former pre-eminence also bears an informing relation to a pervading sense of dissatisfaction in his life that was as idiosyncratically psychological and emotional as it was bluntly political. Such powerful emotions, of nostalgia for past happiness and of bitter reaction against the present, emerge in Wister's most famous novel in a series of affective divides among sentimentalized romance, angry polemic, and withheld scenes of violence. These disjunctions produce a narrative far more complicated in its formal methods and thematic effects than most critics have recognized.

While the novel is at the most basic level the story of the cowboy hero's courtship of Molly and his defeat of his enemies, three unnamed figures play an important role in the narrative structure: the authorial voice, the first-person narrator, and the reader, whom the author addresses; only the first-person narrator is a character. The author's intermittent addresses to the reader remind us why this hero has a national importance. *The Virginian* figures the reader implicitly as feminine – as one who, like Molly, cannot see how democracy is about natural born "quality" as opposed to equality and who is courted to fall in love with the cowboy hero. For the novel to work on both a polemical and an emotional level, the feminized reader must effectively consent to her own inferiority. Yet the polemicizing narrator who courts us is also suggestively feminized by his attraction to the Virginian. To the extent he is aligned with Wister himself, this bachelor narrator reveals how ambivalent Wister was about fulfilling the heterosexual marriage plot. While the frontier purportedly produced its greatest character traits precisely without women, *The Virginian* needs feminized figures (Molly, the narrator, and the reader) to consent to the romance and perpetuate its hero's values. There is thus a telling paradox in Wister's figuration both of the reader and of the Virginian's masculinity. Wister's social ideology stands against majority views, those of the "bystanders" or the "equality," and yet his narrative depends upon bystanders (the narrator and the reader) in order to form a consensus about the Virginian's heroism. The Virginian's quality, in other words, is like the tree falling in the forest: it needs ears (and hearts) to sound its virile heroism. Indeed, his "independent" value depends upon Molly's, the narrator's, and the reader's romantic attraction to him and deference to his authority. Yet deference to feminine sensibility is one reason why the narrator selectively withholds vision of the violence involved in building the Virginian's character, particularly in a scene in which the narrator is present but refuses to watch the lynching of Steve, but gives us a vision of the honeymoon, a scene in which the narrator-as-character is entirely absent. The novel caters to a sensibility figured as feminine while denigrating it at the same time.

After seeking the Virginian's approval and intimate confidence throughout the novel, the narrator is left to play voyeur on the Virginian's honeymoon in the form of an omniscient narrator. On the honeymoon, the Virginian sees a small animal (a beaver) and imagines that it asks him, " 'What's the gain in being a man?' " He adds, "But . . . the trouble is, I am responsible. If that could only be forgot forever by you and me!" (p. 425). Addressed to Molly, the Virginian's words are curious, since she does not have to assume the responsibilities of being a man. They might as well be addressed, as so many of his most intimate confidences elsewhere are, to the second person missing from the scene, the narrator. It is as if Molly has taken the narrator's place at the moment when the Virginian questions the masculine aims the novel everywhere else supports. Once he is married, that is, the Virginian calls into question the gendered difference that otherwise drives this marriage plot. At one brief, but key, culminating moment, Wister seems to doubt the gendered grounds upon which his novel stands, as if he would take the formula out of the Western genre he was to shape.

Why would Wister give his novel an ending that its masculine ethos does not require? Wister's wish to perpetuate his racial beliefs informs the novel's ending as much as the conventional sentimental reconciliation that, as Christine Bold argues, authors of popular Westerns exploited after Cooper.[9] The "bachelor" West that Owen Wister celebrated and literarily memorialized was for him a double-edged sword. It created the true American and represented the greatest happiness he had personally known, yet the brief era of the cowpuncher was ineluctably supplanted by the national imperatives of family and civilization, the very responsibilities which Wister's literary hero momentarily longs to escape on his honeymoon and which Theodore Roosevelt – to whom Wister dedicated *The Virginian* while Roosevelt was president – considered the subject upon which any other subject's importance absolutely depended.[10] "Wilful sterility" in marriage was for Roosevelt "the capital sin, the cardinal sin, against the race and against civilization," one he ranked as "not one whit better than polygamy,"[11] because marriage had not only no virtue without reproduction but corrupted the meaning of both marriage and the civilization of which it was the cornerstone. It is in regard to the assured perpetuation of racial traits that on the last page of the novel, Molly's great-aunt, the Yankee matriarch, tells Molly and the Virginian that she will have the nursery ready for their next visit: "And so it happened that before she left this world, the great-aunt was able to hold in her arms the first of their many children" (p. 434). By this ending, Wister figures the perpetuation, through marriage and procreation, of the sense of innate superiority that was born on the all-male, individualistic frontier – all for the sake of his version of American democracy.

Yet Wister's anti-democratic sentiment was as much a reaction against his bitter nostalgia for a romantic life he could not claim for himself as it was a reaction against his class's loss of power; his longings for the nomadic, bachelor West were in conflict with the national imperative of marriage. The imperatives of convention are transmitted, according to Wister, by "bystanders," which include those reading masses who made him a success. Yet insofar as his bachelor narrator speaks for him, Wister was also such a bystander, courting and denigrating himself at the same time in order to marry his notions of Anglo-Saxon superiority to heterosexuality for the sake of American democracy. If the honeymoon scene reveals the price of being a (national) hero, that price, for this novel, is the affective gulf between marrying for love and marrying for race and nation. While the Virginian's marriage would seem to domesticate him, it is more accurate to say that domesticity allows the masculine individual to fulfill imperial imperatives – and at the expense of personal longing. Wister married off his hero not because he romanticized marriage in any private sense (his parents' marriage alone gave him little reason to) but because there would be a diminished national significance to what the frontier produced if it could not be reproduced.[12]

This chapter looks at how Wister's retrospective longings and conflicted points of view affected his narrative methods. The divide between a romanticized "nomadic, bachelor" West and the responsibilities of the "housed, married West" was never emotionally (or even literarily) bridged by Wister, and in *The Virginian* it shows. Not only is the most sustained romantic devotion in the novel the eastern tenderfoot narrator's toward the Virginian, but the most genuine, poignant emotion is reserved for the Virginian's feelings for his fellow nomad (gone bad) Steve, whom, in the name of honor, he hangs for stealing cattle. His honeymoon with Molly, in contrast, has the feeling of a hypertrophied sentimentalism. Molly functions in a political endgame in which the personal is sacrificed and violently silenced. That the novel's ending questions the masculinist aims that undergird the novel's nationalism is not surprising when one considers that there is a divorce throughout the novel between private affect and national imperative – or between the personal and the political. This divorce mirrors the formal division of the novel between first-person narrative and forms of omniscience. Wister's ideology – his subordination of the lower classes, women, and non-Anglo-Saxons to a select, naturally aristocratic class of Anglo-Saxon men – is most broadly understood as a reactionary response to the decline of his class and the rise of labor, immigrant classes, and the newly wealthy. What has not been given sufficient critical attention are the affective disjunctions and formal narrative problems regarding point of view that result when he translates his ideology into fiction. "Point of view," understood narratively and politically, is key to understanding how the narrative structure of the novel works in consort with Wister's ideological beliefs. Even though the novel's narrative structure is the result of Wister's botched attempt to make his previous short stories cohere into a novel and even if he had succeeded in creating a more consistent narrative voice, the narrator-author's intrusions in the text – when he addresses the reader not only in the preface but at critical junctures in the novel – yet make narrative fiction serve fictionalized polemic.[13] Wister's narrative methods enact by proxy the presumptuousness of his elsewhere more explicitly racial ideas, ideas that propel the marriage plot and turn that plot into national allegory. The inconsistency of those methods exacts an aesthetic cost to the novel's formal and affective integrity related to the social costs, and arguably for him the personal costs, of Wister's ideology.

The greatest paradox of *The Virginian*'s fate in literary history and popular culture is that, even more than is the case with Turner's frontier, it should be so embraced in a democratic society as if in inverse proportion to the narrowness of its author's racial ideology. Soon after the novel was published in 1902, writes Wister's biographer, the author "was the idol of the popular crowd which he so disdained."[14] Wister's Anglo-Saxon racism is not, as Jane Tompkins writes, "spelled out in capital letters" in the novel.[15] It is spelled out, however, in his earlier essay "The Evolution of the Cow-puncher" (1895) and in his subsequent novel *Lady Baltimore* (1906), which drove Theodore Roosevelt to write a scathing fourteen-page response to Wister on White House stationery.[16] That novel romanticized the southern aristocracy and denigrated the innate intelligence of African Americans (both aspects drawing attack from Roosevelt) after Wister grew disenchanted with the West because he saw it as a seedbed for populism. Even by the time *The Virginian* appeared, its author had moved on: having romanticized the West because it had nothing to do with his upbringing in the eastern establishment against which he briefly rebelled, he then romanticized the South of his slave-holding ancestors.[17]

In part because the marriage plot serves the novel's underlying polemic, the ending has struck many readers and critics as forced and overly sentimental – even as a "betrayal" of the myth of the bachelor cowboy hero that the Virginian otherwise embodies.[18] Henry James told Wister that his one, perhaps "perverse," reservation about the novel was the happy ending, in the epigraph above: "I should have made [the Virginian] perish in his flower & in some splendid and somber way."[19] In addition to thinking the heroine a failure, Wister's mother complained that the last chapter about the couple's honeymoon and future married life was "superfluous," and Wister agreed in part with both claims, but insisted, "I should write it the same way over again."[20] While Tompkins argues that the Western excludes everything domestic from its worldview, she reads *The Virginian* as a complicated case that "states so openly the counterargument to its own point of view" when the Virginian, on his honeymoon, questions the purpose of masculinity.[21]

At the beginning of the novel, the Virginian asks another question related to his last one: "What's the use o' being married?" This question, in the opening chapter "Enter the Man," is to be expected of the bachelor cowboy, yet the scene actually ridicules not marriage per se but marriage for such unsuitables as Uncle Hughey. The scene effectively points to the superior suitability, when the time will come, of the Virginian's own marriage. The novel is thus framed by the Virginian's two questions, one that would seem to question marriage and the other that calls into question the aims of masculinity that make the Virginian's marriage socially valuable, as he goes on to become a member of the corporate class.[22] One way to answer the novel's framing questions is to look beyond the man to the future nation that Wister wants him to figure. The personal sacrifices in assuming the responsibilities of being a man and of marrying are justified, for Wister, by their capacity to reframe the meaning of democracy through the ascendancy (and continued descendants) of a new, naturally aristocratic class.

Metaphors of germination and birth mark Wister's view of how "quality" finds expression over against the "equality." What is key about the West's relation to natural, born quality, for Wister, is that, as a laboratory for shaping and testing character, the environment will benefit only those born with the right qualities. While the natural aristocrat can adapt to changing conditions, his ability to adapt is innate or natural, not acquired. In the year *The Virginian* appeared, Wister made this point explicitly in his essay "The Open-Air Education," in which he cites the case of a farmer's boy "from good rustic stock" who is sent away from home for "a little cowboy life in the healing air of the West" but who, unlike the well-born Wister, quickly cries for home and leaves. "Open-air education could not make a man of this luckless weakling, because there was no man in him to make. I am afraid that men, like poets, must be born so ... We may be sure that nothing ever comes out of a person save that which was originally in him ... Books, travel, open air, all these things are merely fertilizers and if there is no seed in the field no sprouts will appear."[23]

One sign of the Virginian's innate superiority is his ability to adapt to the new conditions of the West to which he has migrated. It is essential not only that he has come from somewhere else, but that he derives from a state associated, as Slotkin points out, with a natural aristocracy.[24] To be equal to any situation, in other words, is to prove one's quality over the equality – the urban masses but also the eastern establishment that is, precisely, *too* established in its ways. In this sense, the narrator-as-tenderfoot at the novel's beginning is Wister's self-indictment of his eastern self before he learned to shoot a bear or sleep under the stars. Arguably the Virginian's most significant adaptation, however, especially as it separates him from the bachelor narrator, is his final willingness to marry. A foreshadowing of the novel's marriage plot constitutes the first chapter of the novel, in which the Virginian's first words, as he teases Uncle Hughey for his repeated marriages, are an interdiction against such a plot and set the stage for his final adaptation to new conditions: "Off to get married *again*? Oh, don't!" (p. 3) "It ain't again," says Uncle Hughey. "Who says it's again? Who told you anyway?" The Virginian replies, "Why, your Sunday clothes told me, Uncle Hughey. They are speakin' mighty loud o' nuptials [...] Ain't them gloves the same yu' wore to your last weddin'?" (p. 3). At this point, the narrator steps out to the rail platform to see the man he overhears and whose story he will narrate. It is the narrator's first act of courtship, serving as mediator between the reader's and (later) Molly's desires for the irresistible Virginian. In this mediation, the narrator's attraction feminizes him when translated heterosexually.

Lounging there at ease against the wall was a slim young giant, more beautiful than pictures ... Had I been the bride, I should have taken the giant, dust and all.

He had by no means done with the old man.

"Why, yu've hung weddin' gyarments on every limb!" he now drawled, with admiration. "Who is the lucky lady this trip?"

The old man seemed to vibrate. "Tell you there ain't been no other! Call me a Mormon, would you? ... Then name some of my wives. Name two. Name one. Dare you!" (p. 4)

The Virginian then demonstrates his adroitness at humiliating an old man of legendary unsuitability for marriage by raising a litany of tall tales about canceled engagements: to a woman whose doctor ordered a Southern climate; to one who got hanged; to one who got married to someone else the day before Hughey was to wed her; to one who claimed to have lost her memory. Uncle Hughey can only defend himself by saying, " 'Where's the wives in all this? Show the wives!' " In another attempt to defend his failure to make it to the altar, he reverses the national argument for procreation and grumbles, "This country's getting full of kids . . . It's doomed" (p. 5). The Virginian finally urges him,

"Oh, don't get married again, Uncle Hughey! What's the use o' being married?"
"What's the use?" echoed the bridegroom, with scorn. "Hm! When you grow up you'll think different."
"Course I expect to think different when my age is different." (p. 6)

The Virginian, who warns Trampas in the next chapter to smile when Trampas insults him, knows how to leaven his jibes with humor. More importantly, he knows how he will change his own mind about marriage, as one who adapts to new conditions. Tucked into this dialogue is the surest evidence that he will: the narrator's profession of seduction by this giant "more beautiful than pictures." *Had I been the bride*: by this claim, the narrator seduces the feminized reader as the Virginian will seduce Molly. Contrasted with the litany of women who found it all too easy to resist Uncle Hughey, the narrator's assertion of a helplessness saved only by his gender situates the Virginian's marriage to Molly as something beyond free choice, in the realm of an imperative. It will constitute a forced choice in the manner that Wister's evolutionary model for the cow-puncher is, in the socially Darwinian sense, inevitably foreordained by that which "slumbers" in the Anglo-Saxon.

As author, Wister not only orchestrates the nationally symbolic union between his characters, but also carries the affective investment in the novel's marriage plot as the eastern, tenderfoot narrator he so closely resembles. The narrator is more memorable than the Virginian's love interest precisely because he is won over by the Virginian from the beginning. He is the affective gauge that tells us Molly is next. Much of the novel involves the narrator's gradual coming-to-equality with this man of quality, proving his worth to the Virginian over time, by learning when to speak and when not to, for example, or how not to show fear. The narrator is not so much the eastern, aristocratic arbiter of superiority, as Slotkin suggests, as he is the Virginian's tutee in naturally aristocratic behavior.[25]

Yet the elision of author and narrator makes that distinction moot. More and more, as the narrator omnisciently narrates the Virginian's story and as the Virginian ventriloquizes the narrator/Wister's views, the bearer of innate superiority and the tutee of that superiority mutually constitute each other and become ideologically indistinguishable.

The narrator provides erotic descriptions of the Virginian that have no equivalent in his descriptions of Molly. For this reason, Forrest Robinson has called the narrator "Molly's leading, if unannounced, competitor in love."[26] Many critics have commented on these passages in which the narrator compares the cowboy's movement to "the undulations of a tiger, smooth and easy, as if his muscles flowed beneath the skin" (p. 2) and in which he says he has "never seen a creature more irresistibly handsome" (p. 212). Indeed, the romantic ardor he feels for the Virginian is translated in heterosexual terms: "Had I been a woman, it would have made me his to do what he pleased with on the spot" (pp. 215–216). The narrator twice reminds the reader that he is not a woman. Robinson argues that the narrator "envies Molly her triumph, and . . . his envy, in turn, flows into and informs the management and tone of his narrative."[27] Indeed, his envy sends him voyeuristically to the couple's honeymoon, in abrogation of his fictional self: the narrator bleeds into author in an excess of vision.

As we have seen, during the honeymoon, though it is mandated by a heterosexual plot, the Virginian questions the very imperatives that sent him there: "What's the gain in being a man?" The Virginian's unexpected question and desires on the honeymoon have been interpreted as a wish to return to innocence or to an earth-mother, a wish that verges toward oblivion as the Virginian desires "to become the ground, become the water, become the trees, mix with the whole thing. Not know myself from it. Never unmix again." Looking at Molly, he demands: "Why is that?" (pp. 425–426). What he questions, tellingly, is the gendered structure of human identity and relations. The passage reveals more than just the price of being a hero or the desire to become a little boy again. Having finally acceded to marriage, the Virginian expresses a wish to lose *all* human and sexual identity in his wish "never to unmix again" from an undifferentiated natural world. The natural order, however, is the model for the Virginian's socially Darwinian evolution as a cowpuncher who has had his Anglo-Saxon blood awakened in him on the frontier. Having finally mated with his suitable counterpart, then, the Virginian seems to relinquish the evolutionary fight, much like Edna Pontellier at the end of Kate Chopin's *The Awakening*. And like Chopin's heroine, the Virginian seems to want to escape the imperatives of gender roles, domesticity, and civilization. But whereas Edna's escape is from marriage, the Virginian escapes into it. The innate ability to adapt to the imperatives of civilization, the honeymoon suggests, has its (natural) limits.

While Wister succeeds on the level of plot in wedding the North and the South after the Virginian's courtship of Molly, the emotional believability of that marriage depends upon the success of the narrator's courtship of the reader. Slotkin argues that the courtship structure defines the hero's relations with the male narrator, who must be won over by the Virginian's superiority.[28] Yet the crucial courtship that supersedes even that one in importance is between the narrator and the reader. The reader is an explicit figure that the narrator often addresses, breaking away from his role as a character. What interests me is not so much the fact that the Virginian courts Molly to share what is essentially Wister's point of view, but Wister's attempt to court the reader, a reader he simultaneously figures as someone too unthinking to see things as they are: "Forgive my asking you to use your mind. It is a thing which no novelist should expect of his reader," he interjects at one point (p. 372). Whereas Turner's rhetoric asks the reader to "stand and watch" the procession of civilization over two centuries, the genre of the novel creates problems for that kind of historical sweep, given the need for particular characters and settings. Yet in an effort comparable in its visionary ambition to Turner's, Wister situates himself as first-person narrator, third-person limited and omniscient narrator, and as author. The reader is thus oriented to points of view that feel authoritative individually, but that collectively undermine the novel's persuasiveness and produce telling elisions and blind spots, especially regarding the moments of violence that Wister's ideology ultimately makes recourse to, as Lee Mitchell has explored.[29] While *The Virginian*, like any novel, depends upon imaginative energy and a capacity to bring things to vision, Wister presumes that most of his readers naturally do not have clear eyesight. The novel's values can only be seen as true, in a self-reinforcing way, by those with the natural eyes to see them as true. And yet the novel vies for the reader's consent as few novels do.

Wister did not just admire Roosevelt; he desired his presidential powers. Omniscience in *The Virginian*, while incompatible with first-person narration, acts as the wishful literary equivalent of executive power or of the presidential bully-pulpit. "Let the best man win! That is America's word. That is true democracy. And true democracy and true aristocracy are one and the same thing. If anybody cannot see this, so much worse for his eyesight" (p. 125), the narrator polemically explicates for the author, with a force like that of Roosevelt (who writes, "surely anyone can see this" in the first epigraph above). "If anybody cannot see this": the political presumption here is inseparable from the narrative presumption involved in a first-person narrator who often reports on things he cannot have seen or heard in his role as a character. It is that overtly polemical nature of the novel – with the voices of narrator and author blending indistinguishably into each other – that damages the literary quality of the novel even as it authorizes its national allegory, rededicated as it was in 1911 "to the greatest benefactor we people have known since Lincoln," Theodore Roosevelt.

The narrator of *The Virginian* shares with other first-person narrators or central characters in this study – Cather's Jim Burden and Niel Herbert, for example, or Fitzgerald's Nick Carraway and Stegner's Lyman Ward – a position of bachelorhood, divorce, or marital unhappiness that produces an almost voyeuristic investment in others' marriages, marriages loaded with western significance. Unlike Cather, Fitzgerald, and Stegner, however, Wister lacks any self-consciousness about the distinction between his role as author and narrator. In his address "To the Reader" before the novel, Wister describes his relationship to his fictional creation with a paternal simile that suggests just how personal this fiction is: "Sometimes readers inquire, Did I know the Virginian? As well, I hope, as a father should know his son" (p. xi). The simile is apt: Wister transformed his bachelor days into literary offspring, a transformation not unlike that of the Virginian's transition between his former love for his best friend Steve and his subsequent devotion to Molly, with whom he will have "many children." The author's giving birth to his literary creation fulfills in a different form Roosevelt's imperative to perpetuate the race and its civilized values. In the same year that Roosevelt published "Race Decadence," in which he praises the happiness of marriage and family in the epigraph above, Wister published a collection of his Western tales that he titled *Members of the Family* – the family, that is, of his western offspring.

Wister's use of a procreative simile to describe his relationship to the real-life figure of the Virginian publicly heterosexualizes a same-sex friendship characterized by romantic ardor. The depth and quality of the author's affections for other men – and of one man's affections for Wister – are apparent in his biography. This deep emotional core in Wister's life helps to explain how his fiction works narratively and why his ideology splits the differences among love, responsibility, justice, and violence in the cause of national and heterosexual imperatives. As Krista

Comer has argued, if *The Virginian* "consolidates the new twentieth-century heterosexual imperative, it also consolidates the struggle *against* that imperative," or at least suggests such a struggle.[30] The unsatisfying, sentimental resolution of *The Virginian* resolves things both personally and politically for Wister. While the Virginian commits acts of violence explicitly against Molly's wishes, she is only the ostensible, and hetero-sexualized, figure of capitulation before the hero's sense of moral imperative. The others are Wister himself and the reader he figures. Seeming archetypically to support the cause of patriarchal honor and marriage, violence between men and conflict between a man and a woman in this novel serve alike to keep love between men just out of sight, that which falls outside of heterosexual marriage and the national cause of reproduction, as the Virginian on his honeymoon by implication longs to escape.

Wister weds marriage and nation in his novel and beliefs only insofar as he keeps from readers' immediate view what he sacrifices on the altar of Western marriage for the sake of national significance. For Wister, such sacrifice likely involved the repression of something between homosocial desire and same-sex love. It is unlikely that, even if Wister had not killed off these feelings but "gotten to know himself," as Jane Tompkins wryly puts it, either in Europe studying music or among his fellow nomadic, bachelor cowboys, he would have ultimately avoided the "housed, married" life he came to know.[31] Evidence of Wister's desires for the same sex has primarily been located in those textual moments when the narrator, with whom the author aligns himself, describes the Virginian's beauty or imagines himself as a woman easily seduced by him. Tompkins and Blake Allmendinger also read this possibility into the special relationship between the Virginian and his friend Steve, who is the only one to call him "Jeff" and who knew the Virginian "awful well."[32] I would add to these suggestive passages other suggestive facts and silences in Wister's life and in Darwin Payne's biography of the writer that suggest same-sex desire. Consideration of such desire not only provides interpretive bridges for mysterious moments in Darwin Payne's biography, but helps explain the affective and perspectival imbalances in the novel. Wister reveals the "hidden" and more genuine emotions to characters who are bystanders, and hides the most sentimental emotions from every character but the Virginian and Molly, while presenting them in full view to the reading masses, as if he were capitulating to them.

These biographical moments mostly involve the aptly named George West, who was the original inspiration for the Virginian. Wister met West in 1887, on his second trip to Wyoming, when West was one of his guides. A correspondence immediately sprang up between them. In his first letter to Wister shortly after Wister returned to Cambridge for law school, West described in detail how he went hunting for horse thieves who had stolen thirteen head from him and more from neighbors. One of the aggrieved parties persuaded West that stern measures must be taken and that they must capture them and return them for vigilante execution. The result of this search is not known, but it stirred Wister's imagination. Wister's biographer writes that "If Wister had been captivated by West's mastery of the outdoors, so had West obviously been captivated by the charm of this cultured Easterner." West thanked Wister for a quilt he had presented to him, and he hoped the report was untrue that said that the other guide, Jules Mason, was to receive an even greater gift of a six-shooter. "It irritated West," writes Payne, "that Mason was already claiming full credit for the success of their hunting expedition." West vied not only for Wister's affections, but for his continued financial support, and over the next few years, Wister's support came in a series of large loans to help West build a cabin and develop his ranch. West, however, had persistent financial troubles, and his letters to Wister requesting more aid were laced with longing: "Well it won't be long before we will be out in *our mountains* again," he wrote in 1890 (emphases original).[33] After a visit in 1891, Wister wrote his first western story, "Hank's Woman," a story I will return to, in which Wister based the main character Lin Maclean on George West. The eastern tenderfoot describes him in the first version of the story as the one "whom among all cowpunchers I love most."[34] In the 1900 version of the story, after Wister had married his wife Molly, this line is omitted and the Virginian replaces Lin McLean as the central character. Thus began the erasure of George West from the public record about the personal sources for the Virginian.

Shortly after the Johnson County "war" of 1892 that also served as inspiration for the vigilante justice in *The Virginian*, a war in which the author was on the side of the large cattle ranchers, Wister decided not to go through with a planned hunting expedition with West. The time was not propitious, since Wister was also an outspoken friend of imprisoned vigilantes and could not "easily resume his relationships with common cowboys and noted badmen." Though the precise reason for cancelling the trip is not clear, Payne writes,

Curiously, however, instead of writing a letter, he made a round trip of some five thousand miles to tell West in person. His friends were puzzled that he would take such a journey only to turn around and come back, and indeed a hint of mystery exists as to why he did . . . On July 11, Wister's train rolled into Cinnabar,

Montana, and there on the platform stood an expectant George West. Wister was reluctant to admit that he was cancelling the hunting trip and returning East that very afternoon. But, as they walked up and down the platform, he at last managed to tell West. They drank beer and talked for the rest of the afternoon, and at 6:15 p.m. Wister boarded the East-bound train for the return trip.

While some have suggested that the trip was an act of bravado to prove he was not afraid to go West in the midst of the Johnson County War, another explanation Payne offers is that Wister insisted on paying West the $75 fee for his services for the hunting trip, "and he may have wanted to do so in person," since West had already arranged to take time off and was "as usual in financial difficulty." Yet, especially given the fact that Wister described this nine-day round trip as one of "almost unalloyed pleasure and content," it seems something much more personal and self-interested was involved. West's letters to Wister following this trip mixed financial with emotional need and offered expressions of love. West complained that his part of the country seemed less and less important to Wister and, as Payne describes it, "if his friend were no longer to spend summers there, West was not certain he cared to stay himself," reminding Wister that at one time they had discussed becoming partners. The constant requests for money began to annoy Wister, who asked West, like a father to a son (though they were the same age), to account for what had happened to the money. West responded that, were it not for Wister's advice, he would have left cowboy life two years earlier to work on the railroad. Wister was "so swayed that he cancelled all West's debts." Overwhelmed, West wrote to Wister that his letter "sent a chill" over him. "You are good, Wister and a Christian if there are any on earth . . . Yes, you are a friend to me & the best I have ever had or will ever have I know. I never thought one man could love another as I have grown to love you." Still, the requests for money continued, and eventually Wister refused.[35]

Why should a man, whose politics did not support hand-outs to the incompetent, be so eager to respond to and to see, so briefly at the cost of nine days' travel, a man who continually asked for money he never repaid? Moreover, the same man who inspired the Virginian wrote to Wister in 1900, as if he were the model for Steve also, "I was arrested for cattle stealing, and gave bond." That year, West married a refined Massachusetts woman who had studied at the Boston Conservatory of Music. Wister served as best man, and the Wests visited Wister and his new wife Molly in Philadelphia. Upon returning to the cabin Wister financed for them, West wrote, "I do wish you could see me in my new house . . . When evening comes and Mrs. West [is] at the piano singing some sweet soft air while I am lying on an easy couch dressed in some of the nice clothes that you have sent me[,] I cannot help thinking that life is sweeter to me than to any other man." West's own good fortune, he declared, was largely due to Wister. "I love you for it," he wrote. It was at this time that Wister composed "the best pages I have ever written," the honeymoon scene in *The Virginian*. Years later, Wister acknowledged some of the actual individuals who had inspired the Virginian, though none of them, as Payne observes, was from Wyoming, and all of them he had met after he created the character. "The one cowboy to whom Wister obviously owed the greatest debt he never mentioned . . . Wister's omission of the man who was his first and most impressionable western hero is striking," writes Wister's biographer. Payne offers two explanations for this omission: first, to tie the Virginian too closely to an individual would detract from the character's imaginative power; and second, Wister had become disenchanted with West because of his requests for help. I would offer a third: too closely for Wister's own comfort, the eastern tenderfoot's ardor for the Virginian resembled Wister's devotion to West – or perhaps more pointedly, West's devotion to Wister: "When I clearly see what you have done for me I must acknowledge you as my god, for I know that *you* have saved me."[36]

In the next thirty years, West wrote Wister two letters; there is no evidence that Wister reciprocated. After sixteen years of not writing, West wrote in 1918, "Wister: I want you to remember this, that with all my faults I love you as I did years ago, and shall always want to see you when you come to Seattle." (West had been warned by his cattle associates that if he did not leave Wyoming, he would be shot.) Then in 1934 came the last letter: "I think of you every day, when I go about my work as a janitor in an apartment house." Payne writes that "[a]s far as West was concerned, there was no question about it – he himself was the Virginian. Ironically, this man, whose supposed lack of self-control had brought a breach in the relationship with Wister, never publicly claimed the honor. Only his close friends and relatives heard the story." West died in 1951, at the age of ninety. He and his wife had no children.[37]

Wister's approach toward this real-life Virginian, who, like Steve, stole cattle and squandered others' property, is quite different from the way in which the Virginian metes out unforgiving justice to his own best friend in the novel. Another curious episode in 1917 suggests Wister's softness toward a handsome young man who was accused of theft – and of borrowing, like a talented Tom Ripley, Wister's very identity:

Wister's young French valet disappeared in Wyoming with many of Wister's possessions. The valet, a French Army veteran named Charles Bret, packed about one thousand dollars worth of Wister's clothes in his employers' luggage and fled to Boston, where he rented a suite of rooms at the Hotel Savoy and posed alternately as a count and as Wister himself... Finally, though, his bad checks caught up with him, and he was arrested one day... Wister suggested that charges against the handsome young man be dropped if he would reenter the French Army. Bret preferred to stand trial. Wister urged in court that the punishment not be unduly severe, and Bret was sentenced to prison for one year.[38]

Wister's biographer does not stop to speculate here why the writer who has his hero lynch his best friend should have been so lenient toward this thief. Was Wister trying to make sure the young man was not asked to testify in the first place about their relationship? Omitted from Wister's biography is what the novel itself barely conceals: a type of love not legitimated by law that makes the execution of justice awfully hard to bear. When the Virginian is recuperating from the attack against him by Indians, he cries out in the presence of Molly and other women: " 'Steve!' the sick man cried out, in poignant appeal. 'Steve!' To the women it was a name unknown – unknown as was also this deep inward tide of feeling which he could no longer conceal, being himself no longer. 'No, Steve,' he said next, and muttering followed. 'It ain't so!' he shouted; and then cunningly in a lowered voice, 'Steve, I have lied for you' " (p. 289). The Virginian unwittingly reveals a "name unknown" that calls up an otherwise hidden "deep inward tide of feeling." The cunning claim "I have lied for you," suggests the Virginian's desire to break even his code of honor to spare his friend's life in the execution of extra-legal justice. But if the Virginian was modeled on George West, the fictional character literally lies for Wister's friend by displacing onto Steve the figure of the cattle thief and bachelor who knew "Jeff," as the Virginian says to the narrator with a sob while "utterly overcome," "awful well" (p. 343). Lying in the name of love is what the Virginian secretly longs to do. What is so telling about this bedside scene is that it is women as bystanders who hear this poignant appeal. Even more than the women, to whom the name is "unknown," the readers are in on the secret: we know more than "Jeff" seems to know himself about the costs of being a hero.

Wister seems to have understood both the liberties worth killing for and the liberties worth dying for having taken – as Steve does when he resigns himself calmly to his death – when he wrote in 1911, "all government, all liberty, reduces itself to one man saying to another: you may do *this*; but if you do *that*, I will kill you."[39] Although Molly threatens the Virginian by saying that if he kills Trampas, "there can be no to-morrow for you and me," Wister has her marry the Virginian anyway after the fatal shoot-out, not only because the man must be master to the woman, but because the Virginians of the world must kill the Steves and Trampases, and will not achieve their nobility and perpetuation without doing so. In this sense, the convention of marriage is only acceptable if the Virginian is not blackmailed into accepting the conventional morality Molly represents. On the honeymoon, the Virginian reveals the "secrets of his heart" to Molly as he begins to resemble a boy of nineteen: " 'What I did not know at all,' he said, 'was the way a man can be pining for – for this – and never guess what is the matter with him' " (p. 426). The Virginian's brief hesitancy in ambiguously naming what he has longed for, without having guessed before what was the matter with him, gives the admission the quality of a false confession and the marriage of this otherwise far-seeing individual the quality of a conversion. While the novel in the end seems to support Roosevelt's idea that no happiness is greater than the happiness of husband and wife who have children, at the end of his life Wister personally felt otherwise: "No, I don't want to see any of that country again. Too much nostalgia for past happiness. I have never enjoyed anything more than those camping days in Wyoming."[40] Once again, Wister, who could otherwise see things "objectively" and without the aid of bystanders, could not bear to look – to the past, to the place where he was most happy and free.

In 1902 when his novel appeared, Wister wrote, "Oh, the blackmail that we pay to convention! the petty, cowardly tons of blackmail! . . . The bystanders are always with us; whenever we take an unusual step we peep and squint to see how the bystanders are looking. In fact, it is chiefly through the eyes of bystanders, and not our own, that we look at life."[41] While the Virginian would seem to kick against convention and the gaze of bystanders, curiously enough it is because of the eyes of others that he feels compelled to fight Trampas: "If folks came to think I was a coward – . . . My friends would be sorry and ashamed, and my enemies would walk around saying they had always said so. I could not hold up my head again among enemies or friends" (p. 409). This contradiction can be explained simply: the masculine gaze sees things objectively; women see things personally and subjectively. Wister continues,

Let nobody suppose that I suppose convention is an unmitigated evil. We all of us know that it is an imperative necessity; but I do not purpose to let it bleed me of my principles, my pleasures, or my purse, or in any way whatever rub me out . . . How, then to get rid of the bystanders? How to see things as they are and not as somebody else sees them?[42]

*We all of us know that it is an imperative necessity.* Wister's admission describes the imperative of his novel's ending when, though he has bucked female convention about violence and equality, the Virginian follows convention and marries. To "see things as they are" is to see them through the eyes of other men who measure masculine honor. Wister's answer to his question about gaining independent and objective eyesight is for young men to go to the open air of the West and be tested, as he himself did in acquiring some semblance of independence from his parents and their conventional imperatives. To consider Wister's views about "things as they are" apart from the bystanders' perspective, together with the fact of the Virginian's concern about how he will be regarded by other men, is to see how a presumedly objective point of view in *The Virginian* is purchased at the denigration of female subjectivity – and at the cost of Wister's most personal feelings. Since the novel depends upon a feminized subjectivity – the reader's and the narrator's as well as Molly's – to grant the Virginian his qualities, it is the narrator, suggestively, who is denigrated by the very structures and aims of masculinity the novel supports.

As he was struggling with his decision not to study music in Europe, in 1885 Wister wrote, "Were I surer of my powers, – or rather were my powers sure – I think I should not now be in America, but wandering with musicians and other disreputable people – having kicked over all traces. [But] a fortunate grain of common sense self knowledge . . . says 'You're too nearly like other people to do more than appreciate & sympathize with revolution' – thus I remain conventional.' "[43] Even Wister's decision to marry came through the persistence of others. Still single in 1895 at the age of thirty-five, Wister attended a birthday party for Winthrop Chanler, who, seeing Wister's large belly, recommended some "boudoir gymnastics." As Wister's biographer recounts it, "It was past time, he said, for Wister to take a bride. A few days later, Elizabeth Chanler raised the subject again, and Wister discussed it with enthusiasm, confiding with her 'more than I've ever told to any one.' " Payne adds without elaboration or explanation that up to this point in his life Wister "had purposefully decided against marriage. Now, however, he had concluded that he should marry."[44] To the extent that Wister's sense of calling to write about the West served a deeply personal need, including his need to serve the national purpose through the literary birth of a racial type, it may be that it provided a sense of romantic transition where there may otherwise have only been an affective rupture: when, in 1898 on the day the US declared war against Spain, Wister assumed the responsibilities, as his family and era thought imperative, of marriage and family – and wedded and raised children with Molly, the daughter of his second cousin, once removed.

This about-face is reflected literarily in dichotomous representations of marriage written before and after Wister's own. The last chapter of *The Virginian* figures as the marital Eden to the marital hell of Wister's first published western story, "Hank's Woman" (1892). Yet in both the story and the novel's honeymoon scene, what follows marriage is a drive toward oblivion, a desire for the swallowing up of sexual difference either in death or in an elemental return to pre-human nature. The story depicts, in grisly form, precisely the racial and cultural *unadaptability* of its characters to marriage out West: the drunken, "black" frontiersman Hank and his new religious bride, an Austrian woman. As revised in 1900 to include the Virginian, "Hank's Woman" inspired the dialogue in the first chapter of *The Virginian*, when the hero mocks marriage, and is alluded to in the novel. (In both the story and the novel, the Virginian comments, "Nothing's queer . . . except marriage and lightning.") The 1900 story is framed, significantly, like *The Virginian*: in his first literary appearance, the Virginian tells Hank's story to an eastern narrator. But while the Virginian knows the characters he talks about, he, like the reader, the narrator, and everyone else in the camp, does not witness the story's culmination in marital violence when Hank shoots his wife's crucifix – a sign of European civilization and of religious devotion completely alien to him – and his wife smashes his skull in with an ax out of rage and despair at her ill choice in marriage. In not representing the violence that follows marriage, the story mirrors the withheld scenes of violence in *The Virginian* that precede marriage. The story not only seems to represent Wister's views about racially suitable types, but his fear of marriage, whereas the novel represents his regret at what has been killed off after he married. The story as revised in 1900 is seen through a group of men's voyeurism and dismay in witnessing the marital misery of the only couple in the camp but in not (fore)seeing the outcome. Indeed, the story's main events are presented in a relentlessly subjective fashion. As Lee Mitchell describes similar moments in *The Virginian*, "it is as if the very possibility of objective description were being denied."[45] If masculinity is aligned in Wister's beliefs with the ability to see things objectively, "as they are," and women are associated with subjectivity, then the men in "Hank's Woman" are suggestively feminized when faced with this mismatched marriage, as if their unmarried status limits their ability to see things objectively.

The Virginian's inexperience in marriage is aligned early on with the narrator's: "Have yu' studied much about marriage?" he asks the narrator. " 'Not much,' I said; 'not very much.' " This exchange is immediately followed by the kind of reversion to boyish play that Tompkins argues *The Virginian* secretly longs for: " 'Let's swim,' " the Virginian says. "Forthwith we shook off our boots and dropped our few clothes."[46] After the swim, the narrator writes,

We dried before the fire, without haste. To need no clothes is better than purple and fine linen. Then he tossed the flap-jacks, and I served the trout, and after this we lay on our backs upon a buffalo-hide to smoke and watch the Tetons grow more solemn, as the large stars opened out over the sky.
"I don't care if I never go home," said I. (p. 7)

While rejecting the domesticity of "home" and preferring relaxed nudity (in the company of men) to "fine linen," the narrator and the Virginian re-create domesticity in sharing the cooking responsibilities. The scene is a more natural version of the Virginian's and Molly's honeymoon, when the newlyweds lie by the water and the Virginian longs to swim like a little wild animal. In both the story and the novel, nature takes on the clothes of domesticity before the responsibilities of marriage and reproduction take over; this substitution naturalizes domesticity between men as a pleasant contrast to the later, unnatural violence in Hank's marriage, a soothingly subliminal substitute for the "real" (heterosexual) thing. In "Hank's Woman," such naturalized domestic motifs are seen when the narrator says that "glazed laps" of snow-fields shone "like handkerchiefs laid out to dry" (p. 3) and when the Virginian says the waters by Pitchstone Canyon are "green as the stuff that gets on brass" and trickle "along over soft cream-colored formation, like pie" (p. 21).

Contrasted with these descriptions of a naturalized, all-male domesticity are the images that surround Hank and his wife Willomene, which are anything but soothing. Mismatched by Willomene's desperate circumstances and religion and Hank's lust, race, and drunkenness, the couple represent the clash between a European woman and a "little black" man who, unlike the Virginian, does not know better than to take advantage of a blind but "good" woman (pp. 16, 11). Marriage was "but a little

thing to Hank – agaynst such a heap of advantages" (p. 12), surmises the
Virginian. Berating her for her ignorance of horses, Hank takes her on a
trail along Pitchstone Canyon, which emits a "queer steam" from its cav-
ernous depths, down in which, the Virginian explains, "is caves that yu'
cannot see. 'Tis them that coughs up the steam now and agayn . . . And
when it comes that-a-way risin' upon yu' with that fluffy kind of sigh,
yu' feel might lonesome" (pp. 20, 21). Though the Virginian knows how
unhappy this marriage is – "when he'd come home and see her prayin'
to that crucifix he'd always get riled up," he says – the reader never hears
a word from Willomene. What is key is that the voyeur-bachelor knows
more than the married protagonists ever tell – yet he is not given to see
things as they are or as they happen. The story ends when, upon returning from a hunt and having left Hank and Willomene alone, the men
of the camp see, at first with difficulty, the visible signs of what finally
explodes between the married couple, leaving both of them dead. At this
point in the story, the marriage is just about all the men think or talk
about – or look at. They share glasses as they look at the now lonely
camp and newlyweds' cabin from afar, in a passage filled with as much
detailed information as ambiguous appearance and guesswork:

The Virginian took the glasses. '*I reckon* – yes, that's Hank. . . . he's comin' in out
o' the brush.'
    Each of us took the glasses in turn; and I watched the figure go up the hill
to the door of the cabin. It *seemed* to pause and diverge to the window . . . It was
*too far to discern*, even through the glasses, what the figure was doing. *Whether* the
door was locked, *whether* he was knocking or fumbling with a key, or *whether*
he spoke through the door to the person within – *I cannot tell* . . . I was handing
the glasses to the Virginian for him to see when the figure opened the door and
*disappeared in the dark interior*. As I watched the *square of darkness* which the door's
opening made, *something seemed to happen there – or else* it was a spark, a flash, in
my own *straining eyes*.
    But at that same instant the Virginian dashed forward upon his horse, leaving
the glasses in my hand. (pp. 32–33, emphases added)

All the men follow, as now a woman's figure appears, committing unknown acts. When they arrive at the cabin, the *fait accompli* is visible
through a series of clues:

There hung the crucifix, with a round hole through the middle of it . . . The
cabin was but a single room, and *every object that it contained could be seen at a glance;
nor was there hiding-room for anything*. On the floor lay the axe from the wood-pile;
*but I will not tell of its appearance*. So he had shot her crucifix, her Rock of Ages,

the thing which enabled her to bear her life, and that lifted her above life; and she – but there was the axe to show what she had done then. (p. 35, emphases added)

Wister's style of narration-by-elision when the crucial, plot-turning acts of violence occur is here apparent. What we do not know, are not given to see ("I will not tell of its appearance") is the violence that had simmered under the surface of this interracial marriage, worrying every man in camp, and that has already erupted. It carries both the sense of inevitability and the inscrutability of the working out of a natural law. The Anglo-Saxon voyeurs cannot see, up close, the natural causes at work, only their effects.

As they follow the trail of a woman's footsteps that leave the cabin, they come upon the scene that "tells" the story and yet that leaves much to guesswork. As they approach Pitchstone Canyon, the narrator writes,

... at first *I failed to make out* what had set us all running.
"*Is he* looking down into the hole himself?" some one asked; and then I did see a figure . . . leaning strangely over the edge of Pitchstone Cañon, *as if* indeed he was peering to watch what *might be* at the bottom.
We came near. But those eyes *were sightless*, and in the skull the story of the axe was carved. (pp. 37–38, emphases added)

The figure that is not easily made out seems to be looking "as if" he was "peering to watch what might be at the bottom," but its eyes are "sightless," imitating the characters' obscured vision and the scene's opacity. But "the story of the axe" – indeed the story of this marriage – is carved in violence that we do not witness as it occurs. What the figure seems, finally, to be looking at is the figure of Willomene below; the narrator "staggered at the sight" of "Hank's woman, brought from Austria to the New World. The vision of that brown bundle lying in the water will never leave me, I think. She had carried this body to this point; but had she intended this end? Or was some part of it an accident? Had she meant to take him with her? Had she meant to stay behind herself?" There is no answer from the dead, but from the canyon "a giant puff of breath rose up," a sigh that seems to ventriloquize Hank for McLean, who points at his body: " 'He's talkin' to her! . . . See him lean over! He's sayin', 'I have yu' beat after all' " (p. 38).

The husband's right to proclaim such final victory over his betrothed is repeated in *The Virginian*, comedically rather than tragically, and with an excess rather than a dearth of objective description, as if the triumph of the heterosexual imperative marks the mastery of objective reality and the turning away from the feminized subjectivity (and feeling) of the bachelor cowboy's life. In this formative story, the landscape naturalizes and swallows up the bottomless violence, along with its precise contours of intent and motive, that terminates this marriage plot; the "story of the axe" is visual, not narrative. At once subliminally domestic and the sign of domesticity's demise, nature has a prescience beyond that of any character's capacity to know, as silent as Willomene and as unpredictable. While Hank's body is brought to burial by the men, Willomene's unreachable body is "left in such a vault of doom, with . . . no heap of kind earth to hide it. But whether the place is deadly or not, man dares not venture into it" (p. 39). Neither do the Virginian or the narrator, in this story, dare to enter into marriage. Since the story naturalizes homosocial domesticity, fear of marriage in "Hank's Woman" is a fear of a different "natural law," that of heterosexuality, and a fear of female sexuality. When marriage triumphs at the end of *The Virginian*, the Virginian tellingly longs for a nature anterior to heterosexual difference.

"Hank's Woman" can be read to represent Wister's misogynistic fear of the female body, but also of a feminized landscape that is marked, like the woman's body, by death. But in light of the novel it anticipates in its characters and concerns about marriage, the story also can be read as a corollary to the one Wister makes in *The Virginian* about marriage between racially suitable types. While the novel, as Slotkin argues, suggests that violence is a reserved right for a particular class of Anglo-Saxons on the national domestic scene against the laboring masses, violence erupts in "Hank's Woman" in the scene of domesticity when the interracial married couple come from unsuitable and incompatible classes or types. (In the 1892 story, Lin McLean decides "[a] native American woman could have managed Hank so he'd treated her good and been sorry instead of glad every time he'd been drunk.")[47] Willomene's violence, in other words, while it is a logical extension of her marriage's unsuitability, is irrational, unsuccessful, and gives evidence of the need for social order, while the Virginian's violence – against Steve and Trampas – is rational, successful, and enforces social order. Moreover, the Virginian's violence is the prelude to his marriage, or more precisely to Molly's submission to him in their ideological debate, while Willomene's violence is the postscript to a marriage doomed by the clash of races and cultures. In both cases, the narrative structure places one or more men, but always the eastern narrator, in the voyeuristic position of witnessing and interpreting these almost laboratory-like experiments in social order. At the end of the 1900 version of "Hank's Woman," the Virginian "corrects" the moral of the story that Lin McLean draws from it:

"Well," [McLean] said, taking an offish, man-of-the-world tone, "all this fuss just because a woman believed in God."

"You have put it down wrong," said the Virginian; "it's just because a man didn't." (p. 40)

In this early story, revised shortly before the publication of *The Virginian*, Wister has the Virginian espouse something associated with women – religion – precisely as a curb and corrective to male lawlessness and desire; this is the conventional way he resolves the matter. Religion is that which sanctions the law that sanctions marriage, according to the values of Wister's civilization; to reject it, as Hank does, is to open up marriage to a violence that knows no bounds. Haunted by Willomene's unburied and thus unsanctified body, and feeling, as one might expect of him, no desire to attend Hank's burial, the narrator comes to Pitchstone Canyon, where he finds the Virginian, who "had set up the crucifix as near the dead tree" above Willomene's body as it could be planted (p. 39). In *The Virginian*, in contrast, masculine honor legitimates the violence that precedes the marriage – and the Virginian and Molly stand as far apart in their view of such violence as Hank and Willomene do in their view of religion.

Wister's work thus holds two contradictory ideas together: on one hand, certain universal values enacted in the religious rituals of marriage and burial are upheld while, on the other, the naturally aristocratic cowboy's sense of justice requires no universal consensus or practice to be valid – it is, if not extra-religious, extra-legal. This contradiction between grounds for conduct and value is, however, resolved in an illustration the narrator offers the reader late in *The Virginian* in order to explain how the Virginian's lynching of his best friend Steve, outside of legal jurisdiction, is not immoral, as Molly would have it. (This passage precedes her submission to the Virginian in marriage.) In this illustration, Wister-as-author usurps the role of first-person narrator to ventriloquize Judge Henry in his effort to persuade Molly that the lynching was justified and right. The awkward narrative means used to advance this view, in other words, enact the view they advance. The author is aligned in his sense of right not only against one of his characters, but against, he presumes, his reluctant readers as well. Yet this propounder of "objective reality" depends upon the contingencies of perspective to make his case.

The paragraph begins with third-person omniscient narration that orients the reader to the Judge's argument against a view of the lynching as a crime, a view that the narrator assumes the reader shares with Molly:

Judge Henry sat thinking... He did not relish what lay before him ... He had been a stanch [*sic*] servant of the law. And now he was invited to defend that which, at first sight, nay, even at second and third sight, must always seem a defiance of the law more injurious than crime itself. (p. 370)

Admitting everything the reader or Molly might think she sees clearly at first, second, and third sight, that there is no justification for lynching, the paragraph then shifts into first-person and then, at the end, authorial voice. What occurs narratively, in other words, is the exposition of a subjective view (Judge Henry's) as, gradually, an objective or authoritative one beyond the constraints of character, including the narrator's. These are the aesthetic costs involved as Wister expounds a minority viewpoint against a majority that includes his sense of the reader: we begin with a situated individual within the text ("Judge Henry sat thinking") and conclude with a polemical call to the politics of Wister's day. As the third-person omniscient voice describes Judge Henry's moral dilemmas, the narratorial and then authorial "I" step in to resolve them:

There come to him certain junctures, crises, when life, like a highwayman, springs upon him, demanding that he stand and deliver his convictions in the name of some righteous cause, bidding him do evil that good may come. I cannot say that I believe in doing evil that good may come. I do not. I think that any man who honestly justifies such a course deceives himself. But this I can say: to call any act evil, instantly begs the question. Many an act that man does is right or wrong according to the time and place which form, so to speak, its context; strip it of its particular circumstances, and you tear away its meaning. Gentleman reformers, beware of this common practice of yours! Beware of calling an act evil on Tuesday because that same act was evil on Monday! (p. 371)

This passage is one rare instance when Wister addresses readers figured as men, and yet his association of reformism throughout the novel with women's suffrage, and his deriding of the female reformers in the parable of Em'ly the Hen, would seem to emasculate these "gentlemen." That concluding admonition covers over the moral divagations that precede it, as Wister moves from authoritative declamation ("There come to him") to subjective doubt ("I cannot say") to an assertion about the relativity of context. The moral or contextual difference between Monday and Tuesday in this passage echoes the geographical difference Wister invokes at the beginning of the novel in "To the Reader": "Had you left New York or San Francisco at ten o'clock this morning, by noon the day after tomorrow you could step out at Cheyenne" (p. x). It also recalls the relativity of place in Wister's admission, when he chose not to study music in Europe, that were he surer of his powers, "I should not now be in America but wandering with ... disreputable people" and acting in revolutionary ways. The different world of the West, like the world of Europe, is one in which, as context changes, morality must change also. But while Wister seems to be arguing for the specificity of times and places and the relativity of moral contexts, his own sense of right here narratively transcends the specificity of his fictional settting, as the "I" becomes that of an author-polemicist's and not a narrator's, situated in 1902 and not 1874. While he views morality as dependent on context, he puts his fiction's context aside – thus reminding his readers that this argument is a fiction of his own making. While most good novelists and playwrights depend upon a suspension of disbelief through the unresolved clash of worldviews and values that seem to imitate the clash of values in the actual social order, Wister presumes the need, because he feels he knows precisely why the social order is misguided, for authorial intervention in making his fiction make sense.

Having shifted the narrative "I," Wister introduces the second-person to/as the reader: "Do you fail to follow my meaning? Then here is an illustration," he writes, as he cites the case of a man walking across his neighbor's lawn on a Monday and then walking across it the next day when there is a "No trespassing" sign. "Do you begin to see my point? Or are you inclined to object to the illustration because the walking on Tuesday was not *wrong*, but merely *illegal*? Then here is another illustration which you will find a trifle more embarrassing to answer" (p. 371). Wister reveals here not so much the limits of a legal code as his presumption of an absolute moral code in marriage that supersedes even the different contingencies of western context and that we can all, presumably, "see." In this illustration, setting is universal, and the consensus about the absolutely sanctifying act of marriage enables – in Wister's mind at least – the author to persuade his readers of the relativity of all other moral codes. Indeed, by the end of this authorial intrusion of shifting "I's" and "you's," there is a consensus of "we."

Consider carefully, let me beg you, the case of a young man and young woman who walk out of a door on Tuesday, pronounced man and wife by a third party inside the door. It matters not that on Monday they were, in their own hearts, sacredly vowed to each other. If they had omitted stepping inside that door, if they had dispensed with that third party, and gone away on Monday sacredly vowed to each other *in their own hearts*, you would have scarcely found their conduct moral. Consider these things carefully, – the sign-post and the third party, – and the difference they make ... Forgive my asking you to use your mind. It is a thing which no novelist should expect of his reader, and we will go back at once to Judge Henry and his meditations about lynching. (pp. 371–372)

The moral code regarding pre- and post-marital sex is the one code, significantly, beyond question; that is, the one by which he can assume that all of his readers would grant his argument logic. And yet that code is dependent upon a bystander: that figure Wister bemoaned in its conventionality and yet here the one figure upon which his argument rests. The status of "the third party" is not only legally critical in the act of marriage and rhetorically critical in Wister's defense of extra-legal justice, but is structured into the novel's narration. The eastern narrator performs this function of third party, extending all the way to the honeymoon. When that narrator becomes author-addressing-reader, the "third party" becomes two parties rolled into one: both judge and jury. While many have noted that *The Virginian* celebrates an individualistic hero so self-determined that he can say no to even the pleas of his sweetheart who threatens not to marry him, few have taken stock of the fact that, narratively speaking, the Virginian is not allowed a single act of significance without the narrator peering, at the least, from off-stage. He is the one whose values Judge Henry and the Virginian speak in concert with. Yet in the end the narrator falls out of the marriage plot and has no role to play. The marriage legitimates the Virginian's national importance and completes the novel's national allegory in part by divorcing the Virginian from the narrator's affections. The triumph of marriage and the suppression of same-sex feeling give the novel its "nationality." For it ultimately does not matter what is "really" in the narrator's heart: it matters what he would do if he were the bride.

The law of marriage is thus not subsumable under the laws of popular government – or of the reformers – that Wister feels free to disavow. It is a law in line, rather, with those immutable values that will save democracy. The Virginian is not seen, then, as obeying a law of the land in formally marrying his bride, but in following a law of his own second nature, after he has demonstrated his exemption from existing presumptions about legal justice. In the conversation between Judge Henry and Molly, which will help to woo her to the altar, the "civilized" nature of the lynching of Steve is identified with the West as a region determined to avoid the barbarism of the South. This "son of the South" will thus redeem the nation from southern barbarism by exercising lynching in a different form out West and ultimately by winning over his northern bride. Judge Henry makes the following distinction:

"I see no likeness in principle whatever between burning Southern Negroes in public and hanging Wyoming horse-thieves in private. I consider the burning a proof that the South is semi-barbarous, and the hanging a proof that Wyoming is determined to become civilized. We do not torture our criminals when we lynch them. We do not invite spectators to enjoy their death agony. We put no such hideous disgrace upon the United States. We execute our criminals by the swiftest means, and in the quietest way." (p. 374)

The South's barbarism does not lie in the fact that all-white juries take the law into their own hands – the criminality of blacks put to death is here assumed – but in the non-aristocratic way in which black suffering is displayed, as Slotkin has pointed out; hence the "genteel" way in which the lynching of Steve is narrated through the narrator, who cannot bear to watch more than the preparations. The key distinction in this passage, tied to the regional and racial distinctions, is that between public and private, a distinction that informs the narrative regulation of feeling throughout the novel. It is one more curious paradox that the sign of the Virginian's civility is that his violence is not given to public view, in a novel that everywhere else seems to exceed the limitations of the first-person narrative point of view it establishes at the start. In that sense, the narrator is linked to the reader as among those "not man enough" to watch. Tompkins reads the lynching of Steve as representing the necessity of killing off that which the western hero must abjure, such as femininity, emotion, and transgressive behavior – all in the name of the social order and his marriage into it. When one of the men who are about to hang him urge Steve to drink some coffee, the narrator writes, "These words almost made it seem like my own execution. My whole body turned cold in company with the prisoner's . . . I put the blanket over my head" (p. 334). If femininity is being killed off, the narrator as a feminized figure would be lucky to escape his own execution. It is as if he survives by not looking, especially at the costs of becoming a man who marries and who is severed from the other man he loves.

At once feminine and the denigrator of femininity, limited in what he can (bear to) see but omniscient, disdainful of third parties yet acting as one, Wister's narrator suggests more than just the author's own frac- tured sensibility as a man who subjected himself to the imperatives of a civilization he was born to uphold, but who longed to escape civilization, arguably because of something inborn. The novel's narrative structure, with its disjunctions of affect and perspective, suggests that the episte-mological means by which "justice" is measured and meted out for the sake of a national imperative depend upon the eyes of those that such justice is blind to: the democratic majority. What is remarkable about the world of *The Virginian* is that so much violence serves as the prelude to marriage and hence that so many other codes of morality and feeling – including not only Molly's against lynchings and shoot-outs, but also the Virginian's "inward tide of feeling" for Steve – should be subordi-nated before the altar of marriage for the sake of a nation's racial future out West.

# CHAPTER FOUR

# Polygamy and empire: Grey's distinctions

Like *The Virginian*, the immensely popular novels of Zane Grey had enormous influence on the development of the Western. Although Grey's work is best known for its formulaic elements such as the gunslinger, one of the curiosities for today's readers of his most influential and successful Western, *Riders of the Purple Sage* (1912), is the villain: a Mormon polygamist. Early reviewers noted the historical distinctiveness of his antagonist, but contemporary criticism of the novel has given it relatively little attention.[1] Grey's first novel to deal with Mormons, *The Heritage of the Desert* (1910), like the 1915 sequel to *Riders*, is contrastingly sympathetic toward and understanding of Mormons, given his personal experience among them.[2] The immediate cultural catalyst for Grey's reversion in *Riders* to a demonizing stereotype, which was arguably key to the novel's huge success, was an anti-Mormon magazine crusade in 1911 that Grey was well aware of and that revived paranoia about polygamy. I will discuss this crusade in the first section of this chapter, along with the cultural logic behind that immediate context: the history of Mormon and American tension that would make of that brief, revived fear of polygamy such a potent factor in the novel's reception. Far from being a substitutable figure in Grey's novel, the polygamous Mormon was a specific repository for Grey's readers, as it had been for decades for Americans, of the contradictions and anxieties inherent in American beliefs about racial and sexual identity (and the others such identity is constructed against) and of the relationship between the law and religious freedom. The Mormons figured negatively in these categories' relation to empire-building not simply as an other but as a quasi-ethnic group that was not quite other, one that, as Terryl Givens argues, was "not subject to the same means of exorcism as communities racially, culturally, or geographically distinctive" and that produced "an anxiety of seduction perhaps unique in the American experience of otherness."[3] Indeed, the Mormon distinction, which made it a much demonized group in American politics and culture up to the time of Grey's novel, came eventually to make little difference as an effective other once the end of polygamy – and rumors of its continued practice – allowed the Mormons to become identifiably "white," in the period's moral and ethnic senses, and thus American, a process that merits comparison with the history of the Irish in America.[4] Set forty years before it was published, Grey's novel records this transition: "I've known many good Mormons," says the hero Lassiter, "but some are blacker than hell."[5]

As the wealth of explanatory criticism on the formula Western shows, its ideological and cultural origins are far more complex than the simple formula itself. This chapter argues that in the case of one of its founding practitioners, the Western formula's function – and a key to its popularity – is not simply to demonize an other but also to resolve American contradictions about religious, sexual, and racial identity by casting the American hero and Mormon villains in distinct but eerily similar roles in which they enact a family drama, and in which the whiteness and womanhood of Grey's (virtuous) Mormon heroines are at stake. That family drama is in its largest cultural significance the drama of America justifying to itself its own history of conquest, since the designs of empire are to a large degree predicated upon the idea that the conquered are both other (sexually, religiously, racially) and yet culturally "familiarized," or made ideologically serviceable and assimilable, for the conquerors. In the case of Zane Grey and Mormon polygamy, the ghosts of what America had transformed were revived in a manner that would ensure their disappearance from the Western formula, once the Mormon distinction was no longer freighted with much difference. The Mormons, in other words, served as a transitional object in American identity-formation, as Americans shifted from viewing them through much of the later nineteenth century, primarily based on their polygamous practices, as a quasi-ethnic other who joined with Indians in hostile conspiracies, to viewing them as white Americans once they adopted monogamy.[6] Grey wrote his novel at just the right moment, when nostalgia about the distinctiveness of Mormon polygamy began to replace paranoia about it; when, in other words, Mormons were no longer seen to threaten "whiteness," "womanhood," "Christian civilization," or the American empire.

In the three sections below, I will explore the history of this paranoia about Mormon polygamy and how American culture pruriently identified with its presumedly transgressive nature; how Mormon difference was constructed according to the imbricated distinctions of ethnicity, gender, and religion; and how the symmetries and asymmetries between

American and Mormon imperial designs produced respective paranoias that also inform Grey's novel. In order to understand Mormon sexual difference – in which whiteness and womanhood are the corruptible terms – representations of Mormon sexuality relied on various non-white ethnic categories to emphasize the threat it posed not just to marriage but to white, Christian civilization, of which marriage was considered the cornerstone. The sense of cosmic significance that Grey's novel instills in the struggle over the marital fate of the virtuous Mormon heroine Jane Withersteen arguably derives as much from the long history of this cosmically freighted rhetoric as it does from Grey's mystical landscapes. Grey's novel is also fascinating for the way in which Gentile and Mormon identities are not just irreconcilably opposed but equally undergo cross-fertilizing transformations, such that Mormon difference is made more familiar, and thus ultimately less threatening, at the moment that this happened historically. American paranoia about this confusing and complex identity figured into both the designs of American empire and the designs of Grey's novel. Omniscience in Grey's novel instills a sense of "helpless capitulation" to a set of norms, in Lee Clark Mitchell's phrase, that imitates the Mormon empire's capitulation, with the ban on polygamy in 1890, to American imperial designs, for it was ultimately the distinction between Mormon and American empires that made all the difference historically for Mormon assimilation and for the popular reception of Grey's novel.[7]

*Riders of the Purple Sage* serves this cultural assimilation by typologizing its characters. Lassiter says to Jane, "mercy and goodness, such as is in you, though they're the grand things in human nature, can't be lived up to on this Utah border. Life's hell out here ... I'm going to try to hide you somewhere in this Pass. I'd like to hide many more women, for I've come to see there are more *like* you among your people ... An' remember this – some day the border'll be better, cleaner, for the ways of men *like* Lassiter!" (p. 272, emphasis added). Grey's rhetoric establishes fixed, analogous types – Gentile American men like Lassiter, redeemed Mormon women like Jane – within a border region about to undergo historical transition and religious and legal transformation. By retrospectively setting the novel in 1871, however, Grey posits the rescue of Mormons from polygamy after federal pressure had already coerced them into officially abandoning the practice in 1890. In culturally shaping the moral and sexual identity of the Mormon for an American readership, the work of fiction follows the work of law in the latter's coercive shaping of the Mormons' future place in the American nation, and follows the 1911 journalistic crusade in its revival of paranoia about polygamy. Jane's dilemma between the oppositional claims of Mormon and Gentile men, and her inability to keep her land *and* her freedom, resembles the no-win situation in which Mormons found themselves in the years leading up to their church's ban against polygamy: practice religious freedom and face destruction or give up the cornerstone practice of the religion and join the nation. Between a rock and a hard place, Jane faints into the American Lassiter's saving arms. The fall of Balancing Rock, which closes off Deception Pass "forever" at the novel's end and thwarts the pursuing Mormon riders, allows Lassiter to hide Jane and to close a chapter on southern Utah before a better and cleaner era begins, implicitly leaving to others the resolution of historical struggle.

In the contest over presumed social universals that Grey's novel engages, grounded on the American side in the conflation between federal law and the "natural" law governing the sexes and on the Mormon side by invocations of religious freedom, a woman's body, soul, and possessions are both battleground and sacrifice. Jane is possessed by her American savior only to be dispossessed of her Mormon father's land and inheritance. Like all the contradictions in this novel, the fact that Jane resists the Mormon elders who want her land only by allowing Lassiter to take her away and leave it forever (at least until the sequel) only makes sense when viewed against the evil Mormon elders, perhaps the only characters who never contradict themselves. The crime of which Tull and his colleagues are guilty is quite simple; at the novel's opening, Venters puts it succinctly: "You want her all yourself. You're a wiving Mormon. You have use for her – and Witheriteen House and Amber Spring and seven thousand head of cattle!" (p. 5). Metonymically connected to land and cattle, Jane is in the end forced to cede both to the Mormon elders in her absence. The fate of Jane's womanhood is the microcosm of a larger legal and national destiny that Grey's readers understood had overtaken Mormonism. When Venters exclaims to Tull, "you want her all yourself," it is not so much polygamy but exclusive, legitimate rights to a woman and her land that upsets Venters, who is not immune from wanting a woman all to himself.

PERSECUTION AND PRURIENCE

A cartoon in the 30 April 1881 issue of *Harper's Weekly*, entitled "A Distinction Without a Difference," contains the following dialogue:

*Justice:* As the laws now stand, Mr. Jonathan, we can punish a Gentile bigamist, but in the case of a Mormon polygamist they appear to be inoperative. Is that right?

*Mormon:* I am not a criminal. Polygamy is a part of my Church creed. No interference of State with Church, you know. I –

*Jonathan:* Stop, sir! Your plea is but a sham, to cover a heinous crime that should be tolerated no longer. If the laws are inadequate, they must be seen to. Nearly twenty years ago I wiped out slavery; now it is about time to attend to you.[8]

One year after this cartoon appeared, federal laws were "seen to" in what had become and still stands as the most intense and prolonged campaign waged against any religious group or practice in American history. The Edmunds Act of 1882 and the Edmunds–Tucker Act of 1887, which was upheld by the Supreme Court in 1890, disfranchised all polygamists, took control of Utah's public school system, abolished the Mormon territorial militia, abolished female suffrage, and disincorporated the Mormon Church, escheating its properties, except for meeting houses and temples, to the United States. In 1887, voters were required to swear to uphold the Edmunds Act of 1882, not even advising others to engage in unlawful cohabitation. Wives could be called to testify against their husbands, witnesses were compelled to attend trial without subpoena, and prosecutions for adultery were permitted without complaint by a spouse.[9] By comparing slavery with polygamy, the cartoon makes no distinctions in order to demarcate the Mormon practice as worthy of a kind of civil war to be waged in the name of protecting American civil liberties and justice, although Mormons perceived the campaign against them as violating both. As the 1856 Republican Party platform put it, polygamy was, with slavery, one of the last "twin relics of barbarism," a sentiment echoed by President Grant in 1871, who decried Mormons as "barbarians" and "repugnant to civilization and decency."[10] Beginning in 1852 when the Mormon Church publicly announced its core religious practice, polygamy was the distinction in that religion that arguably made the greatest difference between religious freedom and legal censure, or between American tolerance and intolerance, toward the Mormons. And the proscription against it made all the difference, ultimately, for Utah's admittance to the Union in 1896.

Statehood brought with it tacit American assumptions about future Mormon behavior, and a corresponding suspicion and paranoia that Mormons could not be trusted morally or politically. Eager to put the past behind them, but scarred by years of anti-polygamy rhetoric that they implicitly and contradictorily had to accede to after the ban on the practice, Mormons continued to fear the government's power to investigate, even as they sought to prove themselves changed and trustworthy. Yet some Mormon leaders continued the practice after 1890, which helped to set the cultural stage for the reception of Grey's novel. In order to gain sympathy for the new Utah while simultaneously criticizing American practices toward the Mormons, S.A. Kenner described in his church-sanctioned 1904 history *Utah As It Is, With a Comprehensive Statement of Utah As It Was* the "long-drawn-out, drastic, dangerous epoch" that was marked with "political, legal and illegal procedure of unusual and far-reaching proportions" – and that "is all over now." His recounting suggested that the period's psychological effects remained, even as he claimed the "epoch" was over: "Raids and raiders, systematic prosecutions and persecutions of a class, hounding, spying and vilification on one hand; with demands for proper interpretations of law, requests for such indulgence as accused people elsewhere have all along been given, and a dogged, perhaps at times unwise determination to stand by what they believed to be their constitutional rights in upholding certain assailed tenets of their faith, on the other – these things are but a memory, and it is fading fast."[11]

Yet during the next seven years before Grey wrote his novel, the memory did anything but fade, as both Mormons and non-Mormons revisited their respective paranoias and their divergent views of what the separation of church and state meant; for Mormons, governmental noninterference in their religious practices, and for other Americans, an end to "theocratic" rule in Utah. When a coalition of protesters wrote in 1904, the same year Kenner's history claimed "it is all over now," that Utah's Senator Reed Smoot should be barred from holding office because he was also an Apostle in the Mormon Church, Congress embarked on an investigation into Smoot and the church that "may have been the longest and most thorough investigation of any religious body in the history of the United States."[12] Rumors of polygamy's continued practice circulated following the investigation of Senator Smoot, who eventually kept his seat, in a steady stream of articles in the years up through 1911 in publications such as *The Independent, Collier's, McClure's, Pearson's, Cosmopolitan,* and *Everybody's* magazine.[13] One year before Grey's novel was published, Theodore Roosevelt echoed a long-standing American sentiment when he warned that the continuation of polygamy would "secure the destruction" of the Mormon Church itself.[14] That same year,

Maude Radford Warren wrote of her travels in Utah for *The Saturday Evening Post*. A Mormon woman named Mrs. Finley, who gave stump speeches in 1904 for the Democratic Party, told a number of Mormon women "that if the Republicans got in there would be another Smoot investigation, and that all of them might be haled into court again. One woman got up and said she could not go through such agony a second time."[15]

In the midst of this anti-polygamy fever, Grey wrote his most popular novel. While preparing for his 1911 trip to Utah, during which he did his research for *Riders*, Grey wrote to his Mormon guide David Dexter Rust that "I shall not write anything about the Mormons that would hurt anybody's feelings... I see them as a wonderful people, and so I shall write of them." Relative to his first Mormon novel, his treatment of Mormonism in *Riders* proved to be demonizing, but not relative to the anti-Mormon magazine crusade: "If you could read what is being written now in three magazines about the Mormons," he wrote to Rust, "you would be pleased with my point of view." Grey was well aware not only of the anti-Mormon articles that year but of the lucrative potential of anti-Mormon sentiment; he went on to argue that by writing favorably about Mormons, he would lose money rather than earn it: "As I will not make any contract with a magazine to roast the Mormons, I'll have to pay my expenses [for the 1911 trip] out of my own pocket. If I wanted to make any such contract I should get $2500 tomorrow for a trip."[16] *Riders of the Purple Sage*, of course, made him a wealthy man; in formulating that novel, Grey may have been divided between friendship and the desire for financial success, as the magazine crusade continued.

Grey's novel helped codify the formula Western around a historical specificity that had, by the time of the Progressive era, borne the weight of rumor, hysteria, and stereotype, and that had been enmeshed in decades-old debates not only about religion but about race, sex, and the territorial, jurisdictional future of the nation. While *Riders of the Purple Sage*, like many silent films on the subject, simplifies the image of the Mormon polygamist that had been for decades various, wide-ranging, and often contradictory in its negative associations, the novel's popularity in 1912 derived in part from that cultural history. In contrast to the shifting cultural representations of Mormon villains in the latter half of the nineteenth century, in Grey's novel it is the heroes and heroines – both Gentiles and virtuous Mormons – who undergo transformation, especially regarding gender, in their escape from the unchanged

"Mormon menace" (to borrow the title of John Doyle Lee's 1905 book). Grey's depiction of Mormonism became more nuanced and tolerant in his less popular 1915 sequel *The Rainbow Trail*, which his wife called one of his "thinking novels," as the anti-Mormon magazine crusade waned after 1913.[17]

Part of the entertainment value of the stereotyped Mormon villain lay in the fact that it made possible in literature what had been eradicated in reality by politics: a prurient peek into the (exaggerated) Mormon polygamous difference, which Mark Twain famously parodies in *Roughing It.*[18] That polygamy endured for over a half a century, argues Louis Kern, "suggests that Gentile critics were both repelled and attracted by [it] and that it was but a distorted mirror of the imperfections inherent in their own sexual relationships." Or as Givens puts it, "it is precisely the transgressive nature of polygamy that excites both envy and rejection. The supposed virtue of exposing 'the moral leprosy' of Utah gives at the same time opportunity to luxuriate in all the seamy details one is excoriating."[19] This is precisely the double gesture Grey wrote into the 1915 sequel to *Riders*. In *The Rainbow Trail*, the Protestant Minister Shefford seems for a time to assume the role, if not the sexual activity, of a Mormon polygamist when he visits a sealed-wife village, which the 1918 movie poster for the quickly adapted Fox Pictures production called the "Adamless Eden."[20] "He was surrounded and made much of," writes Grey. "He had been popular before, but this was different . . . A dozen or twenty young and attractive women thrown much into companionship with one man. He might become a Mormon. The idea made him laugh. But upon reflection it was not funny; it sobered him."[21] The scene's muffled prurience might well have been a cause for nervous laughter in 1915: the clean-living reformist Protestant thrown into the harem. "The thing was provokingly seductive," writes Grey. "It was like an Arabian Nights' tale. What would these strange, fatally bound women do? . . . Already eyes flashed and lips had smiled" (p. 117). Just as the Gentile Lassiter usurps the role of suitor from the Mormon elders in *Riders of the Purple Sage*, Shefford usurps the role of polygamous patriarch who has a choice of women: "In the afternoons there was leisure for him and for the women. He had no favorites, and let the occasion decide what he should do and with whom he should be . . . It was not a game he was playing. More and more, as he learned to know these young women, he liked them better, he pitied them, he was good for them" (p. 119). Shefford is permitted to play this game, of course, only because he does not cross the sexual boundary and remains appalled by polygamy: "The crimes in the name of religion! How he thought of the blood and the ruin laid at the door of religion!" (p. 120). In effect, the American hero, whether Lassiter or Shefford, has it both ways, to extend Forrest Robinson's study of the Western: both seducer and savior, both enforcer of moral codes and liberator from religious codes.

That Grey's hero has it both ways structurally imitates the symmetrically opposing arguments between Mormons and Americans over polygamy, and suggests that readers may have been nostalgic for a transitional era of unresolved tension in which Mormon difference was preserved as a threat to rescue people from. Frontier regions, Grey knew, provided this backdrop of dramatic contrasts as places that were, one could say, not yet completed, just as the territory of southern Utah in 1871 was a border region both in the sense that it was a federal territory and not a state and in the sense that it was populated by both Mormons and Gentiles. Michael Colacurcio's discussion of Hawthorne's "My Kinsman, Major Molineux" explores the kind of political and psychological ambiguity that Grey establishes in this border region. Colacurcio argues that "the political ambiguities of eighteenth-century Boston provide, for Hawthorne, precisely the sort of 'neutral territory' he needed for such a tale . . . he learned to let disputed or non-aligned real-estate stand for those neutral times when the bewildered psyche does not know if it is 'here or there.'" *Riders of the Purple Sage* is often bewildering to the extent that it is symptomatic rather than selfconsciously critical of a cultural psyche that does not know if it is "here or there" – or now or then. In the end, this "historical" novel retreats into the landscape in an escape from the world altogether, as Lee Mitchell has observed.[22]

The fall of Balancing Rock in *Riders* is a gate of escape from the novel's anxiety about and dependence on history, even as it imitates the Mormons' desire for seclusion in their flight to Utah away from persecution. As Kenner's history put it in 1904, almost as melodramatically as Grey might, the Mormons had "sought seclusion for the purpose of being secluded, and so conditioned that the waking hours would be free from dismay and the sleeping ones from nightmare."[23] Grey's novel preserves in another form what federal pressure had changed: unassimilated Mormon difference. The rescue of Jane points to the virtue of future Mormon assimilation and American acceptance, which the less popular sequel also records, even as an implicit cultural nostalgia for Mormon peculiarity enables the novel's dramatic tension. Indeed, in 1901, John Fiske had lumped Mormons "together with buffaloes and red Indians as those American spectacles best known to travelers from abroad."[24]

PECULIAR PEOPLE: WHITENESS, CHRISTIANITY, WOMANHOOD

You're false to your womanhood an' true to your religion. (Lassiter to Jane, p. 131)

Although *Riders of the Purple Sage* draws upon some conventions of the captivity plot, there is nothing conventional about Jane's "captivity" as an unmarried woman who owns her own land and cattle. Captivity plots most often involve racial or ethnic difference, but Jane describes her purported captors as "my people" – people who were themselves often imprisoned for polygamy. If anything, it is the Gentile Lassiter who is ethnically other in this setting, and it is the seclusion he ultimately shares with Jane in Surprise Valley that resembles captivity as much as escape. The culturally presumed Mormon ethnic difference is key to understanding how the novel's "seclusion resolution" is not a captivity but a rescue and why the plot should have Jane lose her inheritance. Jane's transformation is enabled by the cultural flexibility of Mormon ethnic identity as the "not-quite Other." Givens argues that to attribute quasi-ethnic status to a new religious minority, a cultural process in which literature plays a major role, "is to participate in a process by which threatening proximity has been transformed into manageable difference."[25] The reification of Mormon religious difference into ethnic status involved, for much of the latter half of the nineteenth century and even into the twentieth, a confused amalgamation of non-white stereotypes.

Writing in *Cosmopolitan* in 1911 during the anti-Mormon magazine crusade, Alfred Henry Lewis exploited the national anxiety with immigration and white slavery to argue that by bringing female converts from overseas, Mormonism threatened "the whiteness of American womanhood." Throughout the latter half of the nineteenth century, the most persistent criticism made of Mormon polygamy was that its threat to monogamy placed civilization in peril. That sexual threat was, significantly, frequently aligned with and perceived as a racial – i.e., non-white and non-western – threat to white America. The Republican party's 1856 pledge to rid the nation of polygamy and slavery was "salted through," as B. Carmon Hardy argues, with racial and sectional implications. In light of the widespread belief in Mormon disloyalty to the United States and the racial politics of Manifest Destiny, the unassimilated Mormon presence in the Utah territory was perceived to threaten not only the nation's homes but the racial and sexual health of the nation itself. "If [polygamy] be tolerated as a local institution," said a critic in the 1850s, "it must be tolerated also as a national institution, and stamp its impress forever upon the national character." One Chicago journalist argued in 1880 that the country could solve a double problem by shipping all of its Negroes to Utah; the same Chicago paper, the *Chicago Evening Journal*, urged the nation to take care of its Indian problem by colonizing tribes among the Mormons. As late as one year after *Riders* appeared, a special commission on Mormonism established by the National Reform Association, in response to rumors of persistent polygamy, made its report and invoked the following rhetoric: "If Lincoln were still living he doubtless would say: 'The national house divided against itself will not endure. No nation can endure very long with its homes part polygamous and part monogamous, with its marriage system partly Moslem and partly Christian.' "[26]

Comparisons between slavery and polygamy were accompanied by comparisons of Mormons with blacks and other non-white people. Reflecting the assumed linkage between sexual and racial health, Mary Chesnut wrote in South Carolina in 1862 that there were "no negro marital relations, or the want of them, half so shocking as Mormonism." After the Civil War, Utah polygamists "were cast with blacks as animal and profligate" and pointed to as evidence of disregard for nature's laws. Repeating Chief Justice Morrison R. Waite's 1879 association of polygamy with non-Western peoples, John A. McClernand of the Utah Commission referred to it in 1889 as an " 'Asiatic and African pestilence,' sure to stultify the nation's genius." Some called polygamy Buddhist and Mohammedan, while one female critic in 1880 asked how any proper woman could live with a man whose religion encouraged him to marry Indian squaws. Another common argument was that polygamy produced physiological decline. The polygamous offspring degenerated into a new species, according to one 1861 account: "the yellow, sunken, cadaverous visage; the greenish-colored eyes; the thick protuberant lips; the low forehead . . . [all] constitute an appearance so characteristic of the new race, the production of polygamy, as to distinguish them at a glance." The child of polygamy "was simply a white negro."[27]

The Mormon graphic image preceding Grey's writing often relied heavily on associations between Mormons and other non-white ethnic minorities. Illustrations in magazines would often associate Mormons with Jews, Chinese, and Indians (with whom they were often, based on some history, considered on good, even conspiratorial, terms), as well as with blacks. One Mormon baiter in 1897 in Missouri wrote, "The Lord intends that WHITE FOLKS, and not Mormons shall possess that goodly land." In the 1897 "Frank Merriwell Among the Mormons or The

Lost Tribe of Israel," Frank Merriwell, the embodiment of American values, comments, "He seems to be a white man . . . even if he is a Mormon."[28] The confusion over Mormon racial identity was sometimes brought about by transferring onto the lusty polygamist the popular belief that Africans and African Americans had a peculiarly potent sexuality.[29] After the announcement concerning polygamy in 1852, the black-Mormon connection seemed irresistible; into the twentieth century, Mormons were often illustrated as blacks, sometimes making it impossible to identify the true target, whether Mormon or black. In 1905, one of the "Coon Songs" of popular culture, songs used to ridicule blacks, was entitled "The Mormon Coon." The cover to the lyrics shows a black, bearded Mormon man surrounded by six wives, three white, one black, one Chinese, and one Indian (see figure 3).[30]

A *Life* magazine cartoon in 1904 entitled "Mormon Elder-berry – Out with His Six-Year Olds, Who Take after Their Mothers" shows a Mormon father hand in hand with his many children of various caricatured races (see figure 4).[31] Societal anxieties over miscegenation are clear. In this cultural context, the sexualized battle between Gentile and Mormon in Grey's novel must also have had racial overtones, so that the substitution of Mormon for Indian as the alien Other, in Lee Mitchell's argument, does not entirely de-racialize, or keep entirely alien, what in Grey's novel is a conflict over a purportedly white woman's body, soul, and property. Warning her of the Mormon conspiracy, Lassiter says to Jane, "The cottonwood grove's full of creepin', crawlin' men. Like Indians in the grass" (p. 145). In light of the accumulated cultural meaning surrounding the ambiguously non-white, non-western, nationally threatening Mormon polygamist from which Grey's heroine is rescued in *Riders*, Jane's fate is connected not only to the preservation of monogamy and the American home, but also, implicitly, to the racial future of the American West and the nation at large.

Just as Mormons and Gentiles make contesting claims on Jane's body, soul, and ranch, so do the "new" Mormon Joe Lake and the Protestant minister Shefford vie, though amicably, for Jane's adopted daughter Fay's body, soul, and fate in the sequel to *Riders*. But another, more subtle claim is made in *The Rainbow Trail* for the racial identity of this mysterious, saving woman of the desert, a claim that only has meaning given the ambiguously non-white status of a plural wife; Grey writes, for example, that the "sealed" wives are "as blind in their hoods as veiled Arab women in palanquins" (p. 199). (The year *Riders* appeared, Bruce Kinney published a popular text called *Mormonism: The Islam of America*.)

Figure 3 "The Mormon Coon" Songbook, 1905. Published by Sol Bloom.

The fact that Fay is rescued from such a (Muslim) fate by Shefford suggests the possibility that she has been implicitly rescued as white, but only if her whiteness is in doubt to begin with. (The fact that Grey was one-thirty-second Indian on his mother's side may only partly explain his

Figure 4 "Mormon Elder-berry, Out with His Six-Year Olds, Who Take after Their Mothers." *Life* magazine, 28 April 1904.

creation of characters like Fay or the half-Indian, half-Spaniard Mescal in *The Heritage of the Desert*.) Gender and racial identities in this novel, as in *Riders*, are confused only to be reinstated, providing the queer thrill of the strange and new in the West. In *Riders*, Fay is a little girl who "sees things as they appear on the face," according to Lassiter, who adds: "An Indian does that" (p. 225). Climbing rocks and hills with Fay, Shefford "imagined she must be like an Indian girl, or a savage who loved the lofty places and the silence" (p. 128). Fay's wildness is thrilling and "strange" to Shefford, who reaches "for the brown hand stretched forth to help him leap," which gives him "the fear of a man who was running toward a precipice and who could not draw back. This was a climb, a lark, a wild race to the Mormon girl, bound now in the village, and by the very freedom of it she betrayed her bonds" (p. 129). Seeming to "embrace the west" (p. 129), Fay seems to represent the frontier's freedom to break the bonds of custom, in Turner's formulation, but she is also, suggestively, of a "wild race" in their wild race together, and she has broken the bonds to her appropriate race: the frontier's freedom should only go so far. What is fearful to Shefford is arguably not simply sexual love but an implied miscegenous love that dares not speak its name: "To Shefford it was also a wild race, but toward one sure goal he dare not name . . . she was standing on the summit, her arms wide, her full breast heaving, her slender body straight as an Indian's . . . Shefford instinctively grasped the essence of this strange spirit, primitive and wild" (p. 129).

Fay's ambiguous Indian identity, however, is brief enough to tantalize but not enduring enough to shock: quickly the sun dies out, and "the girl changed as swiftly . . . The whiteness stole back" (pp. 129, 130). Fay's whiteness is a point of repeated reference in the text. She is named after the lily "of a whiteness purer than new-fallen snow"; Fay has "the same whiteness" (pp. 126, 127). "How white her skin!" thinks Shefford (p. 124). "She's so white you can look through her," says Joe (p. 199). Clearly, these and many other references to her whiteness are meant to symbolize purity, but the odd occasional comparison with an Indian seems to suggest that while Grey wants to reassure his readers of her racial identity, he also lends to Shefford's desire an illicit thrill known only in the western desert. This illicit quality is sanctioned, of course, by Shefford's saving her: "She was free. She was innocent," we are told after Ruth, "white and resolute," covers for Fay in her escape from the sealed-wife village. Alone and free, Shefford and Fay embrace, and Shefford "became suddenly alive to the warm, throbbing contact of her bosom, to her strong arms clinging round his neck, to her closed eyes, to the rapt whiteness of her face" (pp. 342, 343). The Mormon "black plot" in *Riders* is thus a threat to precisely *white* womanhood and to the "natural" law governing the sexes, a law that the work of fiction, nevertheless, loves to flirt with endangering: the natural seclusion of Jane, Fay, and Lassiter is significantly not "sanctified" by marriage. Grey's adulterous affairs may have inspired this pushing of the envelope. Stephen May even speculates that Grey's "prurient interest in Mormon polygamy" may have influenced his philandering early in his career. On one hand, polygamy "shocked his Protestant sensibilities; on the other it excited a libidinous need in him . . . Grey began to feel some justification for traveling with women friends" away from his wife. "After all," May writes, "his Mormon friends engaged in plural marriages and yet led highly moral lives; why shouldn't he?"[32] *Riders* risks ever more ambiguous distinctions between absolute moral codes. While the protagonists' union is sanctified by conventional values (one man for one woman), the ending also upends them as Jane's sexual virtue is implicitly corrupted, by 1912 standards, in the process of being saved. In the sequel, this contravention of sexual norms is suggestively dispelled when Fay reports to Shefford that in Surprise Valley, "Uncle Jim and Mother Jane talked less as the years went by" (p. 227). The Surprise, it turns out, is that they did not live happily ever after.

Grey's fiction not only "steals back" the white identity Mormons already had but much of their religious and cultural identity as well. John Cawelti has argued that for Grey's characters, "sex and religion are strangely intermixed. Sexual passion is treated as a semimystical moral and religious experience."[33] The same can be said of the Mormons. The fact that in Grey's novel sexual energy, nowhere circumscribed by conventional marriage, is mystical and cosmically transformative, etched in the landscape itself, shares with Mormonism a (heretical) departure from Christian notions of Original Sin. One of Mormonism's most dramatic departures from historical Christianity was, and is, its insistence that human sexuality, as practiced in "sealed" marriage, imitates divinity and is necessary for the highest exaltation. Whereas plural marriage was viewed as licentious by mainstream culture, Mormonism perceived it as a sacred covenant that would allow for eternal progress. Both the non-marital union of Jane and Lassiter and Mormon plural marriage are meant to be means for salvation even as they each fall outside of the legitimating function of conventional marriage.

The secularization or de-sacralizing of the Mormon religion is concomitant with a spiritualizing of the western landscape in which Grey's characters wander in the desert as if they were usurping for themselves the mythic contours of the Mormons' physical and spiritual journey to the New Zion. In *The Rainbow Trail*, for example, Shefford "seemed to be born again" in the desert, a place where, he believes, " 'I shall find a God and my salvation' " (pp. 58, 211). The fact that the Mormon flight from persecution followed the contours of the Israelites' journey as Moses rescued them from slavery adds a Biblical resonance to Lassiter's rescue of Jane from polygamy's slavery. Grey's myth of the West captures the American imagination to the extent that it denudes the Mormon imagination of spirit or sanctifying legend, and it does so, in *The Rainbow Trail*, in a very Mormon fashion: by finding in the American Indian an ancient and sacred culture. "I've been in the desert long enough to know there *is* a God, but probably not the one your Church worships," says Withers to the soul-searching Protestant Minister; "Shefford, go to the Navajo for a faith!" (p. 55). Yet the refrain of an Indian prayer returns the reader to Mormonism. "Now all is well, now all is well" (p. 141) echoes the refrain of the most famous Mormon pioneer hymn, "Come, Come Ye Saints": "All is well, All is well."

This cultural borrowing from a demonized group in the service of what is arguably an American genre is a curious twist in the history both of the "Mormon menace" and of the Western, but it is not surprising when one considers how archetypally American, and not just how peculiar, Mormons were in the nineteenth century. In search of freedom to worship as they believed, they exercised the independence that came to characterize the image of the frontier American and also resembled the Puritans in their flight to the New World. It is because their distinction was so similar to Americans' own sense of divinely sanctioned, exceptional mission in the West that they were so divergently perceived. As James B. Halsey wrote in the *Era*, a national literary magazine, in 1903: "It is hard to find anything between extravagant eulogy from its devotees and sympathizers on the one hand, and fierce denunciation and abuse from religious despisers and Gentile prejudice on the other."[34]

The Mormon threat was social, political, and economic – hence ideological, a threat of a competing national myth or allegory, as conveyed in depictions of Brigham Young as the horned Moses (see figure 5).[35] The theological precepts of Mormonism placed it outside mainstream Christianity and even outside American political ideology, even though it seems to imitate the Puritan mission and covenant. Jan Shipps has argued that the Mormons signaled a departure from Christianity as certain as the early Christian church's departure from Judaism.[36] Believing, like the early Puritans, that they were the new chosen people, that the

Figure 5 "Situation of the Mormons in Utah." *The Wasp*, 1 February 1879.

American Indians were lost tribes of Israel, and that the prophet was in charge of developing the Kingdom of God on earth, the Mormon presence in federal territory constituted not only a different economic system but a theocracy with a differently perceived sense of historical purpose, its own army, and a vast colonized portion of the western half of the continent, stretching in the 1850s from southern California to what is now Wyoming and from Oregon to what is now New Mexico. The Mormons' proposed state of Deseret in 1849 covered one-sixth of the present continental United States.

Though the distinction between Mormon and Gentile power made a legal and moral difference in late nineteenth-century debates about polygamy, in Grey's novels the Mormon and the Gentile are distinct yet intimately related, eerily resembling one another, to the extent that Jane's Mormonism is retained in the form in which Lassiter can share it, leaving the actual tenets and beliefs of Mormonism, and its history, unnarrated. " 'I don't know much about religion as religion,' " a Gentile woman says to Jane, " 'but your God and my God are the same' " (p. 79). The novel wants to maintain a basic Christianity, radically "free of any church or creed" by not knowing "religion as religion," even though distinctions between religions seem to make all the difference. This blindness is due to what the issue of religion disguises: a non-normative sexual practice's disturbing alignment with religious conviction and a religion's alignment with a large territory, so disturbing that the nation abandoned its own civil beliefs in religious freedom in order to break a religion and banish certain consensual sexual relations. Indeed, as Nancy Bentley argues, it was precisely the issue of a woman's consent that so baffled anti-polygamists, who could only imagine, as so many anti-polygamy novels did, that polygamy was equivalent to women's slavery.[37] In the anti-Mormon crusades, before and after Utah's admission to the Union, questions about Mormon political allegiance disguised not only anxieties over religious heresy, as Givens argues, but also the contradictions of American religious intolerance, civil beliefs, and cultural practices: espousing religious pluralism while seeking to alter if not eradicate a religion; fighting in the name of a woman's freedom from "slavery" when those very women often defended plural marriage in the name of women's rights; and demonizing Mormons as culturally and ethnically other even though they were largely white.

Although Jane Tompkins argues that the Western rejects a Christian frame of reference, for Grey's influential novel it is important that the

American hero also be a true believer and not a fanatic if he is to "save" Jane from Mormon fanaticism, else the religious distinctions in this novel would make no difference for Lassiter's heroism. Far from being a "savior as Antichrist," as Tompkins describes him, Lassiter develops a religious and domestic faith in Grey's novel while falling in love with a virtuous Mormon woman, as Forrest G. Robinson has pointed out.[38] Lassiter is introduced to the reader as providentially given to Jane. Speaking with "the arrogance of a Mormon whose power could not be brooked" (p. 5), the elder Tull tells Jane as he is about to whip the Gentile Venter at the novel's opening: "your father left you wealth and power. It has turned your head. You haven't yet come to see the place of Mormon women" (p. 7). But before Tull can whip Venters (or for that matter, put Jane in her polygamous place), Lassiter appears from the West, an "answer to [Jane's] prayer" (p. 8). While in Tull there is something "barely hidden, a something personal and sinister, a deep of himself, an engulfing abyss" (p. 7), the "intensity" of Lassiter's gaze that "held" Jane upon his arrival is an interesting contrast to Tull's evil (and an interesting twist on the myth of Mormon mesmerism), "as if [Lassiter] was forever looking for that which he never found. Jane's subtle woman's intuition, even in that brief instant, felt a sadness, a hungering, a secret" (p. 9).

Situated between the dichotomized, bottomless mysteries of these two men, Jane confesses her anguish to Lassiter: "the men of my creed are unnaturally cruel. To my everlasting sorrow I confess it. They have been driven, hated, scourged till their hearts have hardened. But we women hope and pray for the time when our men will soften" (p. 13). The irony of Jane's confession is that it is addressed to a man who himself has become (naturally) hardened by the "unnatural" cruelty and hate of the Mormons he naturally wants to kill and that Jane will try to soften him, ultimately inspiring him to give up his guns. Lassiter even shares with the Mormons and their "black plot," before he gives up his guns and embraces God and little Fay (who becomes a "religion" to him), a "dark" appearance in his "black leather": " 'Look!' hoarsely whispered one of Tull's companions. 'He packs two black-butted guns – low down – they're hard to see – black agin them black chaps' " (p. 8). Just as the Mormon-killing Lassiter is susceptible to Mormon darkness, Jane herself is susceptible to masculine hardening when she begins to grasp "the truth" and "suddenly there came, in inward constriction, a hardening of gentle forces within her breast. Like a steel bar it was, stiffening all that had been soft and weak in her" (p. 7). The novel thus relies on certain gendered contradictions: Lassiter will be softened while Jane is hardened; guns are necessary but must be made obsolete; Venters is deprived of his manhood without guns, but Lassiter will acquire his full manhood when he gives them up. The gendered contradictions in Jane, like the contradictions in Lassiter, whose heart softens around women and children, resemble the contradictions between Lassiter's assertion that "where I was raised a woman's word was law" (p. 10) and his statement that "Gun-packin' in the West since the Civil War has growed into a kind of moral law. An' out here on this border it's the difference between a man an' somethin' not a man" (p. 132). The distinction between a woman and a gun in this novel effectively makes relatively little difference when it comes to a man's masculinity and moral salvation, even as the grounds for these are "neither here nor there."

Gender shifts, like the fluctuations between hatred and love in Jane against both Mormons and Mormon killers, accomplish in the end a sense that things have been worked through, that customs have been broken – a sense, in effect, of freedom and escape. With the fall of Balancing Rock, the naturalizing of Jane's secure fate away from the "unnatural" Mormons disguises the lines of cultural influence along the trail from Mormon demonization to familiarization. Indeed, the novel ends with things made familiar – and familial – as the mysteries of Bess Oldring's and Milly Erne's identities are solved and the characters form something like a large family reunion. The once mysterious masked rider turns out to be Lassiter's niece, Milly Erne's child, and probably Jane's half-sister if her father had, in fact, taken Milly Erne as a plural wife. While the past returns to make familial claims on individuals, to rein-state the American family and to demarcate it from the polygamous Mormons, Mormon polygamy allows things to become more familiar in the end, such that the narrative gap between Mormon and Gentile is effectively narrowed at the novel's end; they are distinct, yet without real differences. Whereas the characters are revealed to have ties to polygamy, Grey's novel does not reveal its ties to Mormon culture and the culture of anti-Mormonism, naturalized as his sexual cosmology is by the mystical landscape. The Mormon religion's allegory of its own history and des-tiny on the American continent is not only silent throughout the novel – and its claims metaphorically crushed by Balancing Rock – but is in the end subsumed by an American familial epic that strangely resembles it, just on the other side of Deception Pass, a natural gate of escape as mysterious and silent as the unnatural Mormons.

## IMPERIALIST PARANOIA

These elders and bishops will do absolutely any deed to go on building up the power and wealth of their church, their empire. (Venters to Jane, p. 19)

He had felt the shadow of an unseen hand; he had watched till he saw its dim outline, and then he had traced it to a man's hate . . . to the long, far-reaching arm of a terrible creed. That unseen hand had made its first move against Jane Withersteen. . . . For hand in glove with that power was an insatiable greed; they were one and the same. (p. 37)

An 1897 installment of the popular Frank Merriwell series by Gilbert Patten, entitled "Frank Merriwell Among the Mormons or The Lost Tribe of Israel," involved a captivity plot whose stock formula Grey's novel follows. Elder Asaph Holdfast, the Mormon villain, jeopardizes the freedom of a young Mormon maiden to select the mate of her choice because he wants her for himself. Melodramatically, the "all-American" Merriwell rescues her from Holdfast just in time.[39] In an 1857 cartoon entitled "Brigham Young's Preparations for the Defence of Utah – The Result" in *Frank Leslie's Illustrated Newspaper*, the Mormon militia is female, a theme given credibility in part by the Mormon leader Heber C. Kimball's 1857 remark, "I have wives enough to whip out the United States." But when the female troops encounter US troops they "half melt" and respond to Brigham Young's command "Charge!" by running into the arms of the handsome Americans. The Utah War ends when Mormon men are "unable to match the allure of their Gentile counterparts" (see figure 6).[40] Nowhere in Grey's fiction, unsurprisingly, does a Mormon "get the girl."

Drawing on Perry Miller, Lee Mitchell argues that the persistence of the captivity plot indicates just how insecure Americans have felt from the beginning about their cultural identity as something not inherited but achieved. Mitchell adds that Grey's novel appeared at a distinctive moment for American cultural anxieties, "an industrializing, imperializing age of new global power," in which Americans perceived alien cultures as forms of psychic entrapment, "as so deeply threatening to entrenched values as to imperil one's cultural moorings themselves." Westerns arouse the fear of confronting an Other by having its characters "post themselves against forces from without, represented by aliens bent on incorporating all to themselves." Mitchell reads into the novel a particular set of eastern anxieties such as the fear of white slavery and concern about gender roles, but qualifies his argument by saying that the "myriad issues involved in any rivalry with an 'empire

Figure 6 "Brigham Young's Defence of Utah – The Result." *Frank Leslie's Illustrated Newspaper*, 19 December 1857.

builder'" could also be located in readings more exhaustive than his own.[41]

Illuminating as his reading is, it repeats the novel's mystery-inspiring reticence about the distinct nature of the Mormon threat and its cultural difference in American history, particularly in light of the rivalry between Mormon and American "empire building" in the nineteenth century, with that rivalry's attendant symmetries and contradictions. Much of the historical distinction of *Riders of the Purple Sage* gets lost in the process of installing it within a cultural hermeneutic broader than its immediate Mormon villain, which bespeaks a different kind of anxiety, one produced when the identity of the Other mirrors that of the imperial power pitted against it and thus calls into question the grounds of difference upon which a national identity is made. While many captivity plots, like Grey's, can illuminate the psychology of empire, the Mormon Other tells a different and even more complicated story, one in which the Mormon "zealot" or "fanatic" in Grey's fiction adopts the role in history, from the Mormon perspective, of the "over-zealous American citizen, imbued with the institutions of his country, and chafing, no doubt, at the *imperium in imperio* which seemed to become more unbearable the more he thought of it," as Kenner's 1904 history of Utah describes him.[42] Rightly observing that "everywhere, the novel works to instill the sensation of helpless capitulation," of being forced to choose to become what one already is, Mitchell points out the ways in which the novel allays fears of a loss of culture "by recasting the traumatic scene of external threat, to confirm one's culture as not simply a matter of choice but of choice well-made," a recasting and confirmation, I would add, that was perforce adopted by the "new" non-polygamous Mormon of Grey's time.[43] That historical moment recorded both Mormon and Gentile rhetoric affirming – though with less confidence on the part of Mormons and with no consensus about the past – the value of monogamy and the separation of church and state.[44]

I want to perform a recasting of "the scene of external threat" different from Grey's by locating in Grey's sense of the Mormon threat those very American pressures that forced the Mormons to choose their monogamous and normative future. That external threat, the kind that is "bent on incorporating all to themselves," is ultimately not the many "alien" minorities in America's past, but those national, imperial pressures that eradicate or assimilate difference. The cultural work Grey's novel performs is in part to assimilate religious difference and its associated corruptions of whiteness and womanhood by not knowing religion as religion and by not knowing the ways in which the novel's (or nation's) designs identify with Mormon power – hence the novel's silence about the Mormon master plan. The novel thus instills a sense of helpless capitulation not only, on one hand, to Mormon power, and on the other, to Lassiter's power, but also to a set of unarticulated yet structural norms that are innately contradictory and unstable insofar as hero and villain, Gentile and Mormon, and male and female exchange roles and imitate each other, as we have seen. Renato Rosaldo's notion of "imperialist nostalgia" describes a particular form of nostalgia that occurs when a society mourns the loss of what it has itself transformed, especially indigenous peoples and cultures, as we saw in chapter 2.[45] But this nostalgia presumes the eradication of a real ethnic or cultural difference. Alternatively, I want to ask: what emotional or psychic relation to the "not-quite-Other" ensues when imperialist transformation of that Other transforms the imperial Self into something resembling it – or when the "not-quite-Other" becomes all too familiar under imperialist pressure? Modifying Rosaldo's notion, I would describe the sense of helpless capitulation in Grey's novel as an imperialist *paranoia* born specifically of domestic conquest of others who are as genuinely familiar as they are perceived to be strange. Like the oxymoronic forced choice which domestic American imperialism offered minority groups, imperialist paranoia has as its mission to rescue minorities from the all-pervasive threat to majority culture they are simultaneously made to represent. The suspense and mystery instilled in this rescue formula is necessary for its entertainment value and concomitantly disguises the fact that imperialist paranoia already knows that the values the rescuer represents have foreordained the defeat – and the cultural incorporation – of the Other. In turn, Mormon paranoia results not only from an external federal threat but from the internal expectation that the faith must choose to end long-defended religious practice. In this influential case of the formula Western, the trauma of history is recast as a game of suspense in which the outcome is already known, even if it is, particularly in the ambiguous case of the Mormons, not fully understood, especially with regard to presumptive norms regarding whiteness, Christianity, the family, and gender difference. As Givens argues, "to this day, debate continues as to whether Mormons are best understood in terms of their deviance and marginalized past, or as the quintessentially American religion – or even, perversely, both at the same time."[46]

In the same year that Mormonism officially gave up polygamy so that Utah could join the Union, the US census declared that frontier settlement no longer could be said to exist: the consolidation of the American West was nearly complete. Mormonism looms large and threatening in this novel to the same extent that the ideology of Manifest Destiny loomed over the nation. The larger significance of the battle for Jane Withersteen's freedom is suggested when Lassiter tries to make her see what is at stake in her fate. Jane insists, "I'm an absolutely free woman," to which Lassiter somewhat triumphantly replies, repeating national arguments about Mormon women's "slavery," "You ain't absolutely anythin' of the kind" (p. 144). In a passage that seems to blur distinctions between Lassiter's and Mormonism's omniscience and even between Mormon and American imperial designs, Lassiter explains:

Jane, you're watched. There's no single move of yours, except when you're hid in your house, that ain't seen by sharp eyes...When you rode, which wasn't often lately, the sage was full of sneakin' men. At night they crawl under your windows, into the court, an' I reckon into the house...This here grove's a hummin' bee-hive of mysterious happenin's...This all means, Jane, that you're a marked woman...you're to lose the cattle that's left – your home an' ranch – an' Amber Spring...I told you once before about that strange power I've got to feel things. (p. 145)

Jane responds, "What does it mean?...I am my father's daughter – a Mormon, yet I can't see! I've not failed in religion – in duty...When my father died I was rich...What am I, what are my possessions to set in motion such intensity of secret oppression?" Lassiter responds succinctly, "Jane, the mind behind it all is an empire builder" (p. 145). He adds, "They tried you out, an' failed of persuasion, an' finally of threats. You meet now the cold steel of a will as far from Christlike as the universe is wide. You're to be broken. Your body's to be held, given to some man, made, if possible, to bring children into the world. But your soul?...What do they care for your soul?" (p. 146).

The "mind of an empire builder" is here left unspecified: Lassiter's words possibly refer to the Mormon concept of the Kingdom of God on earth, but the master plan, like the empire, is never itself regarded by this novel that seems to reveal everything else; the word "Mormon" never appears in the above passage and the reference to the "beehive" that became Utah's state symbol is ambiguous. (The name the Mormons wanted to give to their territory, "Deseret," is the name for honey bee in the Book of Mormon.) This lack of specificity curiously opens up Lassiter's pronouncements to a meaning quite opposite his own, for if Jane is read to represent Mormonism and its possessions, the mind of an empire builder with a will of cold steel could stand for the federal government and its policies toward the Mormons in the latter half of the nineteenth century, before the Mormon Church was "broken" into giving up polygamy, the "soul" of the Mormon religion. It was not polygamy, said many Mormons in the nineteenth century, but "the milk in the Mormon coconut" that their enemies wanted:

And this, they said, had a familiar ring. The anti-polygamy movement was only an excuse for reenacting the dispossessions of Missouri and Illinois. With or without plural marriage, the Devil had been busy against them from the beginning. In 1887 [Mormon] President Taylor wrote that those behind the crusade wanted both Mormon liberty and Mormon treasure . . . Observing that the Saints could not believe the Edmunds Act singly concerned with their marital behavior, that avarice was its real motive, Phil Robinson paraphrased Mormon attitudes by remarking, "The Gentiles . . . are hankering after the good things of Utah, and hope by one cry after another to persecute the Mormons out of them."[47]

The sense of paranoia that Lassiter seeks to instill in Jane was one with which Mormons were familiar during the period of government investigations beginning in the 1880s and continuing episodically to Grey's time. In the sequel to *Riders*, Grey includes an awareness of the investigations. Minister Shefford asks Presbrey why he says the Mormons close to the Utah line are "unfriendly these days," and Presbrey responds, "They are being persecuted by the government" (p. 15). Just as Lassiter asserts that "at night they crawl under your windows, into the court, an' I reckon into the house" (p. 145), nothing was considered off-limits when it came to searches by government agents for signs of polygamous living; even "bedding was sifted for signs of cohabitation."[48] Whether Mormon or Gentile makes designs, or whether Mormon or Gentile is paranoid, the sense of a looming threat is the same. The distinction between Mormon empire and American empire is perhaps the one significant distinction left implicit and unnamed in Grey's novel, and yet that distinction, historically, is what had made all the difference in the abandonment of polygamy and the gradual assimilation of Mormonism by the time Grey wrote his novel.

*Riders of the Purple Sage* seems as blind to its own myth-making as Jane is blind to the Mormon conspiracy. Elsewhere the Mormon "invisible hand" is described as "a cold and calculating policy thought out long before she was born, a dark, immutable will of whose empire she and all that was hers was but an atom" (p. 134). The description is particularly odd because the novel is set only forty-one years after the founding of the Mormon Church. That this policy was thought out "long before she was born" suggests a history and meaning that stretches beyond Mormonism, well before 1830. Yet the soulless Mormon evil that looms so large cannot creep or crawl into Surprise Valley. Mormonism is not, in the end, nearly as powerful and Jane is not as heroic as the sacred landscape and the hero Lassiter, who is invulnerable, all-knowing, and whose distinction with guns makes all the difference. Lassiter exclaims to Jane, "Since I was a boy I've never thanked God for anythin'. If there is a God – an' I've come to believe it – I thank Him now for the years that made me Lassiter! . . . I can reach down an' feel these big guns, an' know what I can do with them" (p. 240). The partial defeat of the Mormon master plan in southern Utah in 1871 is a victory not only for God and Christianity over fanatical Mormons in Grey's novel, but for the consolidated nation that, by 1912, was already growing nostalgic for those distinctive cultural and historical particularities it had so feared and pruriently enjoyed and that its own master plan had forever altered.

# CHAPTER FIVE

# Unwedded West: Cather's divides

While Owen Wister bemoaned those unequal classes of variously non-Anglo-Saxon Americans and Zane Grey exploited briefly but successfully the evil Mormon polygamist, each of them defining their masculine hero against a denigrated other, Willa Cather's fiction upsets any formulaic expectations about heroism and the West that her settings might initially instill in her readers. If Cather shared with Grey and Wister a romantically nostalgic view of the West, she parted company with them – whatever their other aesthetic differences – by refusing to marry masculinity with heroic power and by refusing to Anglify the western landscape or homogeneously Americanize her characters. ("This passion for Americanizing everything and everybody is a deadly disease with us," she commented in 1924.)[1] Cather's West is distinguished from that of Turner, Wister, and Grey in significant part by the fact that she refuses to synthesize the oppositions – man/wilderness, East/West, men/women – that structure various forms of western nationalism. Across the divides she leaves unreconciled, such terms take on new meaning. While the formula Western enacted its allegories of national unity through the lens of heterosexual romance and marriage, Cather's western marriages (and non-marriages) are allegories of the refusal to do so. Nor do representations of violence in Cather's fiction serve an ideological point in the cause of nationalism. Cather undercut the alignment of both masculinity and marriage with nation-building out West and criticized the most homogenizing forms of Americanization, setting all of this against a Naturalist's landscape that revealed people to be small, distinct, transient, and yet heroically enduring. In contrast to both the homogeneous leveling of an assimilationist culture and the economic inequities created by capitalism, Cather's Naturalist leveling was egalitarian and, by her culture's standards, unrecognizably "American." Her writing implicitly but bluntly acknowledges that the continent cannot – any more than our stories about it – be mastered or honestly put to the service of American beliefs in progress, in national destiny, in capitalism, or in marriage as the cornerstone of civilization. The land and the human interaction with it may be shaped by such material and symbolic forces in Cather's work, but her work suggests that much that was lived remains unassimilated by culture, narrative, or nation.

From our contemporary revisionist viewpoint, Cather seems to have captured an authentic West, with her unassimilated immigrants and harsh environments, more accurately than Wister and Grey did in their romanticized, melodramatic renderings of it. But that is only half the story: Cather's fiction is all at once realistic, romantic, and naturalistic, like the range of human experience in the West itself. Cather's literary West, in which romance and realism run up against each other, is a prism through which Americans' divided sensibilities have found themselves refracted – and in which critics today still read a wide and irreconcilable range of moods and political designs, from optimism to disillusionment, from trans-nationalism to nativism.[2]

The significance of Cather's work lies in how she questioned and reshaped the literary materials and cultural presumptions that surrounded her: the alignment of masculinity with pioneering; the nationalist (and seemingly manifest) significance of the frontier; the belief that religion and marriage were civilizing forces and that Americanization was possible, necessary, and valuable; and Naturalism's belief that nature and culture are more powerful than the individual. That her early Nebraska novels are implicit and sometimes quite ironic commentaries on so many American beliefs yet as seemingly plain and flowingly woven as the Great Prairie is perhaps her most significant and broadest contribution to writing about the West, a body of literature that over the last century has ranged widely between dishonest romance and the cynicism frequently born of even the most honest historical revisionism.

This chapter looks at the development of Cather's western aesthetic and her revision of the specifically western plots of marriage, of violent revenge, and of nation-building. While *O Pioneers!*, *My Ántonia*, and *A Lost Lady* ostensibly have none of the polemics and gender politics of *The Virginian* or *Riders of the Purple Sage*, they all implicitly comment on the effect of western settlement on national identity, Americanization, and gender roles in marriage. All three writers, whatever their different aesthetic merits, engage these social concerns through similar literary means. By personifying the natural landscape and imagistically tying their heroes to the land, they naturalize the social views their heroes exemplify. By mythifying their heroes, they tie their fate to the broader fate of the country, though in Cather's case that country is less certainly America than it is for her male contemporaries. By setting their novels a generation before their first readers, they nostalgically romanticize a disappearing frontier past and thereby implicitly comment on the reader's present. These stylistic and substantive choices are less historical than they are aesthetic and ideological. Cather's distinctive combination of literary impulses needs to be understood within a cultural context in which a few young men from the East – chief among them, Harvard-educated Owen Wister and Theodore Roosevelt – came to claim authority to represent the West as it "really" was for reasons that had less to do with either art or disinterested history than the public might have believed they did. Despite some of the conservatively nostalgic leanings Cather shared with the men who also most notably represented the West for the American public, her work is singular for the fiction of her time about the West. It does not so much tell the truth about real places and people as it satisfies, engenders, and explores our need for fictions about them.

### DISCOVERING THE WEST

Cather's short story "Eric Hermannson's Soul," published in *Cosmopolitan* in 1900, reveals her early awareness of, and even subjection to, the Romantic fantasy about the West for which *The Virginian* became famous. It is also a subtle critique of that fantasy's limits and failures, at a time when she had yet to believe in the West as proper material for art. Cather's story certainly leans more in the direction of popular romance fiction, with regard to tone if not plot, than any of her later Nebraska novels,[3] but the story is also about the untranslatability of experience and the unresolvable gap among differing cultural experiences. Where Wister makes humorous the Virginian's and Molly's cultural differences and comedically brings his characters to the altar, Cather conveys the poignant impossibility of a life shared by her story's romantic protagonists Eric and Margaret: "She was a girl of other manners and conditions, and there were greater distances between her life and Eric's than all the miles which separated Rattlesnake Creek from New York city."[4] Cather engages the materials of popular romances but alters the happy convenience of their conventional plots. While she clearly believes in rendering the romantic impulse, her main interest is the gap between experience and the (often romantic) representation of experience, what one Cather critic has called "the gap between the actuality of things, the lived event, and its subsequent narration."[5] That gap in Cather's work is narrower than the one between Wyoming and the "Wyoming" nostalgically inflated in Wister's memory. Narratives of the West so often participate in, yet deny, this gap, but Cather is, along with Stephen Crane, one of the first major writers about the West after Mark Twain to make it her theme.

The historical distinctiveness of Cather's attitude about the West as a literary subject is clarified when situated against Owen Wister's and Theodore Roosevelt's experiences out West and the fact of their subsequently influential writing about it.[6] Roosevelt graduated from Harvard in 1880, got married, and began a career in law. But in the winter of 1884 he suffered a double tragedy with the deaths of his mother one day and his wife the next, after which he famously wrote that "the light had gone out of my life."[7] This suffering was quickly followed by a political setback, and Roosevelt decided in the summer of 1884 to renounce politics, make ranching his business, and center his life around Dakota, where he went in August on an extended hunting trip. That he associated the wild outdoors with its restorative effects on his childhood asthma added to the reasons Roosevelt looked back on this experience as a saving and defining one. Wister had an experience similar to the man's to whom he later dedicated *The Virginian*. After graduating from Harvard in 1882, Wister considered pursuing his love of music in Europe, which brought him into conflict with his father. Though his father eventually consented, Wister vengefully determined to follow his father's original suggestion and work for the investment firm of Henry Lee Higginson. In the spring of 1885 his health broke down – possibly a nervous breakdown – and Dr. S. Weir Mitchell, who had delivered Wister as a baby, recommended a trip to a ranch in the West as a cure. From that point on, although Wister practiced law until his father's death in 1896, his true career was settled: he would write about the West.

These experiences have echoes – and telling divergences – both in Cather's fiction and in her life. In "Eric Hermannson's Soul," Wyllis Elliot, who "had spent a year of his youth" in Nebraska, revisits the area with his sister Margaret in order to buy cheap land. "When he had graduated from Harvard," Cather writes, "it was still customary for moneyed gentlemen to send their scapegrace sons to rough it on ranches in the wilds of Nebraska *or* Dakota" (p. 26, emphasis added). When Roosevelt ventured his first trip to Dakota in 1883, he took his brother Elliott. In 1884 he made his second trip (like Wyllis Elliot) in search of good investments, and became a part owner of a Wyoming cattle ranch run by a Harvard classmate. In 1885, Roosevelt published his first book on the West, *Hunting Trips of a Ranchman*, which he dedicated to his brother Elliott. That Cather names her character Wyllis Elliot is probably no coincidence, if one also considers the fact that Cather published "Eric Hermannson's Soul" four years after Roosevelt's popular, multi-volume *The Winning of the West* was completed and two years after Roosevelt had become immensely (and theatrically) famous at San Juan Hill in 1898. Cather also inserts her boyish nickname as a youth in her character's name: Wyllis ("Will is") Elliot – effectively identifying herself with this young rancher and relating herself familially to the most famous living American and writer of the West. It also suggests the beginning of Cather's own distinct significance in the literary West.

Such identification serves revision, not simply reinforcement, of Roosevelt's ethos and significance. Cather's story is about the struggle over the soul of the rural immigrant whose name "*Her/mann*son" androgynously rewrites the kind of masculinist ventures for the (western) country's soul that made Roosevelt famous. But it is also, as Susan Rosowski points out, a story of female awakening, in Cather's shift of attention from Wyllis to his sister-savior.[8] In this and other early western stories, one witnesses the beginning of Cather's professional struggle over the literary terrain that the era's most celebrated man seized for both private and public mythology in the decade after the frontier's passing. That terrain for Cather was never male-dominated or -defined, except in the male imagination. Jim Burden is redeemed from the adolescent, performative masculinity that is meant to impress a woman by the woman he is trying to impress. Ántonia, unlike Jim, does not get educated at Harvard but has a greater influence on Jim's tastes than anything else in his life.

Cather's 1900 story portrays its male characters against western type, a type constructed for an eastern audience. "These young men," continues the narrator, "did not always return to the ways of civilized life," but, like Roosevelt, Wister, and the narrator of *The Virginian*, Wyllis Elliot "had not married a half-breed, nor been shot in a cow-puncher's brawl, nor wrecked by bad whisky, nor appropriated by a smirched adventuress" (p. 26) – in other words, he did not live out the popular literary convention for masculine adventure. Instead he "had been saved by his sister" Margaret, the story's heroine, "who had been very near to his life ever since the days when they read fairy tales together and dreamed the dreams that never come true" (p. 26). During their visit, Margaret meets and comes to love Eric Hermannson, the closest physical version of a figure like the Virginian in Cather's work. Eric was "handsome as young Siegfried, a giant in stature, with a skin singularly pure and delicate, like a Swede's; hair as yellow as the locks of Tennyson's amorous Prince, and eyes of a fierce, burning blue, whose flash was most dangerous to women. He had in those days a certain pride of bearing, a certain confidence of approach, that usually accompanies physical perfection" (p. 33).

But here end the similarities to Wister's Virginian and the novel of that name that appeared two years later. As soon as Cather describes Eric's beauty, she adds,

but the sad history of those Norwegian exiles, transplanted in an arid soil and under a scorching sun, had repeated itself in his case. Toil and isolation had sobered him, and he grew more and more like the clods among which he labored... It is a painful thing to watch the light die out of the eyes of those Norsemen, leaving an expression of impenetrable sadness, quite passive, quite hopeless, a shadow that is never lifted. (p. 33)

In her work, Cather shares with Turner an environmentalist interpretation of culture and character, but rewrites his view of the frontier's progressive evolution and its socially homogenizing effects. (Turner did not care for Cather's fiction and wrote to Alice Hooper that Cather was too sympathetic toward unassimilated "non-English stocks" in *O Pioneers!* and *A Lost Lady*.)[9] Whereas the light went out of Roosevelt's life back East, propelling him to seek rejuvenation in Dakota, the harsh Dakotan existence takes the life out of Cather's Swedish immigrant. Eric and Margaret, unlike the Virginian and his eastern sweetheart Molly, do not marry. In fact, we are told early on that Margaret is to marry when she returns East. Whereas the Virginian rubs the taint of eastern civilization out of his bride, in Cather's early manner it is the awkward, rough immigrant who yearns for but falls short of what the East represents. "You are the only beautiful thing that has ever come close to me," Eric says to Margaret. "You are like all that I wanted once and never had, you are all that they have killed in me" (p. 37). In 1918, when *My Ántonia* was published, Jim Burden returns to Nebraska from his sterile life in the East and tacitly acknowledges a similar sentiment to his Bohemian immigrant friend from childhood.

The dialogue between Margaret and Eric, and the feelings in Margaret that Cather describes, read as if Grey and Wister later lifted them: "the strength of the man was like an all-pervading fluid, stealing through her veins, awakening under her heart some nameless, unsuspected existence that had slumbered there all these years and that went out through her throbbing fingertips to his that answered" (p. 40). Because Cather was keenly aware at the time of Frank Norris' success and what she perceived – perhaps enviously – as Kate Chopin's Naturalist failure, *The Awakening*,[10] a story that often reads as if it imitates the sappiness of romantic Westerns fulfills its deeper Naturalist impulse:

All her life she had searched the faces of men for the look that lay in his eyes. She knew that that look had never shone for her before, would never shine for her on earth again, that such love comes to one only in dreams or in impossible places like this, unattainable always . . . All that she was to know of love she had left upon his lips. (pp. 43, 44)

Though Cather's novels would never be as purple in their prose as this story in *Cosmopolitan*, the double impulse to represent the most romantic version of experience with the most brutal recognition of the hard soil upon which it most often falls never leaves her work.

Between the publication of "Eric Hermannson's Soul" in 1900 and the publication of *O Pioneers!* in 1913, a change occurs in Cather's view of the West: it comes to represent rich, authentic life, the life that has "light" in it. Cather turns against the language of popular romance employed in her early work only to romanticize the West in a manner she had previously reserved for eastern and European culture. In effect, she begins to find in the West a rejuvenating source of life and the pull of found identity that Roosevelt and Wister experienced and wrote about. And curiously enough, this turn seems to have come about primarily through an experience similar to theirs. The Nebraskan writer "discovered" the West's restorative powers when she took a trip to the Southwest – her first – in 1912. As if imitating her character Margaret, Cather went to Winslow, Arizona and explored "a new country" with her brother Douglass, who was working on the Santa Fe railroad. She envisioned the trip "as a restorative vacation" since she had been ill for several weeks in early 1912 (and had had a minor surgical operation in Boston in January) and since she associated the Southwest with a return to health.[11] But it became more than that. Having long suffered, in her friend Elizabeth Sergeant's words, a " 'truly gruelling inner pull' " between eastern literary culture and her western background, after she returned and began to write *O Pioneers!*, she found a new "integration and tranquillity" and seemed to "be all of a piece."[12]

It was the beginning of her subsequent identity as an artist. "Cather believed she had discovered her authentic, essential identity in the

Southwest in 1912 and then expressed that identity honestly and openly in *O Pioneers!*," writes Sharon O'Brien.[13] Elizabeth Sergeant cites the fact that Cather composed the poem she later used as the epigraph to *O Pioneers!*, entitled "Prairie Spring," after her stay in the Southwest. "It suggests," Sergeant writes, "that Willa Cather was suddenly in control of inner creative forces which had tended to swamp her and make her dismal so long as she could not use them. The vast solitude of the Southwest, its bald magnificence, brilliant light and physical impact" toned up her spirit and suggested to her that "a new artistic method could evolve from familiar Nebraska subject matter."[14] While Cather's western youth provided the materials for her art, the impulse to employ them came from the release that only an easterner, and not a westerner, is capable of feeling in the "new" country of the Southwest.

One aspect of that trip perhaps more than any other seems to have rejuvenated Cather and helps explain the shift in her work from a view of the West as impoverished and the East as cultured to one of the West as rich with culture and life. She developed romantic feelings for a young man named Julio, who lived in the nearby Spanish Mexican settlement and who exposed her to Mexican love songs, local legends and myths, and a Mexican dance at which she was reportedly conscious of being the only white among "gentle, dark-skinned" people.[15] Elizabeth Sergeant recalls from Cather's letters that he was

a young Antinous of a singer... with a mellifluous name and a few simple thoughts and feelings. His golden skin, his ancient race, his eyes with their tragic gleam – well, he reminded Willa of some antique sculpture in the Naples Museum. Being with him was like living in a classic age.

Here she interrupted herself to apologize. Nothing bored *her* more than to hear ecstatic accounts from friends about the charm of Venetian gondoliers and Sicilian donkey boys. But this was different. His words seemed to come from the Breviary, they were so full of simple piety and directness. He would go anywhere to find wild flowers, or hunt a spring of water, as she would do as a child in Nebraska. But when asked to visit cliff dwellers he was indifferent – "*por qué los muertos, pobrecitos?*"[16]

Here was not only timeless culture but ageless youth, paradoxically but not surprisingly perceived through an Old World cultural lens. Julio's age, gender, language, nationality, ethnicity (and probably sexual orientation) were different from Cather's and she became infatuated with his exoticized difference. Of the hundreds of Cather's letters that Sharon O'Brien has read, the letters about Julio and her experiences in the Southwest convey, she claims, the most romantic exhilaration and, with

rare exceptions, the most tender infatuation.[17] Cather "immediately felt
that she had been reborn" in the Southwest through this encounter.
Writing to S. S. McClure shortly after leaving, "she told him that he
would never recognize her; she was a new person, dark-skinned and
good-humored. She was ready for a different life, she thought; she felt
confident in herself, in touch with fundamentals."[18] Sergeant recalls that
the Spanish Mexican settlement "redeemed the boredom of the desert
and the crassness of the frontier by its whole gentle, homely, free-handed
atmosphere" and that in this region "the grandiose and historical scale
of things seemed to forecast some great spiritual event," something "that
had nothing to do with the appalling mediocrity and vulgarity of the
industrial civilization."[19]

If the contours of Cather's transformative experience seem to share
much with the experiences and stories of Wister and Grey (it even recalls
the rebirth in the Southwest in Grey's *The Rainbow Trail* of the Protestant
minister Shefford, who falls in love with a girl who resembles an Indian),
the experience gave birth to a more complex and distinctive literature
in which the rejuvenation of the West and the exoticized other do not
participate in imperial designs.

OBSCURE DESTINY

In 1896, Cather wrote an essay in the *Nebraska State Journal* on the
American poet "of the dung hill as well as of the mountains." She
was describing Walt Whitman. Writing before she modified her eastern
sense of discrimination, including her sense that Nebraska was not poetic
material, she thought Whitman to be "without an exclusive sense of the
poetic, a man without the finer discriminations, enjoying everything with
the unreasoning enthusiasm *of a boy*" (emphasis added). One could not
call Whitman either good or bad since such judgments were alien to
his world view: "he accepted the world just as it is and glorified it, the
seemly and unseemly, the good and the bad. He had no conception of
a difference in people or in things." His literary ethics, she wrote, were
no more than nature's, with its level playing field. "He did not realize the existence of a conscience or a responsibility. He had no more
thought of good or evil than the folks in Kipling's Jungle book."[20] But
thirty-five years after her statement on Whitman, Cather claimed that
in writing *O Pioneers!* "everything was spontaneous and took its own
place, right or wrong."[21] By the time she took her title from Whitman
and wrote *O Pioneers!*, that which Cather found in Whitman to be both

charming and yet alien to her own aesthetic sense became the "home" style by which she rendered life on the Great Divide. More harshly than in her judgment of Whitman, Cather decried Mark Twain in 1897 as "neither a scholar, a reader or a man of letters and very little of a gentleman . . . nor a man who loves art of any kind." Implying, it would seem, that there is nothing for Art to be found on the frontier, Cather compared Twain's laugh to that of "the backwoodsman" and described him as a "rough, awkward, good-natured *boy*"(emphasis added).[22] Even though their carefree attitude imitates her boyish youth, in her early assessments of Whitman and Twain, she attacks both their subject matter and style for boyishly making no distinctions, including that between East and West.

By the time she sets her second novel on the Great Divide, however, such undiscriminating boys become subjects for her sympathizing art and are joined to a balancing strength in figures like Alexandra Bergson and Ántonia Shimerda. *O Pioneers!* begins, as perhaps no novel of the West ever had, with the image of a male "crying bitterly" and a female coming to the rescue. Emil Bergson's kitten is atop a telegraph pole and his tears are soothed by "a ray of hope: his sister was coming," walking, like a cowboy hero, though in less melodramatic circumstances, "as if she knew exactly where she was going and what she was going to do next."[23] Although Alexandra will not ultimately be able to rescue Emil from boyish passions, in *My Ántonia*, Jim Burden's undiscriminating younger self grows up to recognize gratefully Ántonia's powerful, continuing influence on his adult sensibility. While Cather early criticized Whitman and Twain for their unpoetic lack of discrimination, her art later benefited from their common egalitarian impulse. The fact that she went in 1905 to Mark Twain's seventieth birthday party – where she also met Owen Wister (with likely excitement, according to one biographer) – possibly suggests an appreciation at the time of Twain's leveling aesthetic, the kind that reconciled her divided sensibility.[24]

Despite her seeming personal desire to reconcile her divided sensibility, Cather departed both from what she perceived to be the romantic excesses of women novelists and from what she judged the boyish predilections of the male American literary originals whose freedom to choose their subject matter she may have envied. But in the divide between them, she married romance with reality, youthful passion with sacrifice, and femininity with independence, though not always harmoniously. Like Grey's *Riders of the Purple Sage*, which appeared one year before, *O Pioneers!* represents a woman whose father leaves her land and who has to struggle to keep it. But unlike Jane Withersteen, who gains her freedom from Mormon tyranny only by losing her land, Alexandra Bergson keeps both her independence and her land and prospers on it. "I'll do exactly as I please with the rest of my land, boys," Alexandra says to her brothers (p. 151), and she does so, without a shoot-out, without a man. "The authority you can exert by law is the only influence you will ever have over me again," Alexandra says to them (p. 155). Her fate is not beholden to her wedding, her land is not wedded to empire. More influential than the men in her life is the land itself, the problem of aridity, and her own courage. In the ideological context of both Manifest Density and the Reform Era's Christian rhetoric, Alexandra's prosaically economic claim that "alfalfa has been the salvation of this country" (p. 154) is rhetorically revolutionary: a crop stands in for the Cross, and "this country" suggests a geographic region more than it suggests "America." Sentiment surrounds this woman and her land in Cather's novel, but such affect is divorced from domesticity, nation, and conventional marriage. For all of her noted mythic qualities, Alexandra is particular, distinctive, even flawed; at times uninteresting, at others blind. And the reality of the masculine world in which she must live is acknowledged sympathetically by her future, self-deprecating husband Carl, who says to her, " 'It is your fate to be always surrounded by little men. And I am no better than the rest" (p. 163).

Despite Cather's reversal of female subordination and her unconventional (non)portrayal of marriage, her work nevertheless portrays the frontier as less socially egalitarian than Frederick Jackson Turner liked to believe it was.[25] In Cather's literary West, power, influence, survival, control, and reason are not exclusively masculinity's domain, but neither are human beings free to remake civilization, unconstrained by the Old World. While social custom is broken in *O Pioneers!* – Alexandra is an unmarried, independent farmer at forty, more successful than her brothers – many of the strict social codes of the Old World are in evidence, often to disturbing effect. In their misogynist denunciation of women in business, for example, Alexandra's brothers seem impervious not only to family feeling but to the egalitarian spirit that Turner found on the frontier. "You can't do business with women," Oscar complains after trying to convince Alexandra that only the men of the family can be responsible for the land (p. 155). Whereas Turner argued that the frontier produced composite Americans, Cather's composite picture of immigrants in Nebraska stresses not their Americanness but their ethnic, cultural, physical, and linguistic distinctiveness. Cather neither dramatizes their sense of belonging to America nor downplays the barriers and tensions among immigrant groups. At the same time that she conveys a sense of her characters' quiet but epic heroism, she is unsparing in her portrayal of their unaccountable failures and despair. Cather's description of Emil scything, for example, invokes Alexandra's happy destiny without making its justification any more manifest than the tragedies that outnumber it: "He was not thinking about the tired pioneers over whom his blade glittered. The old wild country, the struggle in which his sister was *destined* to succeed while so many *men* broke their hearts and died, he can scarcely remember" (pp. 75–76, emphasis added). Emil embodies the pioneer's optimism and the kind of leveling Cather saw in Whitman. He cannot remember the pioneers' exhausted, broken lives any more than he can foretell how his life and passion will be cut down suddenly on the grass – and like the leaves of grass – that he scythes.

If Emil is not free to chart his individual destiny, neither is Frank Shabata a free agent when he kills him. Violence in *O Pioneers!* plays no part in heroic development, ethnic conflict, or nationalism. The murder of the lovers Emil and Marie is narrated through the perspective of Marie's husband Frank, whose jealousy and possessiveness take hold of his mind: "He began to act, just as a man who falls into the fire begins to act. The gun sprang to his shoulder, he sighted mechanically and fired three times without stopping, stopped without knowing why. Either he shut his eyes or he had vertigo. He did not see anything while he was firing" (p. 235). The shooting is far less premeditated and heroic than any killing in Grey or Wister – and more realistic and gruesome. And nowhere in Wister and Grey is there comparably grim violence against a woman. Marie does not immediately die: "Suddenly the woman stirred and uttered a cry, then another, and another. She was living! She was dragging herself toward the hedge! . . . He had never imagined such horror. The cries followed him. They grew fainter and thicker, as if she were choking" (p. 236). In the next chapter, the causes of death are clinically detailed. While Emil was shot through the heart, and rolled over on his back and immediately died, for Marie "it had not been so easy. One ball had torn through her right lung, another had shattered the carotid artery. She must have started up and gone toward the hedge, leaving a trail of blood. There she had fallen and bled." (One can hardly imagine a phrase such as "carotid artery" appearing in the work of Wister or Grey.) Yet the grim report on the stained grass "told only half the story."

Incongruously, "above Marie and Emil, two white butterflies...were fluttering in and out among the interlacing shadows; diving and soaring, now close together, now far apart; and in the long grass by the fence the last wild roses of the year opened their pink hearts to die" (p. 241). Murder and natural beauty are conjoined irreconcilably. Framed by natural beauty, the murder is nevertheless not aestheticized, nor does it serve as a parable about honor.

Revising not only the plot of marriage but that of western revenge, Cather has her unconventional heroine forgive Frank Shabata for murdering his wife and her brother. She tells him in prison, "I understand how you did it. I don't feel hard toward you. They were more to blame than you" (p. 260). Yet the novel's epigraphic poem seems to celebrate the Whitmanian youthful passion that brought the slain couple together. While the divide between "good" and "bad" whites in Zane Grey and Owen Wister is arguably already somewhat confused, for Cather's fiction such distinctions in the Western, especially where violence is concerned, lose any meaning. Cather's contrasts and contradictions do not synthesize teleologically into a sense of national destiny and her equanimity does not imply an escape from history or a social prescription. Despite Cather's constantly metaphoric images, such as the scythe, they do not suggest the kind of larger allegorical design of progress installed in "Manifest Destiny," only an allegory of unaccountably unequal fates. The narrative voice that describes Emil scything, for example, suggests no explanation of or moral accounting for the disparate fates it recounts, even though the scene seems allegorically loaded. Cather associates Alexandra with the soil and also privileges her as perhaps the first "human face" to look on the land with "love and yearning" in a kind of double erasure of Indian presence. Yet when the narrative voice adds, "the history of every country begins in the heart of a man or a woman" (p. 64), the romance here is with the land itself, not with a nation or a heterosexual union, and the word "country" in the novel is always ambiguous. Does this sentence mean American history is beginning in Alexandra's heart? Or is this a regional statement? Although there are many nations and cultures referred to in the novel (Mexico, Bohemia, France, Sweden, Norway, Russia, among them), the word "America" never appears; "American" appears suggestively only once in the phrase "American law" (p. 59) and twice in the phrase "American boys" (pp. 108, 137), to distinguish Emil from them. (Recall that Alexandra says to her brothers, whom she calls "boys" even though they are grown men, "the authority you can exert by law is the only influence you will

ever have over me again," p. 155.) While Alexandra thinks Emil is the
one Bergson "who was fit to cope with the world" (p. 191), suggesting
the promise of assimilation, his murder and the likelihood of Alexandra's
continued childlessness call into question the promise of the future. What
kind of history is beginning in Alexandra's heart and what are the signs
of its posterity or continued prosperity? Though Emil's death is often
read as representing the loss of innocent youth, it also represents the
loss of an explicitly non-American boy. Emil is survived by his legalistic
older brothers, who resemble Americans more than he: this is the price,
Cather suggests, of the assimilation thought necessary for survival.

Though her omissions do encourage the erasure of native peoples' dispossession, Cather romanticizes the immigrant experience in *O Pioneers!*
not by linking it to national narratives of progress or to the racialized
rhetoric of Manifest Density, nor even by linking it to the vague promise
of Americanization. Instead, she does so by anthropomorphizing the
land and establishing analogues between people and natural objects. In
one example, Cather writes that the field "yields itself eagerly to the
plow . . . with a soft, deep sigh of happiness . . . There is something frank
and joyous and young in the open *face* of the country" (emphasis added).
In contrast, Emil "was a splendid figure of a boy, tall and straight as
a young pine tree" (pp. 74, 75). As a result of such naturalizing metaphors,
Cather implies that our more essential "nature" is in relation to nature
itself and its cycles of growth and death.

Cather's resistance to the more invidious forms of Americanization
and her celebration of immigrant farmers is also the result of her distaste
for her culture's alignment of masculinity with racialized nationalism, especially through marriage. The "country" of the plains offers a feminized
agrarian alternative to masculine "America." Her Naturalism suggests
not only her belief that Nature will have the last word, but also her desire
that women, less invested in masculine myths and denied power, will have
the last word on narrating the West's true history. When Cather ends the
novel by imagining a "fortunate country, that is one day to receive hearts
like Alexandra's into its bosom, to give them out again in the yellow
wheat, in the rustling corn, in the shining eyes of youth!," the personified
"country" is more land than nation, more nature than culture – yet also
a country more of the future than the present. The natural, cyclical economy of the "fortunate" country that will profit from its past has nothing to
do in the text with capitalism or national progress. Behind the exuberant
prose lies a Naturalist's fatalism that no patriot or booster would coun-
tenance, but that many women of her time might have identified with.

To label this interpretation as a sign of Cather's feminism is to be anachronistic, however, given her later strong ambivalence about women's politics. At her most explicitly political Cather is merely appalled by the "mediocrity and vulgarity" of industrial civilization, and turns to Nature and Region for alternatives. The politics of her art derive primarily from, or at the least exhibit, her understanding that point of view conditions everything and that something always escapes in the divide between historical experience and retrospectively told stories about it. That loss is what nation-building, with its requisite optimism and unifying symbolism, cannot heuristically incorporate.

The epigraphic poem in *O Pioneers!* thematizes the (American) optimism that escapes even the harshest reality, just as the sombre land escapes human will. Divided into two sets of images, the poem begins with descriptions of the "flat," "sombre," "silent," "heavy," and "black" land, the "tired men", the "long empty roads," the sunset "fading," the sky "unresponsive." "Against all this," the poem then situates "Youth, / Flaming... Singing... Flashing" with its "fierce necessity, / Its sharp desire." Cather's gerunds provide a sense of movement and life that the land's blunt characteristics do not. While Youth knows an "insupportable sweetness," the poem implies that the silent land, the empty roads, and the heavy soil are insupportable without that sweetness and the Whitmanian "Singing and singing." But there is no unifying synthesis in Cather's poem to compare with Whitman's, or Turner's synthesis of opposite forces on the frontier. There is no reconciliation or even accounting of the sharply poignant contrast between agriculture and desire or between silence and song. Although Youth receives one more poetic line than the land's gradual cycles and silence, the novel introduced by this poem silences Emil's and Marie's passion and soils the ground with their blood, sacrificing their narratives to Alexandra's larger, more lasting story of survival. Alexandra succeeds and endures regardless of marriage; Emil and Marie are destroyed by it. Cather disavows the purposes to which poetry is put in both Turner and Whitman and the purposes to which marriage is put in the marriage plot: she refuses to synthesize harmoniously what she perceives to be the unaccountable, unconquerable, and brutally exacting contest between ideals and reality, between nature and culture, and between art and experience. It is perhaps due to this refusal that many readers find *O Pioneers!* oddly unsatisfying and that some critics have found it lacking solid arrangement.

Among common readerly dissatisfactions are the character, situation, and fate of the heroine herself. Neither backwoodsman nor cowboy,

neither sweetheart nor suffragette, neither rough immigrant nor composite American, Alexandra is a study in non-assimilation to cultural and
gendered types.[26] As much as Cather seems to depict her heroism – for
standing up to her brothers, for prospering, for being independent – she
pointedly denies her character and plot the formulaic expectations of her
time. As a locus of cultural assumptions, Alexandra is suited to the Great
Divide, which is neither the Wild West nor the East, a region of cultural
discontinuity and cultural transplant, a land both barren and fecund.
As David Laird has observed, Alexandra saves her family only to have
to fight for her own independence against her family: "In the end, her
self-sacrifice in the service of others has accomplished little beyond the
sacrifice."[27] Whereas Turner argued that social constraints were broken
on the frontier and an egalitarian spirit prevailed in order for people to
start over, survive, and prosper, Alexandra breaks the constraints of gender in order to help her family survive, but suffers the constraints of gender with her prosperity. Whereas Turner saw a linear progress for world
civilization through the rapidly recurring cycles of social evolution on the
frontier, the cyclical life on Cather's frontier follows the logic of a zero-sum
game between culture and nature or of the cultural contest between an
individual woman and her demanding social and natural environment.
When Frank kills Emil and Marie for breaking the marital contract, the
reader is left doubting the good of sweet youth and the social point of
Alexandra's forgiveness of their murderer. When the novel ends with
the suggestion that nature's victory is far greater than Alexandra's, the
reader is left to wonder what progress, civilization and even survival either
mean or make. Despite the novel's nostalgic sentiment, a reader would
be hard-pressed to say precisely what the nostalgia is for: Harsh conditions? Loneliness? The murder of innocents? Sibling conflict? In Cather's
"country" nothing is morally unambiguous, there is no progress without
a high cost, and the landscape takes as much as it gives from the people
whose stories it dwarfs and swallows up. No destiny is manifest in Cather's
country, except with hindsight, and even then its significance is unclear.

If Cather seems to offer a wolf in sheep's hide, the duplicity is the
key not only to the novel's critical success when it was first published,
but also to its importance in contemporary American classrooms, given
the country's present interest in a reconceived "real" and "authentic"
West. Today, we now see with hindsight, in the real West nothing is
won without a real loss and the stories of ordinary people are more
moving than narratives of mastery and conquest. Cather was familiar
with those narratives – about women and marriage, about masculinity

and settlement. In *O Pioneers!* she conjoins two irreconcilable stories: one of a woman's non-dramatic, hard-won survival and independence, uncompromised by marriage; the other, of innocents who compromise a marriage and who are murdered for it. The stories seem so mythically familiar that one wants to assume their import is transparent, but it is not. Emil thinks of Alexandra testing her seed-corn in the spring and of how "from two ears that had grown side by side, the grains of one shot up joyfully into the light, projecting themselves into the future, and the grains from the other lay still in the earth and rotted; and *nobody knew why*" (p. 148, emphasis added). Many of Cather's urban, white readers *would* have thought they knew why, if those two ears of corn stood for differently racialized people. Her dominant culture believed that anything in society could be explained, improved, reformed, or assimilated through conventional categories of social identity and moral behavior – categories which valued whiteness, Christianity, masculinity, and marriage. Emil's modest assertion of wonder and ignorance about survival and causality pits two of the same species against each other; there is no categorical distinction that can account for the difference in their fates. Both Zane Grey's story of Mormon defeat and Owen Wister's argument that the Anglo-Saxon race was the cornerstone and conquering builder of civilization are contrasting versions of Cather's small, revisionist parable about a frontier landscape that defied the expectations that most often led people there.

A NATION, HIS DREAM

Romantic western fiction helped create expectations about the West. Although Cather negatively characterized Kate Chopin's Edna Pontellier as belonging to "the feminine type" that "demands more romance out of life than God put into it," *My Ántonia* has often been read as delivering upon such demands. H. L. Mencken wrote that "No romantic novel ever written in America, by man or woman, is one half so beautiful as *My Ántonia*." When the first film adaptation of the novel was made in 1995 for Cable TV, any careful reader of Cather's novel would have been surprised to see how much in love Jim and Ántonia were with each other. The film is suggestively *not* framed by the older Jim's loveless marriage and does not portray other missed loves in his life. When 80,000 copies of the novel were distributed to overseas members of the armed forces in World War II, and certainly were passed through even more hands, it was probably in the spirit of Romance and of patriotism for America's heartland – not to mention in the desire to escape war's reality – that the troops read Cather's novel.[28] Yet for all the Romantic expectations with which readers have greeted and responded to it, *My Ántonia* contains, even more than *O Pioneers!*, a litany of disappointments and tragedies, including Jim's unfulfilled heart, the abandonment of Ántonia, Mr. Shimerda's suicide, the suicide of a tramp in a threshing machine, and a marital murder-suicide.

Guy Reynolds' study *Willa Cather in Context: Progress, Race, Empire* reads Cather's work as fundamentally not about escapism and nostalgia but about racial diversity and the rise and fall of empires. He reads *My Ántonia* as a "radical commentary" for her time "on what it is to be 'American' " – not the narrow English-speaking Protestant, but something more "capacious" and "fluid," an identity that integrates what Werner Sollors calls descent and consent, something both given and chosen.[29] Published before the pervasive Americanization speeches after the war, when nativism got into high gear (and had a legislative impact in Nebraska), *My Ántonia*, Reynolds argues, "reads as a remarkably optimistic text about cultural transmission," in which Cather " 'poeticized' the politics of Americanization, taking the raw material (language learning, immigration, a multinational society) and showing how this all came down to the question of stories; and in so doing Cather showed that simply to *tell* a story can become a political act."[30] What, then, are the politics of telling another person's story? This is the question I want to focus on with regard to Cather's complex narrative as told by the unhappily married narrator Jim Burden, who shares Virgil's Aeneas' burden in transmitting culture in book VIII of the *Aeneid*. For it is Jim Burden's narrative and "his" Ántonia through which we are able to read romance, tragedy, imperialism, and a critique of Americanization. As such, Jim Burden carries a considerable burden of critical significance – and indeed "burden" can mean the main theme of a book.

One of the few critics to focus on Jim Burden's "colossal illusion," which enables the novel's romantic readings, compares him to Fitzgerald's Nick Carraway: "within themselves they carry the seeds of their own disaster or defeat." James E. Miller, Jr. asks,

What happened to the dream – to Jim's dream of Lena, to the larger dream of personal fulfillment? Was his failure in not seeing some connection between the dreams? Was Jim's destiny in some obscure sense a self-betrayal? And is this America's destiny, a self-betrayal of the possibilities of the dream?[31]

It seems odd that such questions would be asked about a novel the United States Military agreed its troops could read during wartime. But such questions inevitably arise from the divide in the novel between Jim's romantic nostalgia, after he marries expediently and becomes a member of the corporate class, and the scores of unhappy endings the novel retells. The questions Miller poses presume the need for allegorical interpretations: whether framed morally or nationally, Jim's particular fate is burdened with larger ones than his own. As Miller argues, "no one with the name Jim Burden could be a totally *un*allegorical figure. He carries with him not only his acute sense of personal loss but also a deep sense of national unease, a *burden* of guilt for having . . . watched with apathy as the dream dissipated in the rapidly disappearing past."[32] One missed opportunity that lends an unease to Jim's narrative is his long absence from Nebraska; his retelling at times reads as self-reassurance that his knowledge outweighs his neglect and ignorance and that his romantic nostalgia relieves his responsibility. Comparing Jim to Jay Gatsby, and arguing against those critics who believe the novel exemplifies Frederick Jackson Turner's recurring social evolution on the frontier, Blanche Gelfant argues that Jim "forgets as much as he remembers [and] substitutes wish for reality in celebrating the past."[33] Guy Reynolds argues that because such critics neglect the theme of liberal Americanization, they read the latter section of the novel "as bleaker than it really is": "In counterpoint to disillusion, Cather writes of a creativity and renewal that is the result of her idiosyncratically pluralist version of Americanization."[34] Cather does believe in such creativity and renewal. Susan Rosowski argues that the final scene of the novel represents a familial form of creativity in which Ántonia participates, while Jim plays the role of the cultural transmitter of an aesthetics of kinship, connecting Jim through mutuality and storytelling, rather than domination, to Ántonia's creativity.[35]

But what gets lost in this transmission? Through her narrator, Cather self-consciously and thematically opens the gap between experience and the representation of experience, which is one definition of what ironic discourse does. The 1918 introduction opens up many gaps, especially that between the novel we are about to read and other versions of Ántonia, such as the first narrator's unwritten version. There are other lacunae, including the text's twenty-year jump between books iv and v, which represents Jim's considerable absence from Nebraska and leaves out any representation of either Jim's or Ántonia's experiences in the years of their greatest maturation and self-awareness. Though it obviously diverges from the genre of popular romance fiction – which is not to say the novel has not been popular or perceived as a romance – *My Ántonia* subtly diverges from the realism it has often been seen to exemplify, unless we mean by realism a modernist awareness of the ironic gap between representation and experience. These modernist tenets can be located in the form and structure of Cather's deceptively "realist" novel: there is no objective truth that can be known; every narrative has blind spots; time, like a whole narrative, is neither linear nor continuous.

Cather's modernist devices serve an implicit critique of western American expansion, with its totalizing and progressivist rhetorical beliefs. *My Ántonia* is both a demonstration of the kind of retrospective and romantic historicizing of the West in popular fiction of the time and a self-contained critique of it. That critique lies in the novel's irony, its allegorization of western dream-making, of the failures of that dream and of western imperialist nostalgia, primarily through the double narrative structure the introduction establishes. Many critics have aligned Jim Burden with Cather, forgetting or neglecting the novel's other first-personal voice; this alignment produces critical readings that stress the novel's romantic nostalgia for the Great Prairie and the central woman who seems to embody it. But Jim Burden, as some critics have observed, is a faulty narrator, sometimes abrupt in his transitions from one story to another and often insensate to the reality of those whose stories he narrates. Cather's introduction serves to allegorize Jim's own storytelling, to frame it, thereby raising the ghost of an untold story. How she does this and why it is important that she does this are suggested by the significant changes that she made to the introduction in the 1926 edition. It is as if Cather were concerned that her original introduction revealed too much about her aesthetic intentions, thereby deflating its romantic effect, or as if it revealed too clearly how her intentions are quite divergent from Jim's. In letters to her editor, it is clear that Cather worried over the introduction even at its first incarnation in 1918. In one letter, Cather explained that the introduction would be the last thing she wrote because she would have to wait to see how far the story told itself before she could know how much to put in it. Five months later, she asked her editor to send the proofs of the introduction as soon as possible in order for her to make comparisons with early chapters of the story, though she did not describe what those comparisons might involve.[36]

This other narrator is an old friend of Jim's who is never identified in the course of the novel, who grew up with Jim in Nebraska, but who, although they both live in New York, does "not see much of him there."[37] Nevertheless, the voice reveals some pertinent information about Jim that culturally contextualizes the retrospective story he is about to narrate. Jim, we are told, is "legal counsel for one of the great Western railways" and is married to a "handsome, energetic, executive" woman who seems "incapable of enthusiasm" (p. x) and has her own fortune, and who involves herself in Progressivist causes and in theater: "She gave one of her own houses for a Suffrage headquarters, produced one of her own plays at the Princess Theater, was arrested for picketing during a garment-makers' strike, etc." (p. x). Jim's marriage is described without explanation as loveless and expedient. Yet Jim has a "naturally romantic and ardent disposition," we are told, which "has been one of the strongest elements in his success." "He loves with a personal passion," the voice tells us, "the great country through which *his* railway runs and branches. His faith in it and his knowledge of it have played an important part in its development" (p. xi, emphasis added). Cather disparages the progressive politics that result from privilege rather than experience. The extra-narrative voice criticizes Jim's wife for not having "much feeling for the causes to which she lends her name and her fleeting interest" (p. x), but Jim's narrative also reveals a frequent lack of sympathy for the stories he signs his name to. Ascribing a name – saying "this is mine" – is often revealed in Cather's novel to lack the affective or authentic interest it should be based upon.

Whatever Cather may have intended her original introduction to convey, she diminished the amount of information given in the 1926 edition. In both introductions, however, Cather sets up an allegory about a white man's influence in western expansion: the railroad is pointedly *Jim's* and seems to have been inordinately influenced by this one man who must, for such a statement to be true, be many men. Just as the railroad is Jim's, so is Ántonia, as the book's title states. These possessives stress not only the relative truth of this romantically disposed narrator's story but the fact of economic possession itself, subtly suggesting a history of western conquest and capitalist development. ("It ain't my Prairie," Lena says, in contrast.) In a passage Cather excised from the original introduction, we are told that Jim is "always able to raise capital for new enterprises in Wyoming and Montana, and has helped young men out there do remarkable things in mines and timber and oil. If a young man with an idea can once get Jim Burden's attention . . . then the money which means action is usually forthcoming. Jim is still able to *lose* himself in those big Western dreams" (p. xi, emphasis added). Jim never directly writes about the world he is chiefly "invested" in: a male world in which dreams become money. He does write, however, about his lost self.

Jim signifies industrial, commercial development, whereas Ántonia "seemed to mean to us the country" of his childhood, ambiguously suggesting Nebraska and America. In a few sentences at the novel's opening, Cather establishes metonymic links among the western railway, Jim, western capital and federal law, western dreams, Ántonia, and the country itself, links that imitate the very railway Jim defends by law and that helped to develop his country. Of the manner of his narrative's presentation, Jim says in the original introduction that he would have " 'to say a great deal about myself... and I've had no practice in any other form of presentation' " (p. xii). When Jim hands his manuscript about Ántonia to the extra-narrative voice, he writes "on the pinkish face of the portfolio the word 'Ántonia.' He frowned at this a moment, then prefixed another word, making it 'My Ántonia.' That seemed to satisfy him" (p. xiii). The "face" of the portfolio Jim writes on is suggestively metaphoric of Ántonia's face and therefore the "face" of "the country." (Cather later excised the telling word "pinkish," suggestive of flesh.) The passage highlights the metaphoric nature of naming itself, the way in which another word – "My" – can make one thing into another. Whereas the 1926 introduction ends with Jim's satisfaction with the possessive pronoun, the original introduction ends with the other narrative voice: "*My* own story was never written" (emphasis added), suggesting that the power to raise capital is aligned with the power to tell the story about this girl who seems to mean the country. Jim "had had opportunities," the first narrator tells us, "that I, as a little girl... had not." "Read it as soon as you can," Jim says to her in the original introduction, "but don't let it influence your own story" (p. xiii). Only with her (unwritten) story, the extra-narrative voice earlier says, "we *might*... get a picture of her" (p. xii, emphasis added).

Who is Ántonia before she is made into Jim's Ántonia? This question is difficult to answer (without referring to the known biographical source); all we have is Jim's retrospective construction of her youth, with twenty years of her life relatively unknown. As the daughter of Bohemian emigrants, she does not speak English when Jim meets her: "She looked at me," Jim writes, "her eyes fairly blazing with things she could not say. 'Name? What name?' she asked... I told her *my name, and she repeated it after me*" (p. 25, emphases added). "She learned a score of words," he continues; "She was quick, and very eager" (p. 26). Ántonia's father gives Jim's grandmother a book with two alphabets, one English and the other Bohemian, and asks her "with an earnestness which I shall never forget, 'Te-e-ach, te-e-ach my Ántonia!' " (p. 27). The language Ántonia learns is the language with which Jim will represent her; she is quoted speaking his tongue. What is left out – her native Bohemia – dies in the narrative with her parents who, unlike Frederick Jackson Turner's rugged backwoodsman, do not become composite Americans. When Mr. Shimerda kills himself, Jim imagines that "it was homesickness that had killed" him and that if Mr. Shimerda could have lived with Jim and his grandparents – if he could have assimilated with an American family – "this terrible thing would never have happened" (p. 97). Yet the reality of this terrible thing is something Jim does not seem to absorb; he seems, in fact, to treat it as only one more adventurous story from his childhood. On the morning when the suicide is discovered, Jim "wakened with a start. Before I opened my eyes, I seemed to know that something had happened . . . I looked forward to any new crisis with delight. What could it be, I wondered" (p. 90). Jim echoes Cather's earlier assessment of Whitman's "boyish" lack of discrimination, and reflects her belief that behind Whitman's optimism was a writer who "did not realize the existence of a conscience or a responsibility."[38] Left alone in the house later that day, Jim writes that "the quiet was delightful, and the ticking clock was the most pleasant of companions" (p. 97). Later, as the casket is built, Jim writes of the "pleasant purring of the plane. They were such cheerful noises, seeming to promise new things for living people: it was a pity that those freshly planed pine boards were to be put underground so soon" (p. 105). Jim's statement does not pity a man his suicide or a family their grief; Ántonia's loss becomes a loss of materials.

Jim is writing, of course, of his impressions as a youth; yet the adult narrator is equally invested in the cheerful sounds of the "plain" and never attempts to reckon himself with or take a moral accounting of the tragic outcomes, the murder, suicide, and insanity that punctuate the narrative and that disturb the novel's pervasive sense of romantic nostalgia. There are numerous, jarring passages in the novel after Jim has reported one tragic story or another. Immediately after reporting a tramp's suicide in a threshing machine, Jim writes disjunctively that "there was a basic harmony between Ántonia and her mistress" (p. 174). After the terror of Pavel's and Peter's story of feeding the wedding party to wolves in the Ukraine, an end to the marriage plot if there ever was one and a burden from which they fled to the frontier, Jim writes that "For Ántonia and me, the story of the wedding party was never at an end. We . . . guarded it jealously – as if the wolves of the Ukraine had gathered that night long ago, and the wedding party been sacrificed, to give us a painful and peculiar pleasure. At night, before I went to sleep, I often found myself in a sledge drawn by three horses, dashing through a country that looked something like Nebraska and something like Virginia" (p. 59). If one thinks of Jim as a crude ethnographer, we can understand James Clifford's argument that all ethnography is inherently allegorical in that it at once presents us with a representation of a foreign reality and continuously refers to a familiar pattern of ideas to make that difference comprehensible – and durable.[39]

While the experience ultimately "ends" Pavel, the story has no end to its imaginative life for Jim. The reality of Peter's and Pavel's experience does not temper Jim's enthusiasm for stories that he makes his own. While the experience becomes a dream to Jim, three days "after he unburdened his mind to Mr. Shimerda," Pavel dies; on the other hand, Peter leaves the country to "cook in a *railway* construction camp where gangs of Russians were employed" (p. 58, emphasis added). That Jim has such faith in "his" railway and that Pavel "un*burdens*" his mind only to die suggests that the adult Jim is somehow implicated in their story and their fates. When, years later, Cuzak tells Jim the story of Wick Cutter's murder of his wife and his subsequent suicide, all to prevent Mrs. Cutter's family from receiving his money and property, Jim writes, "Cuzak gave me a twinkling, sidelong glance. 'The lawyers, they got a good deal of it, sure,' he said merrily." Cuzak tells Jim his own story "as if it were my *business* to know it" (pp. 352–353, emphasis added). In such passages, Cather suggests that Jim Burden, who is at this point a lawyer and whose middle name could well be "white man's" (Cather later excised "Quayle"), is in the business of receiving both material benefits and pleasure from the experiences of hardship and violence he recounts.

The "white man's burden" is only one of the possible suggested meanings of "Burden," yet arguably an important burden or theme of Cather's novel. That Cather might have as her theme a thing not said is not surprising. Surprising, however, is the relative critical neglect of the racist passage in which Jim tells the story of Blind d'Arnault, a mulatto piano player whose concerts break the monotony of the winter months. Jim describes d'Arnault's "amiable negro voice . . . with the note of docile subservience in it. He had the negro head, too . . . He would have been repulsive if his face had not been so kindly and happy" (p. 178). D'Arnault plays plantation songs; Jim tells us that "he was born in the Far South, on the d'Arnault plantation, where the spirit if not the fact of slavery persisted" (p. 179). Jim's descriptions of d'Arnault in this long passage are filled with the most racist of characterizations – the words "animal," "savage," and "barbarous" punctuate this cheerful and disturbing scene, a scene very few critics of the novel choose to discuss, perhaps out of the embarrassing implications of aligning Cather with her narrator and out of a desire, like Jim's, to overlook those aspects of the novel that threaten its romantic nostalgia.[40] If we read this scene as not about the blind mulatto but about the blind narrator, who here calls to mind Captain Delano in Melville's "Benito Cereno," a reading of the entire novel as also an ironic allegorization of the American empire and Manifest Destiny is all the more compelling.

Many names in *My Ántonia* inscribe allusions to colonialism and imperialism. Not only is d'Arnault named for his family's white owners, but even sandbars Jim recalls "with their clean *white* beaches . . . were a sort of No Man's Land, little *newly created worlds* that *belonged* to the Black Hawk *boys*" (p. 226, emphases added) – boys who are not actual Indians. Cather lexically ironizes what proponents of Manifest Destiny assumed: that lands were free for the taking. Cather even names two big bulls after imperialists: Gladstone and Brigham Young, who habitually ram their heads together. "Had they not been dehorned," Jim writes, "they would have torn each other to pieces" (p. 88). The inscription of a nationalist allegory also occurs, not accidentally I would argue, in Ántonia's name: "Shimerda" is an anagram for "His Dream," and Ántonia is an anagram for "A nation," such that the woman Ántonia Shimerda is "a nation" that is begotten of "his dream" and that begins and ends, like America, with an "A." The reason this seems deliberate on Cather's part (despite some critics' excesses in anagrammatical readings of Cather's names) is that she was otherwise particular about every spelling, especially of foreign words and names. (She argued once to her editor that "Mamma" was too sophisticated for her country characters and should be "Mama"; on an earlier occasion she asked if her proof-reader could check up on foreign words with severity.)[41] The fact that the actual female Czech name (Antonie) ends with an "e" – as does the biographical source whom Cather called Annie – suggests a highly particular intention more than it suggests a highly uncharacteristic carelessness with the name of her titular heroine.[42]

Jim is possessed with a romantic idea of Ántonia that obscures and one-sidedly resolves more ambivalent relations of power in the rural past of his childhood and in the business of his adult life in New York. As a child, Jim "hated a superior tone that [Ántonia] sometimes took" with him (p. 41) and at one point writes that he "hated her almost as much" as he hated Wick Cutter, who later murdered Mrs. Cutter. After

Jim kills a snake "left on from buffalo and Indian times," which "seemed like the ancient, eldest Evil" (p. 45) – mythically aligned with woman's frailty – he writes that Ántonia "never took a supercilious air with me again" (p. 48). But when Jim returns to visit Ántonia twenty years later, he tells her children, " 'You see, I was very much in love with your mother once' . . . The boys laughed . . . 'She never told us that' " (pp. 335–336). The power of *My Ántonia* lies in part in Cather's ability so convincingly to render the optimism of the western dream of the past while simultaneously revealing the often brutal materials and currents of self-deception out of which it is made. In this sense, Jim's dream of a nation does indeed "say a great deal about [him]self" (p. xii), a self that so easily gets lost in the divide between the dream and what he cannot admit.

Susan Rosowski reads Ántonia as Cather's optimistic figuration of a highly atypical future American nation: "It is not a separation from or casting off of other cultures. It does not set a New World against an Old World, an American future against a European past or a Native American mythology."[43] Referring to the famous scene at the end of the novel when Ántonia's children emerge from the fruit cave, Rosowski writes, "Making explicit that this scene is Cather's version of the birth of America, Jim reflects that Ántonia is 'a rich mine of life, like the founders of early nations.' "[44] But the word in the novel is "races," not nations: so compelling is the image that it is easy to overlook how Ántonia is both Jim's dream of a nation no longer available to him, and at the same time, for Cather, antecedent to America and what Turner called its "composite" ethnic make-up. What Ántonia gives birth to is Cather's version of the West, one that marginalizes any nation's sense of its own importance by making a simple immigrant farmer more significant than nation, and by making her more significant than her marriage. Jim says at the beginning of the last book, "[Tiny] told me that Ántonia had not 'done very well'; that her husband was not a man of much force, and she had had a hard life" (p. 317). Out of such mundane, even disappointing, materials, Cather weaves Jim's romance of this "rich mine of life" (p. 342).

Through the divide in her allegory of an allegorizing nation that is born of and burdened by the white man's dream, Cather deromanticizes the American empire's history, at the same time that she paradoxically and irreconcilably convinces her readers of its nostalgic allure through Jim's dream of the past. The novel's epigraph, Virgil's "Optima dies . . . prima fugit" ("The best days . . . are the first to flee"), is certainly not an optimistic sentiment, and it does not comport well with either the trajectory of Ántonia's life, as we are given to know it, or notions of American progress. Its fatalism and nostalgia suit, rather, the tragic view of western development, in which Jim and his railway played such a large role. In a retrospective projection that is more obscure than manifest in meaning, Jim says at the end of the novel that "Destiny" brought him together with Ántonia. But if he has been united not so much with his childhood friend as with his dream of a nation, then the destiny Jim discerns is his own. His destiny, in other words, was to help build the railway, which helped unite the country and changed the West, and which he rides at the novel's beginning as he conceives his nostalgic memorialization of "his" Ántonia. Those opportunities which Ántonia never had, or what he calls "the road of Destiny," took them both to "those early accidents of fortune which predetermined for us [both himself and Ántonia] all that we can ever be." Substituting accidents and predeterminations for his own (self)determinations, Jim's fatalism both obscures and shrinks the great distance he has traveled since birth. The train becomes both the progress-oriented means by which he leaves his past behind and the regressive means by which his nostalgia claims him: "I had the sense of coming home," he writes; not to his wife or to anyone else, but "to myself." If Jim is correct to describe man's experience as "a little circle" (p. 360), then what haunts *My Ántonia* is the idea that such a little circle should encompass the meaning of the past, and of a nation.

In *A Lost Lady* (1923), the heroine Marian Forrester's marital fate seems to signify the passing of the old West, at least in the eyes of Niel Herbert. More than any of Cather's heroines, Marian Forrester embodies both the romance of that old West and the disappointment over its passing through her marriage to the aging and feeble railroad man Captain Forrester and her subsequent business dealings with the mercenary Ivy Peters. The two men represent the antipodes of western dreams and exploitation, and Marian's alignment with both of them, especially in his own thinking, is what Niel is hard-pressed to reconcile. Captain Forrester argues, as Frederick Jackson Turner had done in his essays on the frontier republished in collected form in 1920, that the pioneers were dreamers: "A thing that is dreamed of in the way I mean, is already an accomplished fact. All our great West has been developed from such dreams; the homesteader's and the prospector's and the contractor's. We dreamed the railroads across the mountains, just as I dreamed my place on the Sweet Water."[45] Comparing the dream of domesticity with the national, commercial enterprise of the railroad, the Captain weds idealism to pragmatic enterprises as Jim Burden does, giving the dream primary causality. But while the distinction between homesteading and contracting loses its meaning in the Captain's reductive dream, such distinctions are brought into relief through the hard choices and changing circumstances of the Captain's wife Marian, who altogether resists such symbolism and whose vitality lies in her "many-coloured laugh" (p. 68), in contrast to the monotonous repetition involved in the Captain's one-making. The Captain used the "same words. It did not bother him to repeat a phrase" (p. 53). The Captain's dream of Marian also precedes her reality. He regards her as an abstraction and as useful decoration for his property: "I planned to build a house that my friends could come to, with a wife like Mrs. Forrester to make it attractive to them," he explains (p. 51). Later, Niel thinks that "[t]he longer Niel was with Captain Forrester in those peaceful closing days of his life, the more he felt that the Captain knew his wife better even than she knew herself; and that, knowing her, he, – to use one of his own expressions, – valued her" (p. 136). Marian's value throughout the novel, in Niel's view, is based contingently on how men use her; Niel shares the Captain's sense of her domestic value. The comforts of domesticity overcome misogyny for Niel, who although he "had been so content with a bachelor's life, and . . . had made up his mind that he would never live in a place that was under the control of women, found himself becoming attached to the comforts of a well-conducted house." Long afterward, "when Niel did not know whether Mrs. Forrester were living or dead . . . [w]hen he was dull, dull and tired of everything, he used to think that if he could hear that long-lost lady laugh again, he could be gay" (pp. 66, 68).

Like Fitzgerald's famous novel that he wrote under its "spell," as he wrote to Cather, *A Lost Lady* is in part an allegory of the consequences of western development.[46] In both *A Lost Lady* and *The Great Gatsby*, the vast natural landscapes of the West that inspired intense aesthetic wonder are feminized as the corruptible term under capitalist development – and as her last name suggests, Marian Forrester's feminine charm is aligned with the vast forests that will fuel profit. If it was once "enough to say of a man that he was 'connected with the Burlington' " railroad, it is enough, for Niel, to say of Marian that she is connected to Captain Forrester: "Curiously enough," Cather writes, "it was as Captain Forrester's wife that she most interested Niel, and it was in her relation to her husband that he most admired her" (p. 75). Instead of draining his meadows to make them "highly productive fields," Captain Forrester "had selected this place long ago because it was beautiful to him" as a home for him and his wife (p. 9). But this preservation is itself a form of denial about the larger economic forces that will, inevitably, change the West and that Captain Forrester's railroad, like Jim Burden's, made possible. Ivy Peters mocks and feminizes such aesthetic regard for natural resources; Marian later entrusts the Captain's lands to him and he eventually drains them. As a child, Niel points out "contemptuously" to Ivy that a woodpecker Ivy captures "ain't a he, anyhow. It's a female. Anybody would know that." Ivy taunts Niel by responding "carelessly," "All right, Miss Female," as he proceeds cruelly to slit both of the woodpecker's eyes. Both Niel and Captain Forrester want to leave unchanged an aestheticized, feminized nature while Ivy Peters threatens to corrupt it. Niel says to Marian, "'You seem always the same to me, Mrs. Forrester.' 'Yes? And how is that?' 'Lovely. Just lovely'" (p. 37). Niel's aestheticizing presumption that, because of her loveliness, a woman can resist time, or that the old West should resist economic and social change, falls victim not only to the Ivy Peters of the world but to its own lack of realism. Like Gatsby's seemingly imperishable dream, Niel's dream of Marian perishes the moment it confronts temporality – and the moment that the woman who is the object of that dream is aligned with another, careless man. Niel's aestheticizing presumption is, in this novel, self-deludingly complicit in the disappointment Niel experiences over Mrs. Forrester's reality, a reality both personal and metaphorically linked with the old West.

Cather shared the nostalgia that both Turner and Wister felt for a past frontier, uncorrupted by the profit-motive, yet her fiction is at the same time subtly and ironically self-conscious about feminized figurations of western destiny – and the role men play in that figuration – and about the distance between dream and reality. The narrative sympathy accorded Niel's point of view evinces Cather's own nostalgia. Yet while that sympathy seems to suggest that Cather endorses what Hermione Lee, in a reading of the novel that is most consonant with my own, calls Niel's "judgemental aesthetics," the novel shows how Marian's reality escapes and diverges from Niel's framing aesthetic.[47] The Captain and Ivy Peters represent to Niel a historical allegory that produces an irreconcilable disjunction between past and present, between aesthetic idealism and material corruption.

By draining the marsh Ivy had obliterated a few acres of something he hated, though he could not name it, and had asserted his power over the people who had loved those unproductive meadows for their idleness and silvery beauty.

After Ivy had gone on into the smoker, Niel sat looking out at the windings of the Sweet Water and played with his idea. The Old West had been settled by dreamers, great-hearted adventurers who were unpractical to the point of magnificence; a courteous brotherhood, strong in attack but weak in defence, who could conquer but could not hold. Now all the vast territory they had won was to be at the mercy of men like Ivy Peters, who had never dared anything, never risked anything. They would drink up the mirage, dispel the morning freshness, root out the great brooding spirit of freedom, the generous, easy life of the great landholders. The space, the colour, the princely carelessness of the pioneer they would destroy and cut up into profitable bits, as the match factory splinters the primeval forest. All the way from the Missouri to the mountains this generation of shrewd young men, trained to petty economies by hard times, would do exactly what Ivy Peters had done when he drained the Forrester marsh. (pp. 101–102)

Niel describes the divide between the frontier and post-frontier Wests that Turner marked and that recent western historians have questioned. Only a retrospective posture makes possible the nostalgic notion that motivations for early western settlement involved only an aesthetic dream and nothing practical. The moment of transition from aesthetic contemplation to profitability is one we cannot witness; we can see only evidence of the profit-motive in the present and hence wishfully imagine that the past spurned it. For Niel, that present evidence and imagined past are allegorically read through the figures of men such as Captain Forrester, Frank Ellinger, and Ivy Peters and their relationship to the same woman.

The way in which Niel jealously guards his own aesthetically idealized vision of Marian imitates the very kind of possessiveness that other men exert over her. That vision produces a divide in his affections as sharp as the divide he imagines between the frontier and post-frontier West. His admiration for her is shattered when he realizes one day that she is having an affair with Frank Ellinger: "In that instant between stooping to the window-sill and rising, he had lost one of the most beautiful things in his life ... This day saw the end of that admiration and loyalty that had been like a bloom on his existence. He could never recapture it. It was gone, like the morning freshness of the flowers ... *It was not a moral scruple she had outraged, but an aesthetic ideal.* Beautiful women, whose beauty meant more than it said ... was their brilliancy always fed by something coarse and concealed? Was that their secret?" (pp. 82, 83; emphases added). Underlying Niel's aesthetic regard for Marian is the misogynist assumption that others' use and exploitation of her, like Ivy's of both Mrs. Forrester and the Captain's marsh, corrupt absolutely and precipitously. In the end, Niel has no imaginative or emotional use for her: "Nothing she could ever do would in the least matter to him again" (p. 162) – though Cather makes it matter for the novel. It is the same with his view of the West. In the end, fleeing from his lost dream, "He was in a fever of impatience to be gone, and yet he felt that he was going away forever, and was making the final break with everything that had been dear to him in his boyhood. The people, the very country itself, were changing so fast that there would be nothing to come back to. He had seen the end of an era, the sunset of the pioneer. He had come upon it when already its glory was nearly spent" (p. 160).

The West's legacy, as historians remind us, is more continuous and more complicated than Niel imagines, and so, Cather's novel suggests, is Marian Forrester's story. She is neither pristine nor corrupted nature, neither aesthetic dream nor nightmare of exploitation. Just as Turner's reading of the frontier's significance is both idealized and doomed at the same time by its finitude, what Niel most holds against Mrs. Forrester is "that she was not willing to immolate herself, like the widows of all these great men, and die with the pioneer period to which she belonged; that she preferred life on any terms" (p. 161). Mrs. Forrester's significance for Niel, in other words, is like the frontier's for Turner: it must be lost to achieve its ideation. Marian is more aligned with her marriages and relations to men than either Alexandra or Ántonia, creating a more explicit, metonymic relationship between marriage and a westering nation. In that relationship, the sign of a man's greatness is his wife's willingness to immolate herself upon his passing, given her function as legitimating adornment to his pioneer dream and property. Indeed, as Hermione Lee describes the shift in Cather's portrayal of women in her pioneering novels, from Alexandra and Ántonia to Marian and *My Mortal Enemy*'s Myra Henshawe, "the focus has shifted from the immigrants to the American 'aristocracy', and from female heroism to femininity. These heroines are 'ladies', socially adept, self-conscious, sophisticated, decorative."[48] It is as if Cather has followed Wister's Molly beyond the wedding to observe her function in Wister's aristocratic West. Yet Marian has more vitality and personality than either of Cather's other two heroines, certainly more than Wister's Molly, and more than the men in Marian's life. Whereas Jim Burden's romantic disposition instills in Ántonia more romance than her life actually has, Niel Herbert lacks the romantic passion that drives Marian Forrester, a passion he finally does not understand. Marian is "lost," most especially, to the young man who early on idealizes her through her connection to a railroad man. When that connection dissolves, so does Niel's hope for her and for the old West.

The divergence between Niel's almost schizophrenic view of Marian and Marian's reality is rendered through a complicated narrative structure. At the beginning of the novel, the narrative voice describes "two distinct social strata" in the prairie States in the late nineteenth century: "the homesteaders, and hand-workers who were there to make a living, and the bankers and gentlemen ranchers who came from the Atlantic seaboard to invest money and to 'develop our great West,' as they used to tell us" (pp. 7–8). Cather associates the narrative voice, and arguably the reader, with the former social group, not with those who invested in a West they claimed to share their possession of, "as they used to tell *us*." The reader is "in" on this knowledge, ambiguously figured in the use of the pronominals "our" and "us." But there is a subtle skepticism here about "our" complicity in the West's development by railroad men. Niel wants to share the Captain's dream, but he is deluded in thinking that the Captain is anything like the homesteaders simply because he owns Sweet Water, which the railroad's profits financed, just as the bankers financed the railroads.

Cather's narrative form strikes a balance between the relative omniscience of *O Pioneers!* and Jim Burden's first-person narration in *My Ántonia*. The bachelor Niel Herbert serves as a Jamesian "reflector"-narrator who observes but never fully participates in the lives of the Forresters. Cather uncharacteristically changed her methods during composition, at one time putting the novel in Niel's first-person.[49] The final result gives the reader the impression of a more objective portrait of Marian Forrester, but one that is colored by Niel's alternating admiration and disdain for her and his contempt for the decadence of the old West. Marian Forrester seems to mark the passing of the frontier yet she survives its passing. She is the continuity between the past and the present that Niel's nostalgia forbids him to acknowledge. She forbids mourning any past through her skills at survival, and this is precisely what Niel cannot bear; he cannot assimilate her later marriages into the pioneer plot his mind writes for her. The last he hears of her violates his notion that she lost her vitality after the Captain died, and even that she never had much without the Captain. Ed Elliott tells Niel of his encounter with her years later: "She seemed to have everything . . . No, she hadn't changed as much as you'd think . . . She asked about everybody, and said, 'If you ever meet Niel Herbert, give him my love, and tell him I often think of him.' She said again, 'Tell him things have turned out well for me. Mr. Collins is the kindest of husbands'" (p. 165).

The novel's "double life," as Hermione Lee calls it, "holds together, with breathtaking dexterity, what Marian is, and how she seems. At every point there is a delicate negotiation, in the tradition of the literary pastoral, between artifice and nature."[50] Marian's name is an allusion to Tennyson's play "The Forresters," in which Maid Marian appears as a moon goddess and turns Sherwood Forest into a new Eden, a pre-capitalist golden age. For the greenwood to remain this Eden, Maid Marian must be chaste and faithful. Niel's lament over Mrs. Forrester's betrayal of the Captain is at the same time a lament for the passing of some pastoral, golden West, as if she is to blame for the West's fallenness. Yet Marian not only refuses to play this role, but seems entirely unconscious of it. Her speech may be charming, but her thoughts are entirely realistic. When she and the Captain face difficult economic times she says, "you haven't time to play any more either, Niel. You must hurry and become a successful man. Your uncle is terribly involved. He has been so careless that he's not much better off than we are. Money is a very important thing. Realize that in the beginning; face it, and don't be ridiculous in the end, like so many of us" (p. 108). Marian reminds Niel of the sacrifices to his youthful self in having to become a man. When he encourages her not to invest with Ivy Peters, she turns to him and says, "But, my dear boy, you know nothing about these business schemes. You're not clever that way, – it's one of the things I love you for" (p. 118). While Niel does not seem to absorb the need for Marian's realism and wants to retain her as ideal, Marian recognizes – and Cather reveals – the very idealism in Niel that frames Marian in the narrative. She also recognizes the cold and critical frame of mind that is afraid of its own disillusionment: "You mustn't be so stiff, so – so superior! It isn't becoming at your age," she says to him (p. 150). As Lee argues, Marian "herself has no time for an idealized pastoral: the Forrester home is just the place she means to leave as soon as she can sell it."[51] "I can't stand this house a moment longer" (p. 73), she says; "That's what I'm struggling for, to get out of this hole" (p. 120).

In the divide between Niel's Marian and the Marian who escapes the allegorizing frame of the old, dying West, *A Lost Lady* demonstrates a fundamental truth about nostalgia, that it denies both the reality of the past that the nostalgic putatively long for and the ongoing connection of the past to the present. In severing that connection – when, for example, Niel imagines Marian as lost rather than continually living and the place of his origin as having "nothing to come back to" – nostalgia drains the present of both its vitality and its historicity. Frederick Jackson Turner and Owen Wister wedded their ideals to a vanished West, as Niel Herbert does, preserving them aesthetically but offering more reaction than guidance to the present. Though she held the profit motive and much else in her time in disdain, and though she continually returned to the past of her youth, in her fiction Cather "made her own version of the never-concluded struggle in the American imagination between romance and realism" and between "pioneering energy and elegiac memorializing."[52] Always more significant than their marriages and yet standing as something less than the embodiments of a western country, Cather's women walk through these divides in the imagination.

# CHAPTER SIX

# *Accident and destiny: Fitzgerald's fantastic geography*

"I suppose the latest thing is to sit back and let Mr. Nobody from Nowhere make love to your wife. Well, if that's the idea you can count me out . . . Nowadays people begin by sneering at family life and family institutions and next they'll throw everything overboard and have intermarriage between black and white."

Flushed with his impassioned gibberish [Tom] saw himself standing alone on the last barrier of civilization.

"We're all white here," murmured Jordan.

I see now that this has been a story of the West, after all –

*The Great Gatsby*

In some of Americans' most durable western stories, idealistic beliefs have often coexisted with accidental or intentional violence, as they do in *The Great Gatsby*, in which three people are killed in a chain of presumed accident and mistaken revenge. The story of marital misery, betrayal, murder, and suicide would not be so familiar or have become so canonized without the nationally allegorical burden it self-consciously bears through Nick Carraway's rendering of it and through Fitzgerald's intricate verbal weaving of capitalist and historical motifs, especially western ones, from Thomas Jefferson to the Nevada silver fields. Marriage and its constellation of jealousies and conquests is the plot-shaping structure through which Fitzgerald dissects the ways that ethnic and class divisions perpetuate both the romance and violence of American civilization. Relations of marriage in *The Great Gatsby* are coextensive with relations of property in the same manner that the torn breast of Myrtle Wilson is coextensive in Fitzgerald's allegorizing web of images with the "fresh green breast of the new world."[1] Myrtle and Daisy suffer, respectively, the economic logic of use-value and exchange-value to the same degree that the breathtaking continent in Nick's closing vision provided both the useful "trees that had made way for Gatsby's house" and the symbolic exchange value for an aestheticized national dream putatively "neither understood nor desired" (p. 140). Yet the novel reveals how fraudulent Nick's fantasy is of a new world neither understood nor desired by the Dutch mercantilists. The fantasy's retrospective posture substitutes a kind of enchanted destiny – the very trees themselves "made way" for Gatsby's house – for historical desires, pragmatic choices, and accidents. As a result, the novel both raises and elides the question of causality, especially in so far as time becomes an object of exchange-value that can be "fixed" in a far different sense from the way in which George Wilson "fixes" cars. Gatsby wants to fix the past and get Daisy back with those beautiful shirts; Meyer Wolfshiem "fixed" the World Series. Each attempt to repeat the past or fix an outcome is an attempt at avoiding accidents and manipulating causality.

Among the results of these intentions is a series of casualties, which fixes Gatsby in his timeless Platonic form, like Turner's frontier American, on the scale of social advance. Tom and Daisy Buchanan, who are elitist by racial and class standards, escape blame and harm in the chain of violence they set in motion: Daisy Buchanan kills Myrtle Wilson, Tom's mistress, unwittingly while driving with Jay Gatsby, the man she had once spurned and who has now built a fortune and an opulent house to win her back. George Wilson, the garage mechanic, murders Jay Gatsby in turn, mistaking him for his wife's lover and murderer, and then George turns the gun on himself. In this novel, which can be read as a response to the Western and to Frederick Jackson Turner's notion that the frontier produced egalitarian democracy, violence among whites marks the cul-mination of class antagonisms in the fight for intra-racial supremacy. While Tom invokes, early in the novel, the "other races" that whites must "watch out" for (p. 14), it is actually the presumptuous second gen-eration immigrant from Central Europe, James Gatz of North Dakota, who is Tom's real threat, both because he wants his wife and because he presumes to buy his way into the Anglo-Saxon American aristocracy. As Fitzgerald so tellingly reveals in the epigraph above, and as Walter Benn Michaels has observed, Tom reads the threat to his marriage first through a class threat to that aristocracy (Gatsby becomes "Mr. Nobody from Nowhere"), and then, ineluctably, through the threat miscegena-tion poses, via interracial marriage, to "civilization" itself. To Tom, as Michaels writes, Gatsby "isn't quite white, and Tom's identification of him as in some sense black suggests the power of the expanded notion of the alien."[2] But Jordan's sardonic reminder that "we're all white here" suggests that what the West produced in Turner's formulation for American civilization – "the chance for indefinite ascent on the scale of social advance" – creates a crisis of distinctions among whites over who is allowed to ascend indefinitely or to the highest degree.[3] If this novel "is a story of the West, after all," as Nick says, it is in part because Tom's "gibberish" participates in a western tradition, as we have seen in Zane Grey and Owen Wister, in which battles over "suitable" and "unsuitable" marriages are battles for America's racial future after the era of frontier individualism.

Far from having been "fused, Americanized" into a mixed race, as Turner would have it regarding the frontier's effects, Fitzgerald's Americans are highly conscious of ethnic and class differences. Whether high or low on the hierarchy of social value, Fitzgerald's characters casually invoke denigrated groups upon which they rhetorically stand in order to raise themselves on that scale. Marriage, or escape from marriage, offers the quickest route up. The "shrill voice" of Mrs. McKee says, "I almost married a little kyke who'd been after me for years. I knew that he was below me . . . if I hadn't met Chester he'd of got me sure." Myrtle Wilson reassures her,

"At least you didn't marry him."
"I know I didn't."
"Well, I married him," said Myrtle ambiguously. "And that's the difference between your case and mine." (p. 29)

Myrtle's "ambiguous" claim suggests marriage is not personal; she renders her husband as exchangeable for an unsuitable type. Marriage is, rather, about property, particularly about the value of one's social property. In this sense, as this chapter will explore, the fact that the novel's narrator falls out of this property structure by having no relation to marriage, raises important questions about how Fitzgerald figures Nick's own "investment" in Gatsby's futile pursuit of one woman and the narrative effects of that investment. Nick may not enter into marriage, but he does enter into others' marriages: he is both exempted from and imbricated in the lines of causal influence that produce the violent events in the novel, especially by arranging the fateful meeting between Gatsby and Daisy. But most importantly, Nick renders Gatsby's dream allegorically and it is into that national allegory of the western dream, which made Gatsby, that Nick finally retreats, his eyes incapable of adjusting to the distortions of his own retrospective vision of the nightmare it has become.

By the time Fitzgerald published in 1925 the first of his two novels which explicitly render "the West" thematically, its rhetorical status as national myth, as an ever-renewable cultural resource, was patently clear. Inspired by Cather's *A Lost Lady*, Fitzgerald may have been taken with how Cather's portrait of Marian Forrester invests her with the meaning of the western American past on the frontier, and he imbued his characterizations of both Daisy and Jay with that kind of allegorical reach through the narrator Nick Carraway. *The Great Gatsby* and *The Love of the Last Tycoon: A Western* indulge this national romance but also examine its social and ideological assumptions.[4] After looking in this first section at the figural and thematic western motifs that Fitzgerald revises in *The Great Gatsby*, I will examine retrospection's function in maintaining the West ideologically as a locus of national identity and destiny, as a way of telling stories that obscures ethnic and class antagonisms, violence, and accidents by imaginarily grounding causality in moralized and romanticized geographic origins. The ideological function of the western dream (of the past and future), as Fitzgerald's fiction demonstrates, is to cause an error in perspective that makes it possible to look back in order to dream ahead and to mistake the accidents of history for fantasy. The chapter concludes by looking at Fitzgerald's last, unfinished work in order to outline the mechanisms of national fantasy that Hollywood still capitalizes upon, the origins of which can be easily, and not accidentally, projected onto the Enlightenment.

While there is no direct evidence that Fitzgerald read Turner or had his ideas in mind while writing *The Great Gatsby*, the novel provides enough textual evidence to suggest the possibility that he had, especially given Turner's publication of his collected essays on the frontier in 1920. Turner's notion that the West offered a "free" escape from economic hardship seems ironically echoed in George Wilson's claim to Tom Buchanan, after requesting money from the man who is sleeping with his wife, "'My wife and I want to go west . . . And now she's going whether she wants to or not" (p. 96). The West's supposedly democratic opportunities are limited in Fitzgerald's novel not only to particular classes but also to particular ethnic groups. In "Contributions of the West," Turner argued that "the democracy of the newer West is deeply affected by the ideals brought by" those "German" and "Scandinavian" immigrants to whom America meant "the opportunity to destroy the bonds of social caste that bound them in their older home,"[5] which is what the ancestrally German James Gatz takes advantage of. But Jay Gatsby is destroyed by the "bonds" of social caste – by a man from the lower class and implicitly, through the text's verbal connections, by the story's "well-to-do" teller, who is in the "bond business." The collision of lower- and upper-class resentments crushes Gatsby in the end. Though they are both from the midwest, James Gatz is not, like Nick, a gentleman who went to "New Haven," and despite his opening claim that he is "inclined to reserve all judgements," Nick's invocation of his "prominent" family and his casual scorn for all that Gatsby represents distinguishes himself from this man with a fabricated ancestral past (pp. 5, 6). Turner's fear that the West was already beginning to resemble the Old World seems fulfilled in the sense of superiority that the midwesterners Nick and Tom evince.

Often unmentioned by critics, the novel's important literary-historical western context and its dialogue with the ideas of Turner and the archetypes of Wister are discussed by Richard Lehan in his study of the novel. Noting that Gatsby models himself on Dan Cody, "a product of the Nevada silver fields, of the Yukon, of every rush for metal since Seventy-five" (p. 77), Lehan also observes that Dan Cody's name encapsulates the beginning and the end of frontier history through its conjoining of Daniel Boone and Buffalo Bill Cody. Lehan argues that the novel "is an almost perfect example of the inverted western": the Jeffersonian belief in an agrarian nation, of an aristocracy based on landed values, which informs *The Virginian*, follows a different fate in Fitzgerald's novel. "Instead of creating himself in the East and going west," writes Lehan, "Gatsby creates himself in the West and goes east. Instead of bringing a kind of Jeffersonian idealism East, he brings with him the last vestiges of frontier rowdyism."[6] In the context of recounting Gatsby's relationship with Dan Cody – "who during one phase of American life brought back to the eastern seaboard the savage violence of the frontier brothel and saloon" – Nick reveals that "really, or at least legally," Gatsby's name is "James Gatz of North Dakota" (pp. 78, 76). Nick implies in the phrase "during one phase of American life" that such frontier debauchery or "rowdyism" is a thing of the past. What Jay Gatsby brings back East may not be, as Lehan suggests, a geographically symmetrical inversion of Wister's values, but rather merely their ironized repetition twenty turbulent years later. Immigrant experience is erased in favor of a seeming "natural aristocracy," and instead of Turner's composite American, the victors to whom belong the spoils are the Anglo-Saxons, Nick and Tom. Wister had argued in *The Virginian* and "The Evolution of the Cow-Puncher" that what distinguishes America from Europe is the former's insistence that an accident of birth should not determine aristocratic character, though only Anglo-Saxons can enjoy this freedom from predeterminations of birth. The Anglo-Saxon's aristocratic character, in Wister's fable, may not be determined by the class he is born into, but his race is no accident. The accident of everyone else's birth offers a future that amounts to a forced choice. Turner had argued, in contrast, that from the earliest days, Scotch-Irish and Germans – both Fitzgerald's and Gatsby's ancestral groups – "furnished the dominant element in the stock of the colonial frontier." The new Americans were, unlike Tom and Nick, "English in neither nationality nor characteristics."[7]

A significant inversion of Wister's plot is that rather than represent matrimony between western hero and eastern sweetheart out West, Fitzgerald's novel has the westerners Jay and Daisy back East accidentally (which, to follow the novel's lexicon, is to say "carelessly" or "casually") kill Myrtle, the garage mechanic's wife, while driving together. Geographic distinctions or directions seem less significant in this novel – in which the "resemblance" of "East" and "West" Egg "must be a source of perpetual confusion to the gulls that fly overhead" (p. 8) – than the absence of any "moral" direction or distinction among characters. Wister placed his novel's moral compass in the Virginian, who causes no accidents and whose conduct always hits the mark. Wister's narrator knows "quality" when he sees it and bemoans "equality," while Fitzgerald's text reveals what "meretricious beauty" was born on "the most insidious flat on Lake Superior" (pp. 77, 76). The real Virginian in the novel is the superior-minded Tom Buchanan, whose social views resemble Owen Wister's:

"Civilization's going to pieces," broke out Tom violently . . . "It's up to us who are the dominant race to watch out or these other races will have control of things.
    [. . .] This idea is that we're Nordics. I am and you are and you are and – "
After an infinitesimal hesitation he included Daisy with a slight nod and she winked at me again, " – and we've produced all the things that go to make civilization – oh, science and art and all that. Do you see?" (p. 14)

Tom's words, "we've produced . . . civilization," suggest a racial identification amongst those present. But this racial identification is, significantly, according to the book Tom is paraphrasing (Lothrop Stoddard's *The Rising Tide of Color Against White-World Supremacy* of 1920), based on a latitudinal direction, not a nation. Tom and Nick are possibly from northern England; James Gatz is also possibly from northern Europe. But Gatsby becomes a threat to, not a part of, the Nordic civilization Tom describes; it's the idea, not the place of origin, that counts. Race, according to Fitzgerald's logical and ironic extension of Stoddard's views, is an "idea," a "northerliness" not dependent on either nation or biology as much as it is on a relative distance from more southerly or easterly parts of the same nation or continent, much as the West is a relative direction more than it is a stable place. Gatsby's failure, in the eyes of Nick and Tom, is caused by the accident of his birth as "James Gatz of North Dakota," the son of a poor immigrant, who is more Germanic than (and just as north-midwestern as) each of them and who wants to create a different past for himself by taking the idea of "natural" aristocratic ascendancy seriously and Platonically springing from his own conception of himself. As Michaels argues, the meaning of the authentic past "has been rendered genealogical, a matter of 'ancestors.' "[8] While Gatsby creates his past, Nick, in contrast, comes decisively from "prominent, well-to-do people," he tells the reader at the start (p. 6). Yet Nick's lineage is only one fictional step removed from Gatsby's, in his belief that they, and not an idea, are the cause of his finer judgment, which in turn reproduces the ideas that define his family's prominence. Indeed, it's only a family "*tradition* that we're descended from the Dukes of Buccleuch, but the *actual* founder of my line was my grandfather's brother" – a man from whom he could not be descended (p. 6, emphases added).

Fitzgerald's critique of both the aristocratic western hero found in Wister and the composite American found in Turner lies in revealing the corrosive effect and fraudulent nature of these allegorical histories that seek to explain social development. The sober, charming Gatsby – with a new name and a great deal of money – cannot yet escape condemnation from the "well born" who should otherwise champion these "American" virtues. While claiming to be one to reserve judgment, Nick wants also to assert his born difference from and his innate moral superiority over the likes of Gatsby and Tom. Nick argues "snobbishly" at the novel's opening that, as Owen Wister would have concurred, "a sense of the fundamental decencies is parceled out unequally at birth" (p. 5). What those decencies are, why they are or are not innate in a particular case, and who it is that "parcels" them out unequally, Nick does not say. The presumption is the point. There is no value system, other than his own valued "line," that this westerner seems to embrace. Indeed, Nick is "*supposed to* look like" his great-uncle, ambiguously suggesting Fitzgerald's intentions, who sent a substitute to the Civil War that tested, as Lincoln argued, the principle of equality. Nick's first name means in one sense "to mate satisfactorily" in order to breed a chosen stock. It is arguably Nick's, not Gatsby's, colossal illusion that determines the narrative's retrospective structure, its suppressions, its memorialization of romantic yearning, its pandering to the western hope. Nick's famous description of Gatsby's

Platonic self-conception also describes Fitzgerald's understanding that Nick's sense of his "innate" decency is not only self-deceiving but asocial, as all unavoidably Platonic beliefs in ethnic and class superiority are. Nick's retrospective posturing – the framing of his narration with visions of his prominent family and of his romanticized midwestern origins to which he finally retreats – serves to elide the more troubling questions of causality and responsibility that the novel's violence raises. In that sense, one that goes far beyond the meaning Nick gives it, *The Great Gatsby* is "a story of the West, after all."

## THE CASUALTIES OF RETROSPECTION

"But how did it happen?"

"Don't ask me," said Owl Eye, washing his hands of the whole matter. "I know very little about driving – next to nothing. It happened and that's all I know."

"You don't understand," explained the criminal. "I wasn't driving. There's another man in the car."

"It takes two to make an accident." (*The Great Gatsby*)

soon after passing the river this morning Sergt. Gass lost my tommahawk in the thick brush and we were unable to find it. I regret the loss . . . however accedents will happen in the best families. (Meriwether Lewis, *The Journals of Lewis and Clark*, 2 August 1805 (spelling original))

Fitzgerald's place and significance in the American literary West is no more accidental and his work is no less intricately planned than the Lewis and Clark expedition or the design on an American dollar bill. The two merit brief examination as exemplary American cases of how prescriptive and retrospective designs or narratives misrepresent the complicated matter of causality and historical event, of "place," names, and meaning. On the green back of the one dollar bill are two circular images set off from each other, the two sides of the Great Seal of the United States, agreed upon by Congress in 1782.[9] On the left, resting on land with a distant horizon, is a truncated pyramid above which a detached, abstracted triangle – which would complete the symmetrical pyramid if it were made of the same "material" as the thirteen layers – encloses the Architect Deity's owlish single eye. That eye represents the cause and wisdom of the order beneath it. To the right of this circle is the American bald eagle holding in its mouth a banner proclaiming *E Pluribus Unum*, a motto of identity, while in its two claws it holds contradictory things: an olive branch and spears. Together, the two images represent the ideas that inspired and dictated the expedition of Lewis and Clark, which not only helped America to claim the western half of the continent as its territorial destiny, but which also, in its planning and purpose, demonstrated Enlightenment beliefs in order, perfectibility, and progress that the young nation was claimed to be founded upon.[10] Like the eagle on the dollar bill, Lewis and Clark carried both peace offerings (gifts, trinkets, beads) and weapons: they offered Indian tribes what would amount to a forced choice by the end of the nineteenth century, just as proponents of Manifest Destiny were later to proclaim western settlement as having been inevitable, if not divinely ordained. Whatever the expedition's human – as opposed to ideological – greatness may have been over its two and a half years, it did not resemble the symmetry and order of the Great Seal of the United States, any more than today's United States reflects Thomas Jefferson's imagined agrarian nation.

Like the nation it represented, the military expedition was optimistically prepared for whatever might happen during its "literary pursuit" (the phrase is Jefferson's), whose "author" directed Lewis and Clark to make a written record.[11] But what the "Great Father" foresaw – a Northwest Passage – was not borne out by what Lewis and Clark found. The *Journals* do not read like Jefferson's orderly instructions and lists; they alternately record moments of excited expectations, romantic idealism, and their repeated deferral, along with the pesky presence of "mersquiters" and the somewhat anticlimactic return trip. Fantasies about future time and terrain give way to messy, difficult experience, both physically and mentally. Phenomena occur, such as distant sounds, whose causes a frustrated, scientific Meriwether Lewis cannot explain. Choices and proclamations are made that are later proven mistaken. Accidents happen, such as the capsizing of the main pirogue containing, among other important things, the journals, which for a moment seem to imperil the mission. On the trek back eastward, Lewis accidentally gets shot in the rear. Had Lewis and Clark written about their expedition retrospectively, as Cather's Jim Burden and Fitzgerald's Nick Carraway do of their experiences, we would have a very different narrative. As it was, Lewis never even satisfied Jefferson's request to publish and circulate them for the enlightenment of the nation.

Despite Jefferson's and Lewis' faith in rationality, containment, and perfectibility, the success of the mission lay primarily in how it failed to affirm some presumptions of Jefferson, after whom Lewis and Clark named a river. Most significant historically was the discovery that the presumedly pyramidal, symmetrical pair of mountain ranges, the Alleghenies and the Rockies, that were thought to form a kind of suspension bridge across the continent were in fact not so symmetrically arrayed, nor did they contain a continuous upstream, then downstream, water route that would greatly benefit American commerce in trading with the East. Jefferson's geography proved to have been largely imaginary, but the expedition, along with the chance Louisiana Purchase, made possible America's future as the world's wealthiest and militarily most powerful nation. Although the expedition proved an ambiguous success, and although Meriwether Lewis, drunk and raving, committed suicide by gunshot at thirty-five, American mythology ever since has portrayed Lewis and Clark as national heroes. Meriwether Lewis, it seems probable, felt otherwise about himself: though he was a "national figure," he had (to borrow Nick Carraway's description of Tom Buchanan) reached "such an acute limited excellence" at an early age "that everything afterwards savour[ed] of anti-climax" (p. 8).

I will return to Lewis and Clark's Enlightenment project with regard to Fitzgerald's last, unfinished novel, *The Love of the Last Tycoon: A Western*, which justifies such a metaphorically historical sweep by its allusions to the even earlier explorers Cortez and Balboa and to the building of the railroad, and which portrays how accidents will interfere with the most "enlightened" and financed vision. On the margins of *The Great Gatsby* looms, like the oculist's blind eyes, the question of how Thomas Jefferson's agrarian myth or the Dutch sailors' new world became the Valley of Ashes over which the advertisement for the oculist Dr. "T. J." Eckleburg seems to reign.[12] This larger national and historical quagmire is related through the novel's imagery and verbal connections to the confusing fact that despite Jay Gatsby's nominal greatness on the title page (and in American cultural iconography, where he looks like the durable Robert Redford), Fitzgerald's novel provides little by which to explain or confirm that stature – especially as he is ambiguously a murderer and unambiguously murdered. (One reviewer complained, "The Great Gatsby wasn't great at all – just a sordid, cheap, little crook [with a] gawdy palace.")[13] Just as Cather's *My Ántonia* provides little to explain Jim's unchillably romantic disposition and his retroactively stated love for the novel's finally "battered" heroine, whom he recalls sometimes having "hated," it is never clear what makes Gatsby "great" to Nick Carraway. Nick tells the reader at the start of the novel that he has an "unaffected scorn" for "everything" Gatsby represents – including, one might logically presume, his "heightened sensitivity to the promises of life," his "extraordinary gift for hope" and his "romantic readiness" (p. 6), the very qualities Turner ascribed to the frontier American. That Jay Gatsby ends up shot dead is irreconcilable with Nick's opening, optimistic assertion that "Gatsby turned out all right at the end" (p. 6). At the start of the novel, the first-time reader does not know that "the great Gatsby" is the son of an immigrant whom he never speaks of or that he modeled himself after a "pioneer debauchee" named Dan Cody, and there is little indication that his end is pathetic, if not tragic. Nick knows all of this and knows what is going to happen to Gatsby, but he lures his readers under false pretenses as Gatsby lures his guests – or as used car salesmen and advertisements lure customers.

Toward the close of the novel, Nick Carraway tells the reader, "I see now that this has been a story of the West, after all – Tom and Gatsby, Daisy and Jordan and I, were all Westerners, and perhaps we possessed some deficiency in common that made us subtly unadaptable to Eastern life" (p. 137). Since the novel has been littered with western motifs, the reader is prepared for the revealing first independent clause of Nick's divided sentence, which suggests the West is not so much a setting as a signification. But this revelation is dimmed by Nick's prosaically unrevealing invocation of geographic origins as a way of explaining causality. Given his outspoken difference from Tom, Daisy, and Gatsby, Nick's suggestion that they all share some deficiency is unpersuasive; it is also conspicuously uninteresting. Nick's hermeneutic suggests "the West" is a real place one can come from or go (back) to, as Nick nominally does at the novel's close; it is from the (Mid)west that he writes his narrative. In retrospect, he sees a western significance in events that did not happen in the West: after all, everything in the novel's present happens in New York. His explanation does not shed light on why this story is "of" the West. Or does it? The paratactic marker divides a statement about significance from an explanation about causality via origins; it does not explicitly link them – that is left to the reader. Nick does not question his rhetorical figures because they serve to close rather than open up meaning. His qualifiers "the great" and "of the West" are employed to suture the flow of verbal, cultural, and historical connections that are the text, to give a name to an identity that has no identity: "the Great Gatsby," "the West," this "new" world. While Nick's compulsively evaluating eye is unable to see either his significant place in the story's events or the relationship between his middle-west and the eastern ash-heap, what Fitzgerald called his "intricately patterned" novel resists Nick's blindness.[14]

This *is* a story of the West, but not because the characters come from there. It is a story of the West because it retrospectively organizes signification and causality onto the imaginary origin contingently named "the West," a name that retroactively constitutes its reference, just as Turner's "frontier" does. Naming is necessary, Slavoj Žižek argues, "but it is, so to speak, necessary afterwards, retroactively, once we are already 'in it.' "[15] Nick leaves West Egg for the place named after what he was already thickly in even before he arrived in *New* York, where he had "that familiar conviction that life was beginning over again" (p. 7), a conviction familiar to any reader of Turner, who argued near the opening of his most famous essay that American social development "has been continually beginning over again on the frontier."[16]

Fitzgerald knew how unstable the term "West" was geographically and culturally as any real site of origin, destination, and meaning. He moved "the West" east so as to incorporate his Midwest and also, like Cather, he demonstrated how retrospective narration alters time, space, and value. Nick recalls asking Gatsby "casually" what part of the "middle-west" he is from: Gatsby replies, "San Francisco" (p. 52). By condensing time and displacing or renaming space, such retrospection about origins or categorical significance misrepresents lived history by arbitrarily linking selected metaphorized events in a causal chain. "Reading over what I have written so far," Nick says, "I see I have given the impression that the events of three nights several weeks apart were all that absorbed me. On the contrary they were merely casual events in a crowded summer and, until much later, they absorbed me infinitely less than my personal affairs" (p. 46). Nick claims to have felt indifferently about random events that only later bear a significant causal relation within his retrospective narration. Their "real" relation as they were lived is both unknowable, and by implication, "infinitely" remote, undeterminable. How then could they ever be made present in a reliable narration? Nick's casual adverbial qualifiers obscure sequence and cause. When Nick writes, dizzyingly, that "*Now* I want to go *back* a little and tell what happened at the garage *after* we left there the night *before*" (p. 122, emphasis added), we sense how the retrospective narrativizing of cause – in this context the story of Gatsby's car killing Myrtle – confuses temporal categories because it has posited in advance an atemporal moral judgment. "I disapproved of him from beginning to end," he says of Gatsby after reporting that he nevertheless told Gatsby he was " 'worth the whole damn bunch put together' " (p. 120), as the title itself suggests in substituting his story for everyone else's. Nick's disapproval is, however, rarely revealed in the text's present. Arguably, Nick disapproves of Gatsby "from beginning to end" only at the end of the novel's violent events and before he writes his narrative.

The positing of moral judgment serves to anchor the chain of causality in an atemporal category, since chronology will not help. Neither *My Ántonia* nor *The Great Gatsby* begins at the beginning chronologically: Jim Burden is on a *moving train* two decades after the novel's events when the second narrator meets him, and Nick Carraway is back in the Midwest, recalling his father's advice in his youth as a way of framing his narration about more recent events back East. At the novel's close, Nick also recalls the "thrilling, returning train rides of my youth" in "my middle-west" (p. 137). (Nick defines his middle-west against one that could only be called Willa Cather's: "not the wheat or the prairies or the lost Swede towns," p. 137.) If the middle-west substitutes for both Minnesota and San Francisco in Fitzgerald's text, "the West," which the text is "a story of," is not only unlocatable as space on the American continent, but consistently defers the origin of meaning. And as with space, so with time: "Do you always watch for the longest day *of* the year and then miss it? I always watch for the longest day *in* the year and then miss it," Daisy says "radiantly," as if she were the sun that would not know the difference (p. 13, emphasis added). "Daisy" derives from Old English "day's eye," a phrase that conjoins time and space in the visible world, and that calls up the heliotropic myth that civilization moves according to the sun's westward course. Fitzgerald's complex imagery suggests a simple fact: one cannot watch the past, including the vast American history that came retrospectively to give spatial names (East and West) to geography, names that belie, in their semantically self-defining, national referents, the relative temporalities and human narratives "in" or "of" the past. Fitzgerald's shift in preposition echoes the distinction between being "of" or "in" the West: one can only name a unifying, categorical significance by not participating in or witnessing what occurs in real space and time. The meaning of a person's or a nation's history, like the desire for it, is continuously deferable and revisable or retrospectively projected onto imaginary stable origins, but it does not occur – it cannot be witnessed – from an authentically temporal, participatory vantage point. "Cause and effect: such a duality probably never exists[,]" writes Nietzsche; "in truth we are confronted by a continuum out of which we isolate a couple of pieces, just as we perceive motion as isolated points and then infer it without ever actually seeing it."[7] The continuum of any history can never be fully articulated, let alone confined to a name, except as iterable ideology. Nick's phrase "of the West" depends upon a named yet silent meaning, a consensual one, to garner the illusion of stability it holds in direct proportion both to its lack of explanatory power and to its unreality. At the least one might say: even if the West is real, the words "of the West" refer to another object independent of that reality, an ideological object that structures a causal chain of national origin and identity.

What their narrators do to locate the origin and significance of their stories, Cather and Fitzgerald complicate by providing the reader portraits of them, and particularly by linking them to capital: in Jim's case, to the development of "his" railroad on which we originally see him; in Nick's case, to his "well-to-do" lineage and his excursion in the bond business. The enthrallment each has for the eponymous hero or heroine can and should be read in the context of the financial means that transport them (back) to the scenes of their stories and that enable their narration. Fitzgerald noted in the thirties that he was "essentially Marxian"[18] and *The Great Gatsby* is a demonstration of how ideology misrepresents the complex matter of causality, just as the ideology of Manifest Destiny, by positing an innate moral superiority in the victors, retroactively justified conquests whose aims were chiefly commercial.

At the beginning of "The Significance of the Frontier in American History," Turner famously notes "the closing of a great historic movement. Up to our own day American history has been in a large degree the history of the colonization of the Great West." The word "great" marks the ideological closure Turner's essay gives to the tangled web of colonization and history he reads. In another essay also republished in 1920, "Contributions of the West," he queries whether the ideals born of the "democratic experience of the West" have acquired "sufficient momentum" to sustain themselves in conditions (of industrialism and monopoly capitalism) "so radically unlike those in the days of their origin." Arguing that the West offered "an exit into a free life" and "the chance for indefinite ascent in the scale of social advance," Turner observes, "Never again can such an opportunity come to the sons of men. It was unique, and the thing is so near us, so much a part of our lives, that we do not yet comprehend its full significance."[19] Turner's essays on the West, which seek to "explain" American development, hurry from one phase of American history to another in order to ascribe significance to opportunities that have now vanished. In "The Problem of the West," Turner seems to imitate the western Americans he quotes James Bryce describing, "each darting hither and thither with swift steps and unquiet mien, driven to and fro by a fire in the heart. Time seems too short for what they have to do, and the result always to come short of their desire."[20] Since he first met Dan Cody, Gatsby's "heart was in a constant, turbulent riot" as he listened to "the drums of his destiny, to destiny itself" (p. 77).

What is manifest about such a destiny – Gatsby's, a nation's – is that it will never arrive in the present: "They knew that presently dinner would be over and a little later the evening too would be over and casually put away," Nick writes. "It was sharply different from the West where an evening was hurried from phase to phase toward its close in a continually disappointed anticipation or else in sheer nervous dread of the moment itself" (p. 13). Space alters the experience of time in Nick's formulation, but if this story is "of the West," space may only alter the sense that things happen differently – either causally or casually – somewhere else. Nick's language suggests a forced choice between East or West: the finality of "accidents" ("casually" primarily means "accidentally") or perpetual disappointment. We don't see the dinner put "casually" away; Nick only anticipates it. The word "presently" points past the present moment, just as Daisy's admission that she is "pretty cynical about everything" (p. 17) and Tom's admission that he's a "terrible pessimist about things" (p. 14) infer in any moment evidence only of pre-existing motives or prefigured ends. Gatsby, in contrast, "believed in the green light, the orgastic future that year by year recedes before us" like an unreachable horizon. "It eluded us then, but that's no matter – tomorrow we will run faster, stretch out our arms farther," Nick writes, as if feverishly crossing space can slow down time (p. 141). Indeed, Turner's frontier creates the American future by reverting to earlier stages of civilization. As in Bryce's description of the western American that Turner invoked, Nick's vision of Gatsby's desire is played out across the continent, but rather than suggest that time might run out, the language suggests an irretrievable past mapped onto obscure space, as if the West, not the East, is the landscape of the past: "He did not know that it was already behind him, somewhere back in that vast obscurity beyond the city, where the dark fields of the republic rolled on under the night" (p. 141).

Which came first: East or West? As Nick's closing, imaginary invocation of the Dutch mercantilists' vision suggests, the West is a historically relative and hence unstable term. The East was only named as such after Americans moved west, lending it a directionality dependent on the West, which no historian has ever adequately located semantically or geographically. "Of the West" could thus mean implicitly "of America," which itself was the West when it became a nation on the eastern coast of the continent. Or it could mean movement away from the past toward the future. Ideologically, "the West" can be harnessed to narrate causality in the troubled and violent history of American social and economic development in order to erase the racial and economic antagonisms that mark it. Did idealism create the West, as Turner argued, or did greed? Fitzgerald's novel questions why we need such a question, suggesting this need is produced by a capitalist world, "a new world, material without being real," in which money, as Marx argued, "forces contraries to embrace," such as optimism and pessimism, idealism and materiality, or creation and destruction.[21] A personal romance with wealth was undoubtedly the donnée of his artistic vision, but Fitzgerald unwove the romance in the telling of it, revealing the extent to which everything is imbricated or circularly "goneggted" (as Meyer Wolfshiem would say) in the American landscape, such that the cause of the American dream's failure lies in its self-blinding success as ideology, in its self-convinced vision of a nowhere that never was.

I draw here upon Slavoj Žižek's *The Sublime Object of Ideology* because he brings together Marxist analysis with readings of symbolic culture, often with regard to American materials. Žižek explores what Marx called the "mystical" quality of money that Fitzgerald's novel is famous for literarily memorializing. Money is "the most fantastic commodity of all," as Ross Posnock puts it in his reading of Fitzgerald's novel.[22] By combining a Lacanian understanding of symbolic culture with a materialist critique, Žižek's study is suited to a novelist whose invested narrator describes "the unreality of reality." Seen as its own fantastic signifier and not as an object in reality, "The West" is, for both Nick Carraway and much of American culture, what Žižek describes as a "knot of meanings": it is the word which "*as a word*, on the level of the signifier itself, unifies a given field, constitutes its identity," the word to which we think " 'things' themselves refer to recognize themselves in their unity." Choosing the Marlboro advertisement campaign as an example of this unifying effect, Žižek writes that the advertisement with its iconic cowboy connotes "of course, a certain image of America . . . but the effect of 'quilting' [the stitching of unified meaning] occurs only when . . . Americans start to identify themselves (in their ideological self-experience) with the image created by the Marlboro advertisement" (pp. 95–96). The advertisement for Dr. T. J. Eckleburg enacts such a self-reflecting relation: the eye advertizes the oculist by being a pair of eyes – what one sees *is* "seeing." It also unavoidably connotes something in the advertisement which is more than the advertisement: that "unattainable something" which Žižek draws out from advertisements for Coca-Cola.

[The ideological] vision of America itself achieves its identity by identifying itself with the signifier 'Coke' – 'America, this is Coke!' . . . The crucial point to grasp is that this device – '*America* [the ideological vision of a land in all its diversity], *this is Coke* [this signifier]!' – could *not* be inverted as '*Coke* [this signifier], *this is* [this means] *America!*' The only possible answer to the question 'What is Coke?' is already given in the advertisements: it is the impersonal 'it' ('Coke, this is it!') – 'the real thing', the unattainable X, the object-cause of desire. (p. 96)

Nick surmises that Gatsby "wanted to recover something, some idea of himself perhaps, that had gone into loving Daisy. His life had been confused and disordered since then, but if he could once return to a certain starting place and go over it all slowly, he could find out what that thing was . . ." (p. 86, ellipses original). The fantasy of locating that original moment of falling in love is atemporal; it is called into being by the unnameable desired object itself, the unreality of which ensures the life of the fantasy. Nick describes how Gatsby's "reveries . . . were a satisfactory hint of the unreality of reality, a promise that the rock of the world was founded securely on a fairy's wing" (p. 77). Followed by a description of both Gatsby's "future glory" and "destiny" and his association with Dan Cody, "a product of the Nevada silver fields . . . of every rush for metal since Seventy-five," Gatsby's fantasies, as Nick imagines them, call up the feverish desire for that most elusive of objects, precious metal, which spawned dreams of future glory and seemed to confirm America's destiny in the West. But it also subtly suggests the complex, even "unreal," relation between materiality and desire, between a "rock" and a "fairy's wing." Given that Nick himself is later haunted and has "grotesque" dreams of a dead woman's jeweled hand, his description of Gatsby's imagination is suggestively a retrospective projection that displaces Nick's own disillusionment with his materialistic fantasies onto Gatsby.

What is it that Gatsby's plenitude of colorful shirts cannot fulfill? What is it in Gatsby that is more than Gatsby, and that makes the man a disappointment? To put the question in a western context, if the California state motto announces "I Have Found It!" ("Eureka!") – 'it' being gold – why should Walt Whitman end his poem "Facing West from California's Shores" with this parenthetical question: "(But where is what I started for so long ago? / And why is it yet unfound?)?" Precisely because a name is radically contingent, Žižek argues, its relation to the object it names is tautological: "a name refers to an object *because this object is called that*" (p. 93).

"The West" is "the West" because others use it to designate the object in question ("this story"). Every name that is part of a common cultural language shares, Žižek writes, "this self-referential, circular moment." Before Whitman poses his question about the object of his unfulfilled desire, he writes of "the circle almost circled," which is literally the globe (if it were flat); yet "West" itself is circular or tautological, because it has no positive consistency. It literally cannot be "faced": "I Face West" is the answer to why "it" is not yet found. The nodal point of meaning is a constituent part of the use of names in language "as a social bond" (p. 93). If the words "frontier" or "West" had a clear, positive referent, they would not serve this function; they would not socially bind their users.

Nick Carraway, who assigns his story to "the West," is in the "bond business," in the business narratively of making connections through retrospection by locating an origin at the end, suggestively, of the novel. "The West" of his and Gatsby's origin, like the Dutch sailors' vision of *their* West, is the unplaceable, shifting signifier that makes "great" the "vast" "fields" of meaning (of the republic) that it constitutes and unifies. Nick's closing retrospective projection is familiar if for no other reason than that the "new world" of "the West" already signifies itself; we are in it. But there is no stability in "the West," of course, as Whitman's poem and western historiographical debates show us. Ideology, however, as Žižek argues, is "the effect of a certain 'error of perspective'" that sees in the designator not its own arbitrary self-referentiality but the source of meaning itself, "a transcendent Guarantee" (p. 99). The ideological error is to see in this designator's lack an exceptionalism from the differential play of meaning, to see a fantasy of Identity where there is radical contingency, where there is history one can neither escape nor face.

"In God We Trust" guarantees, one could say, the guarantee of the dollar bill's credit. The words are emblazoned on every bill; the Great Seal is not. But the Great Seal contains the eye whose purported omniscience is saturated with meaning. In *The Great Gatsby* this eye becomes the oculist's eyes on the advertisement for Dr. T. J. Eckleburg. Wilson tells Michaelis that he had pointed out the window and said to his wife:

"God knows what you've been doing, everything you've been doing. You can fool me, but you can't fool God!"
Standing behind him, Michaelis saw with a shock that he was looking at the eyes of Doctor T. J. Eckleburg, which had just emerged, pale and enormous, from the dissolving night.
"God sees everything," repeated Wilson.
"That's an advertisement," Michaelis assured him. (pp. 124–125)

Michaelis' assurance only serves to reinforce the guarantee of the one-supposed-to-know in Wilson's mind; Wilson stands at the window "a long time, nodding into the twilight" (p. 125). The metonymic connection between commerce and a presumedly omniscient nodal point of meaning points to Nick's construction of causality – a construction that ultimately places himself outside the causal chain. Though Nick sets up the meeting between Daisy and Gatsby, he does not witness it; he sees only its immediate effects. Its further consequences leave Nick "haunted" by an East "distorted beyond my eyes' power of correction," since his eyes are responsible for that distortion and those giant, seemingly omniscient spectacles cannot, in fact, correct them (p. 137). Neither Nick nor the reader has recourse to an all-seeing stance that the novel seems to hold out the promise of in the past or in a projected future.

At the beginning of the novel, Nick is, in his clear-eyed conception, a "pathfinder, an original settler" who buys "a dozen volumes on banking and credit and investment securities" which stood on his shelf "in red and gold like new money from the mint, promising to unfold the shining secrets that only Midas and Morgan and Mæcenas knew." Nick wants to be "the well-rounded man" but argues contradictorily that "life is much more successfully looked at from a single window, after all" (p. 7). The proverb echoes the later image of Wilson staring out the window at the eyes that see everything. Both are looking at the same object, but Nick's success lies, literally, in seeing out the window *money* that holds the same "promise" of omniscience; money holds shining secrets in his imagery. Whether volumes on credit and investment securities or an advertisement for the oculist, both are objectifications of a void, the discontinuity opened up in reality by their promise of significance. "It is the same with gold," writes Žižek in describing the "surplus" which the name gives an object that makes it something more than itself; "we search in vain in its positive, physical features for that X which makes it the embodiment of richness" (p. 95). Such a desire can never be fulfilled; the anticipation in the search can only be disappointed: "when we encounter in reality an object which has all the properties of the fantasized object of desire," Žižek writes, "we are nevertheless necessarily somewhat disappointed; we experience a certain 'this is not it'; it becomes evident that the finally found real object is not the reference of desire even though it possesses all the required properties" (pp. 91–92). In the context of Whitman's question "and why is it not yet found?" and Nick's retreat to the West he had first fled, the "West" produces desire through both its promise and poverty of signification.

Nick's implicated "interest" in a narrative that weaves a currency of both linguistic and economic connections is disguised by his presumption of innocence: "I tried to show by my expression," he writes, "that I had played no part in [Myrtle's] past" (p. 30). But he does play a part in romantically distorting the reality of Myrtle's imprisonment behind Wilson's garage, which he imagines concealed "sumptuous and romantic apartments." Despite his knowledge of the outcome of events and his sense at the time that Tom's "determination to have my company bordered on violence," he retrospectively describes his own romantic projections before meeting Tom's "girl" as if they would absolve him of any complicity in domestic misery (p. 22). This is the paradox of romance itself, whether of a person or a country: the romance can only happen retrospectively as something that was already there. In the present, romance is "concealed." In much of the first half of the novel, before the decisive meeting between Gatsby and Daisy, Nick's narration often conveys the feeling of a pointless present, of something not arrived at or given shape, of things both seen and missed. But the retrospective narrative ascribes central importance to this meeting (it occurs in the middle of the novel), the one narrative event the narrator *planned*, but did not witness. Žižek describes the

basic paradox of love: not only of one's country, but also of a woman or man. If I am directly ordered to love a woman, it is clear that this does not work: in a way, love must be free. But on the other hand, if I proceed as if I really have a free choice, if I start to look around and say to myself "Let's choose which of these women I will fall in love with," it is clear that this also does not work, that it is not "real love." The paradox of love is that it is a free choice, but a choice which never arrives in the present – it is always already made. At a certain moment, I can only state retroactively that *I've already chosen.* (p. 166)

As a title, *The Great Gatsby* suggests an already determined relationship of esteem; it is chosen for us before we can choose Gatsby (or perhaps this could only be the case for the novel's first readers). But within a few pages, when Nick announces his scorn for Gatsby, this love/hate fascination suggests the tortured and ambivalent moral evaluations required to exempt himself from the violent chain of events he is invested in telling. To pander to Gatsby's hopes and disapprove of the man is to reinforce the narrative's sense of inevitability and to configure a principle of corruption that obviates any connection of the narrator to his narrative.

The positing of "pre-existing" categories of desire and evil helps to construct retrospective narratives of causality. On one hand, desire and evil pertain to a free, temporal choice; on the other, because they are viewed retrospectively as *a priori* principles, they never occur in time as something originally chosen. Of Daisy marrying Tom, Nick describes it long after the fact as something desired but not chosen: "She wanted life shaped now, immediately – and the decision must be made by some force . . . That force took shape . . . with the arrival of Tom Buchanan" (p. 118). When viewed afterwards through lenses of mourning and nostalgia, agency and choice – whether with regard to desire or moral responsibility – seem to vanish in the landscape of the past. The novel's preoccupation with what it means to *be* a "bad driver" and its nonrepresentation of the moment when accidents *happen* help to confuse the distinction between a wrong as something already there or as something chosen. The moment of violence literally does not occur in the text: "A moment later [Myrtle] rushed out into the dusk, waving her hands and shouting; before he could move from his door the business was over" (p. 107). " 'See the accident?' asked the policeman (p. 109); "Did you see any trouble on the road?" Gatsby asks Nick (p. 112). Žižek asks, "How can we resolve this contradiction between the 'natural', given character of human Evil and that same Evil as pertaining to a free choice?" Kant's solution, he elaborates, is to conceive the choice of Evil as an atemporal, *a priori* act: "as an act which *never took place* in temporal reality but none the less constitutes the very frame of the subject's development, of his practical activity" (pp. 166–167). By blaming Tom Buchanan's carelessness for all the accidents in the story, Nick posits such an atemporal category, since we cannot isolate the moment this carelessness causes effects. That Nick's disapproval of Gatsby "from beginning to end" resembles his disapproval of Tom suggests that what is prospectively and retrospectively posited are indistinguishable in the "present" of the narrative of events. We cannot see these immoral choices because, to put it one way, the narrator of the story cannot see his own eyes. As Turner described frontier settlement, "Other generations have been so much a part of it that they could hardly comprehend its significance. To them it seemed inevitable."

An *a priori* principle of evil is also, of course, at work in the ideology of Manifest Destiny, which demonizes indigenous peoples in order to exempt Americans from the contingencies and responsibilities of their own temporal choices. Especially when those choices involve the profit motive within capitalism, which objectifies time and renders it manipulable for economic "progress," temporal development becomes fixed rather than open-ended. Fitzgerald suggests how human agency effaces itself in historical crimes under the guise of "opportunity" when Nick learns from Gatsby that Meyer Wolfshiem fixed the World's Series:

"Fixed the World's Series?" I repeated.
The idea staggered me. I remembered, of course, that the World's Series had been fixed in 1919, but if I had thought of it at all I would have thought of it as a thing that merely *happened*, the end of some inevitable chain. It never occurred to me that one man could start to play with the faith of fifty million people – with the single-mindedness of a burglar blowing a safe.
"How did he happen to do that?" I asked after a minute.
"He just saw the opportunity." (p. 58)

"America has always been another name for opportunity," Turner argues, nominating the frontier as the chief source of this regenerating category. Revisionist historians have renamed such opportunities "conquests" and "crimes" because they involved other people.

Nick's positing of atemporal categories of both romance and moral corruption helps to disguise the contradiction between the text's pitting of classes and ethnic types against each other and the novel's romantic tone and reputation. Within Nick's narrative energy, Gatsby's unwitting imbrication in the national idea makes him, indeed, "great": as both sacrifice and ideal, as both "fraud" and fantasy-made-real, he serves a culturally symbolic project of reconciling American idealism and greed. A morally principled response to Gatsby's fall and all it represents does not cause Nick's retreat back into "the West," but rather the reverse: Nick's lifelong retreat into the western dream of escape causes his moral principles "from beginning to end." In *The Great Gatsby*, to "go West" has nothing to do with a magnetic compass and everything to do with a moral compass galvanized by the need to leave the scene of the crime. A sure sense of both romance and wrong purchases the ticket to get there.

*How* Fitzgerald has Nick represent, or rather not represent, the culminating violence of Gatsby's murder and Wilson's suicide reveals Nick's self-exemption from the narrative he writes. His account contains no descriptive knowledge of Gatsby's murder, as if a retrospective refusal of realism here marks Nick's own final escape from reality. At the end of a chapter in which temporal references accumulate, the culminating violence, like Gatsby's body, escapes narration and has no spatial or temporal location in Nick's imagery. The last we are given to see Gatsby on his air mattress in the pool, "he shook his head" in response to the chauffeur asking him if he needed help "and in a moment disappeared among the yellowing trees." Wilson becomes a "fantastic figure gliding toward him through the amorphous trees." There is no subjective witness, no present event available to representation. The chauffeur "heard the shots – afterward he could only say that he hadn't thought anything much about them." Gatsby's end coincides with a decline in perception: "there was a faint, barely perceptible movement of the water," "a small gust of wind that scarcely corrugated the surface." When they gaze at Gatsby's body, only Nick's description of the "laden mattress" on its "accidental course with its accidental burden" suggests the presence of a body and only "a thin red circle in the water" suggests the gunshot. Like the trace of that circle, Nick's imagery – transforming intention into accident, knowledge into imperceptibility – circumscribes the meaning of Gatsby's death, a meaning that Nick stands outside of. Only the gardener sees Wilson's body, "and the holocaust was complete" (p. 126), Nick writes sensationally at the end of the chapter, as if overstated significance could disguise his poverty of particular, sensory observation. Moreover, any narrator who would describe three deaths as a holocaust and the Great War, which he experienced, as "that delayed Teutonic migration," has an odd sense of moral significance.

In the end, Nick does not seem to care so much about Gatsby as he does about the fact that, after Gatsby's death, the East "was haunted for me . . . distorted beyond my eyes' power of correction" (p. 137). He imagines, as if in some "night scene by El Greco," a woman carried on a stretcher: "her hand, which dangles over the side, sparkles cold with jewels. Gravely the men turn in at a house – the wrong house. But no one knows the woman's name, and no one cares" (p. 137), presumably including Nick, whose name, it seems no accident, is homophonically "nick care away." The common "deficiency" he might share with the others may be the "vast carelessness" he judges two pages later in Tom and Daisy. The careless, in Fitzgerald's intricate verbal puzzle, cause *car* accidents; they live "casually." That this carelessness is "vast" ties it to the "vast obscurity" beyond the city where Gatsby's dream rolls on, that obscurity Nick uncaringly retreats to where he will write the narrative that ascribes cause to others' carelessness. Nick's deficiency is suggestively the complacency born of the Carraway household: the comfort of privilege that enables the romance of Christmas "sleigh bells" and the "holly wreaths" that are seen in outline by the window frames of such homes as Nick's (p. 137). It is not eastern life that Nick has found he's unadaptable to, but the larger truth about his romance with the West.

After describing his haunted vision of the woman with no name and the wrong house that the men turn into, Nick visits Jordan, who reminds him of a conversation they once had about driving a car:

"You said a bad driver was only safe until she met another bad driver? Well, I met another bad driver, didn't I? I mean it was careless of me to make such a wrong guess. I thought you were rather an honest, straightforward person. I thought it was your secret pride."

"I'm thirty," I said. "I'm five years too old to lie to myself and call it honor."

She didn't answer. Angry, and half in love with her, and tremendously sorry, I turned away. (p. 138)

Nick's self-deceptions are suggested by the fact that "away" is in his name and by the way the language in the passage imitates the language of his earlier vision of a grotesque, uncaring East: just as the men *turn in* at the *wrong house*, Nick *turned away* after Jordan says that she had made a *wrong guess* in thinking Nick was an honest person. (Recall that in *A Lost Lady*, "In the end, Niel went away without bidding her good-bye. He went away with weary contempt for her in his heart," p. 172.) It may not be the East that has, in contrast to the midwest, "a quality of distortion" (p. 137) – implying ambiguously the capacity to distort – but Nick himself and his distorted Midwest. Nick's date of birth is a few months apart from Turner's paean to (American) western civilization in "The Significance of the Frontier in American History" in 1893. Both Nick and Turner's thesis was relatively unchanged thirty years later despite historical upheaval. "Five years" before this dialogue, the Great War ended, which marked in the minds of many the collapse of western progress and idealism, but which Nick "enjoyed . . . so thoroughly" in his experience of it. Nick's statement suggests both his denial and Fitzgerald's historical conscience. If contradictions and deviations are characteristic of distortion, Nick's self-representations are as grotesque – and as aesthetically durable – as a "night scene by El Greco," in which El Greco's figures "melt indistinguishably" into the environs of the canvas as Nick recalls he did into his midwestern environment while on a moving train (p. 137). Nick's nostalgic dream is indistinguishable in its Platonically reproducible form, like East and West Egg, from his nightmare.

Which came first: West Egg or East Egg?

THE DESIGNS OF THE "REEL" WEST

"We ought to plan something," yawned Miss Baker . . . .

"All right," said Daisy. "What'll we plan?" She turned to me helplessly. "What do people plan?" (*Gatsby*, p. 13)

The event of most significance for Fitzgerald's last novel *The Love of the Last Tycoon: A Western* does not happen in the text, but Fitzgerald had planned it before he died, leaving the novel unfinished. The novel's hero, Monroe Stahr, accidentally dies in a plane crash. History intrudes on the manuscript, which thematically renders history *as* accident, as the accident of Fitzgerald's death. The chance incompletion of Fitzgerald's designed novel may indeed accidentally fulfill its design. An Icarus figure, Stahr nevertheless defies the myth by having "the kind of eyes that can stare straight into the sun," the Platonic ideal that casts shadows on the real world. He "stayed up there longer than most of us," the occasional narrator Cecilia writes, but rather than fall in a mythically causal design, "remembering all he had seen from his great height of how things were, he had settled gradually to earth."[23] As an almost perfect emblem of (American) idealism welded to (American) pragmatism, an airplane becomes the vehicle for Stahr's accidental and – literarily and historically – doubly unnarrated death. Stahr is the Enlightenment man, "a rationalist" belonging to the "late eighteenth century" (p. 119). His death, like Fitzgerald's death and the novel's incompletion, does not have a rational cause or mythic meaning, but happens in spite of myth or reason. In some versions of the myth of Icarus, his idealistic hubris (or his father's) burns him and makes him fall: myth "grounds" causality. Fitzgerald's Monroe Stahr has the social power to live Gatsby's dream and cover the continent. There are no gods or careless people to check him, and his ends are either benevolent or innocuous, even if his means sometimes are not. Nevertheless, with his "common sense," it is enough for Stahr "to do his part, to get his block of stone in place, even if the effort were foredoomed, the result as dull as a pyramid" (p. 43). In his most romantic novel, Fitzgerald projected a casualty that has no discernible cause. Yet the cause of money will clearly outlive Stahr, who is accidentally killed, in Fitzgerald's plans, before a plot by money men to kill him succeeds. Which came first: the accident, or Stahr's usurpation by money men like the narrator Cecilia's father?

An equally ambiguous causal relationship, which suggests how retrospection is also projection, and vice versa, is that between the producer Stahr and the narrator Cecilia. On one hand, Cecilia "takes up" the story as a film reel takes up the film (p. 99) – which is already a representation – and brings the man "to life" (Cecilia was to have been narrating after Stahr's death). More accurately, one could say that Cecilia is both projector and soundtrack, as her name, which invokes the saint of music, and the novel's first sentence suggest: "Though I haven't ever been *on* the screen I was brought up *in* pictures" (p. 3, emphases added). The only thing in a film that is not on the screen but is "brought up" in the picture is the soundtrack, which, by adding aural to visual sensation, gives the illusion of three dimensions and puts the viewer "in" the picture. Yet Cecilia is a product of the films she gives life to: "some of my more romantic ideas actually stemmed from pictures [which] shaped me into what I was" (p. 18).

In *The Love of the Last Tycoon*, Fitzgerald makes explicit what is more subtle in the relationship between Nick and Gatsby. The artist projects onto the hero or the national "story" those public fantasies that the audience already wants in advance, which is a form of narcissism, the kind embedded in the phrase "the West is America." When Narcissus gazes at his reflection, he does not realize he is desiring himself. This misrecognition is central to the myth, and Stahr's condition for producing pictures is "that we have to take people's own favorite folklore and dress it up and give it back to them" (pp. 106–107), such that they do not recognize it as identical to their own. Nick does this in projecting onto Dutch sailors desires born only in the Valley of Ashes (while he does not represent his own experiences in war). Hollywood is the logical extension of the Western fantasy's cultural trajectory: "projection," reproduction, and temporal condensation are characteristic of symbolic culture, and especially important for acculturating a western history that is far too complex for public consumption.

Fitzgerald's final novel collapses the distance and all-important difference between representation and historical (geographic, experiential) space-time in order to thematize filmic representation as ideology. Cecilia's opening remark, "I was brought up in pictures," conflates a life's experience with fantasy and collapses three dimensions into two and decades into repeatable hours – which is also true of the Great Seal of the United States, on which a "dull pyramid" sits beneath the flat surface of a two-dimensionally triangulated eye, bringing to a point of illumination the entire landscape and the "meaning" of America. Fitzgerald literarily effects such a conflation or flattening in order to show that by the time the Dutch sailors' dream has hit the movie screen, the American psyche, like the nostalgic Western hope, is not experienced on the ground but played out repetitiously as fantasy, reproducing itself.

The novel's two chief metaphors enact the fantasy's disconnection from "real" space and time: the movie reel and the airplane. While Enlightenment ideals involve the mechanisms of fantasy, the expedition of Lewis and Clark experienced how space and time – their own mechanisms unfixed and unfolding – resist those ideals. From the Age of Reason to the Age of Hollywood, American ideology as fantasy has been circular and hence anti-historical, never settled on the ground, where anything, including accidents, can happen. Cecilia explains her intentions in revealing her upbringing "in pictures" by saying, "I put this down only to indicate that even before the age of reason I was in a position to watch the wheels go round" (p. 3). That position, if those wheels are the reels of a film projector, would be from the projectionist's booth, not from the seats in the audience. As a producer's daughter and the narrative projector of her own fantasies onto Stahr, this hidden position is precisely what sheds light on the subject. And yet, positioned in the mechanisms of fantasy, she cannot give her story the depth of the real any more than a moving picture or the reflection of Narcissus could: "I was going to write my memoirs once, 'The Producer's Daughter,' but . . . it would have been as flat as an old column of Lolly Parsons." So she learned to accept Hollywood "with the resignation of a ghost assigned to a haunted house" (p. 3). Cecilia's description is more than just dryly humorous: she *is* incorporeal as the agent of our own fantasy, which requires the ghostly assignation of fantasy to the "house" already haunted. "House" is the most common noun in *The Great Gatsby*, at the end of which Gatsby's house is vacant and Nick, who projects his own fantasies onto Gatsby, leaves the East "haunted." Given that an actor appears on a set to play the role of Lincoln, the man who invoked the "House Divided," in *The Love of the Last Tycoon*, the house Cecilia has been assigned to haunt is arguably "America," to which she lends the musical soundtrack, completing the illusion that the figures on the screen are real, and marks it as fantasy.

The metonymic link between Hollywood's narcissistic self-reflection and national (and particularly western) history is made in the text through allusions to Andrew Jackson and Abraham Lincoln, who Turner claimed were preeminently shaped by and shapers of the frontier. Jackson was the first US president to call himself a westerner, because he lived in Tennessee. Fitzgerald's novel opens in this sometime "western" region, in the midst of "that sharp rip between coast and coast," which Cecilia ceases to sense only when they "had left those lonely little airports in Tennessee" (p. 4): lexically undifferentiable, the coasts are identical to the same impossible extent that Narcissus is identical with his image. Because of a storm, Cecilia and the Hollywood producers with whom she shares the flight have to land in Nashville, Jackson's hometown. Cecilia guides our reading of this arrival into American history: "airports lead you way back in history like oases, like the stops on the great trade routes" (pp. 7–8). While waiting for the storm to clear, Wylie White suggests taking everyone "out to The Hermitage, Home of Andrew Jackson," to which Schwartze replies, "Where is this Hermitage? . . . Far away at the end of nowhere?" (p. 9). Schwartze, who "is obviously a man to whom something had happened" (p. 7), whose name suggests "black," and who eventually kills himself – the novel's first casualty – questions White's Jacksonian "utopia." Yet Cecilia has called this "mid-America" (p. 8), suggesting that this nowhere, the home of Jacksonian conquest, falls into the self-reflexivity of the "coastal rich": "We were the coastal rich, who casually alighted from our cloud in mid-America," Cecilia says (p. 8). "Casually" implies that the rich are careless, their arrival precarious, accidental, even capable (verbally) of producing casualties. Were this "accident" to have a real cause other than the casual weather, were this arrival to be made not "casually" but "causally," one would reverse almost ocularly "su" to "US." The verbal inversions in Fitzgerald's prose suggest that America's ideological self-reflexivity sees a Narcissus-like reflection that "causes" desire, but that is misrecognized such that what looks like "us" is actually an accident, even a casualty; and it is Narcissus' desire for his reflection that eventually kills him.

That narcissism occludes reality is inherent in the myth of Narcissus, who fails to love other beings. Fitzgerald connects this narcissism verbally to the national project of Jacksonian western conquest, with its attendant obliteration of the human reality that comes between it and its vision of itself. Cecilia observes, "presently the taxi turned down a long lane fragrant with honeysuckle and narcissus and stopped beside the great grey hulk of the Andrew Jackson house" (p. 11). The text then enacts and reinforces the inversion of narcissistic self-reflection when, after Wylie defines "America's tenth president" as "the victor of New Orleans, opponent of the National Bank, and inventor of the Spoils system," Cecilia soon follows this remark with an image of Narcissus: writers, she says, are "like actors, who try so pathetically not to look in mirrors. Who lean *back*ward trying – only to see their faces in the reflecting chandeliers" (p. 12). The textual pattern of images thus enacts the ocular reversal, like a film projector's, of the visual image: narcissus-Jackson, Jackson-narcissism.

If Andrew Jackson is the man of action without principle, then Abraham Lincoln is, in Fitzgerald's structure of allusions, the Nemesis to Jackson's Narcissus, just as Monroe Stahr is the Nemesis of the Hollywood tycoons interested only in money. Cecilia makes frequent observations of Stahr's capacity to look beyond the money motive and demonstrate kindness and idealism. And Fitzgerald connects the tycoon with Abraham Lincoln, stripping them both of mythic origins: "Stahr like Lincoln was a leader carrying on a long war on many fronts. . . . Stahr was an artist only as Mr. Lincoln was a general, perforce and as a layman" (p. 107). Speaking to the fascistic Prince Agge, Stahr explains what "the unity" of a script is: "Stahr hesitated – his face was grim except that his eyes twinkled. 'I'm the unity,' he said. 'Come and see us again'" (p. 58). Stahr's use of the plural pronoun suggests what the two letters can stand for: the United States, *E Pluribus Unum* (as the ribbon in the eagle's beak proclaims on the Great Seal of the United States). Encountering a black man on a beach in Malibu who is "unaware that he rocked an in-dustry" when he tells Stahr that he never goes to movies because "there's no profit," Stahr later re-evaluates his aims as a producer. He submits proposed pictures in his mind "to the Negro and found them trash. And he put back on his list a difficult picture that he had tossed to the wolves, to Brady and Marcus and the rest, to get his way on something else. He rescued it for the Negro man" (p. 96). As Nemesis, Stahr is interested in righting a wrong, creating a more just balance; unlike Narcissus, he recognizes other people, even if he is never able to bring "the Negro man" to the "pictures" of America's "favorite folklore."

Fitzgerald's narrative demonstrates, however, how this recognition of America's real social make-up is limited by the self-replicating privilege that makes it possible (for a white man). Fitzgerald personally knew this as a participant in Hollywood, albeit one who became intensely disillu-sioned with the place. By employing Cecilia as narrator, he demonstrates the socially self-referential nature of even the most beneficent vision. Cecilia cannot tell the reader about the "real America" – an oxymoron of sorts – but only about the "reel" America that is projected. But she is also, significantly, positioned in the novel's other central metaphor: "the world from the airplane I knew," she writes (p. 3). Nick Carraway, on the ground, can only see the difference within his social fantasy between himself and Gatsby, while from a gull's perspective, East and West Egg are hard to distinguish. From her heightened position, where she "ran into" Stahr on the airplane, Cecilia is hard to distinguish from the star of her picture. Fitzgerald provides textual parallels between the two so odd that they can only suggest a mirroring almost as perfect, though as inevitably distanced, as the image of Narcissus is from the man or as the simultaneous soundtrack is from the screen's light. On the plane at the novel's opening, Cecilia wraps her gum before putting it into the "ash-holder" (p. 4), which the stewardess observes is a sign that someone is "nice." Later, "Stahr rolled his gum into its wrapper and put it in an ash-tray" (p. 57). Cecilia admits being "head over heels in love" with Stahr halfway through the book (p. 67). (In Ovid's version, Echo is in love with Narcissus and survives his death, just as Cecilia was to have survived Stahr's.) But she earlier admits that some of her more romantic ideas stemmed "from pictures": "It's more than possible that some of the pictures which Stahr himself conceived had shaped me into what I was" (p. 18). Cecilia feels romantic toward the creator of her sense of romance and self, yet her sense of romance "creates" the picture of Stahr. And the narrative creates Stahr in the image of the narrator when he reproduces her action with the gum. The two "projected" characters also share personal loss: Stahr, his first wife; Cecilia, her sister. While unconscious loss may cause narcissism, it may be this recognition of loss that prohibits narcissism, a structure that Cecilia and Stahr's relationship, like that between Narcissus and Echo, can never become.

Self-reflexive fantasy is called into being, in Fitzgerald's imagery, not by personal loss but by money, just as the Dutch sailors' vision is born of Nick's experience near the Valley of Ashes or as Gatsby's mansion is born of frontier debauchery. (And it is in an "ash" tray that Cecilia and Stahr place their wrapped gum.) Where Gatsby must be about "his Father's Business" while his real father is on the novel's periphery, Cecilia is the actual child of Stahr's antagonist Brady, the money man behind pictures. Children of fantasy would not be such without the money that enables fantasy yet that both corrupts it and is a sign of the fantasy's corruption, as Fitzgerald, himself a child of fantasy, understood. Fitzgerald's "Marxian" leanings and his understanding of the role of ideology as fantasy in America suggest as much: like the eyes of Dr. T. J. Eckleburg, ideology blinds the subject to the Valley of Ashes below; it subjects Americans to the fantasy of a social reality that does not exist.

The particularly American and western character of this fantasy's self-reflexive gaze is clear in the novel not only through allusions to Jackson and Lincoln, but in its nearly obsessive interest in "tracking" the continent. Just as East and West Egg are "almost perfect" ovals indistinguishable from above, there is an almost perfect reflexive symmetry in *The Love of the Last Tycoon: A Western* between not only Cecilia and Stahr but spatially between East and West and temporally between the early explorers and Stahr's pragmatic, visionary version of the Hollywood tycoon. Cecilia uses the characteristics of the Pathfinder to describe Stahr: though he had not much of an education, "he had a long time ago run ahead through trackless wastes of perception into fields where very few men were able to follow him" (p. 18). In the airplane, Stahr "was looking down at the mountains," and he says to the pilot:

"Suppose you were a railroad man . . . .You have to send a train through there somewhere. Well, you get your surveyors' reports, and you find there's three or four or half a dozen gaps, and not one is better than the other. You've got to decide – on what basis? You can't test the best way – except by doing it. So you just do it."
  The pilot thought he had missed something.
  "How do you mean?"
  "You choose some one way for no reason at all . . . You see?" (p. 20)

In surveying the continent and in his approach to laying down tracks, Stahr does away with basic presumptions upon which Enlightenment ideals and the ideology of Manifest Destiny – indeed, the national exploration and conquest of the continent – were founded. Recognizing the inevitability of gaps and the inability to presume right or wrong, Stahr rejects reason as the basis for action. Having lost his wife, Stahr knows accidents can happen even in "the best families," just as an airplane accident was to have happened to Stahr without reason.
  Fitzgerald's intricately planned last novel thematically and accidentally abjures the intricate plans that lay behind the building of a nation, a nation that wanted to believe there was a good and right reason why it had crossed and conquered a continent. Stahr is a man of action, but he is also, like Jim Burden, who puts ideas and capital into action and develops a railroad, a melancholy man. Stahr knows what Joan Didion, who knows her Fitzgerald, reads into the mansions of Newport, Rhode Island – a town, she argues, which is "curiously Western." Newport is a "homiletic, a fantastically elaborate stage setting for an American morality play in which money and happiness are presented as antithetical" (p. 212). "Who could fail to read the sermon in the stones of Newport?" she writes. "Who could think that the building of a railroad could guarantee salvation?"[24] Fitzgerald understood the deeper moral dis-ease at the heart of American conquest. In his rejection of immanent, ordained causality, Fitzgerald's last hero understands what Didion writes in "On Morality," within a collection of essays filled with accidents, casualties, and forced choices. Arguing that it is all right to act, to make choices in the world, Didion writes,

It is all right only so long as we . . . do not confer upon anyone any *ipso facto* virtue. It is all right only so long as we recognize that the end may or may not be expedient, may or may not be a good idea, but in any case has nothing to do with "morality." Because when we start deceiving ourselves into thinking not that we want something or need something, not that it is a pragmatic necessity for us to have it, but that it is a *moral imperative* that we have it, then is when we join the fashionable madmen, and then is when the thin whine of hysteria is heard in the land, and then is when we are in bad trouble. And I suspect we are already there. (p. 163)

Didion's Jeremiad rejects the moral certainties upon which early American Jeremiads relied. Frederick Jackson Turner's Jeremiad marks a modern, western form: he knows he is nostalgic for the frontier and he cannot be sure how something that is vanished is any guide for the future. Nick Carraway expresses vague moral certainties after he knows what has happened to Gatsby's dream, so all he can do is go back – to the past, to the midwest, to himself. Jim Burden does not write about his unhappy present and so he celebrates a past he yet finds "incommunicable." Western history, like American history, has demonstrated to millions who lived it that anything can happen to human beings in time. For that reason, particularly at times of political crisis and social change, writers and readers of the American West have turned to an imagined past for direction. In the 1960s, when Joan Didion became suspicious of the word "morality," the backward western glance offered little escape from domestic discontents.

CHAPTER SEVEN

# Promises and betrayals: Joan Didion
# and Wallace Stegner

Writing during the sexual revolution of the 1960s, Joan Didion and Wallace Stegner bring this study to an appropriate close, to the transitional moment when the dissatisfactions over female options in the gendered West have reached breaking point, and when the battle between the sexes begins to be decoupled from nationalist narratives of western significance in much of the region's literature. What begins to flourish more broadly in this period is not only the representation of female autonomy and non-white subjectivity, but a thoroughgoing critique of the ongoing rhetoric that makes marriage the structuring principle in symbolic nation-building. The work of Didion and Stegner demonstrates that the impulse to find a usable western past can produce some surprisingly destabilizing results. The ambiguous relationship between past and present in their work unsettles any critical attempts to make the past conform to an ideological or mythic standard that can be used either to reflect or to construct the critic's present. In their refusal to predict the future they resemble Turner and reflect a pessimistic reading of Turnerian western significance. But Turner believed in a teleology of the frontier promise that transcended the particularities of those individuals who experienced settlement, the spiritual meaning of which they were not aware. In contrast, the nonprogressive meaning of the frontier for Didion and Stegner, who see a continuing trail of broken promises that connects the past with the present, extends only as far as the imagined lives of their particular characters do. They are no more, and no less, than the particular choices, often molded by prevailing national faiths, that they and others have made, and there is no surplus of narrative or authorial vision that can answer for them. In their tolerance for the ambiguous lessons of the past, Didion and Stegner provide a literary and historiographical set of questions in which, as it were, a diagnosis of the ailing West's "geography of hope" emerges. To what degree are we selective in our reading of the past; do we filter out aspects of the past that speak to more unsettling present states of mind? Is romanticism a cause of failure, and if so, is realism a sufficient antidote? Is there an ethics of ambiguity? If the western past is a story of heartache, what, if anything, are we to take constructively from it? In the literary Wests of Didion and Stegner, the emotional range of marital experience from the tentative blush of hope to suicidal despair reflects a nation's attempts to come to terms with the narrative question, as Didion puts it in an early story, "How exactly did we get from there to here?"[1] Their fiction addresses that question but provides no easy answers, least of all for those afflicted with memory. If there is an answer, it is the causal error in the frontier belief that the West offers a new life, a chance to begin over again, *tabula rasa*. For those westerners, from Turner's individual to the symbolic orphans of Haight-Ashbury, who seek a clean break from the past or who have utopian impulses, history offers no shelter from its painful claims.

The *"quintessentially romantic"* impulse behind westering and other social movements, *"the kind that recurs in times of real social crisis,"* provides the thematic bridge, for Didion and Stegner, between the 1960s and the era of the pioneer. *"The themes are always the same,"* a psychiatrist tells Didion in her title essay "Slouching Towards Bethlehem" (1968) from a collection that ruminates on western character: *"A return to innocence. The invocation of an earlier authority and control. The mysteries of the blood. An itch for the transcendental, for purification. Right there you've got the ways that romanticism historically ends up in trouble."* As Max, one of the orphans of Haight-Ashbury, tells Didion: "'living off the land is the thing . . . we gotta get out somewhere and live organically.' 'Roots and things,' Sharon says." Jefferson's vision of an expanding nation of yeoman farmers; Turner's safety-valve; Emerson's transcendence of historical contingency: such ideational forms of escape provide the thematic leitmotif for both Didion and Stegner in the ongoing history of the American West. For many of their characters, drugs and alcohol are means easily at hand to participate in an American historical tradition of numbing out, breaking from the past, wishing beyond reason for something new to happen. In the ever-increasing length of history's shadow, however, confidence in happy western endings – or even in knowing how one wants things to turn out – is falling apart. So is the idea of the West itself.

Steve is troubled by a lot of things. He is twenty-three, was raised in Virginia, and has the idea that California is the beginning of the end. "I feel it's insane," he says, and his voice drops. "This chick tells me there's no meaning to life but it doesn't matter, we'll just flow right out. There've been times I felt like packing up and taking off for the East Coast again, at least there I had a *target*. At least there you expect that it's going to *happen.*" He lights a cigarette for me and his hands shake. "Here you know it's not going to."

I ask what it is that is supposed to happen.

"I don't know," he says. "Something. Anything."[2]

The teleology of Manifest Destiny has become an edgy, nameless desire without an object in this passage from "Slouching Towards Bethlehem."

Wallace Stegner's Lyman Ward, the reactionary frontier historian and narrator in *Angle of Repose* (1971) whose wife abandoned him and who delves into the past of his grandparents, has nothing but disdain for such wayward sixties youths. Yet his temporal exploration shares similar motives with their geographic explorations – and with the ideological explorations of the young people he disdains in *Angle of Repose*. Reaching backwards through time is another way in which to discern an approaching future, if one can see things as they appeared to those in the past. The Doppler effect is for Lyman Ward the scientific analogy for this experience of time past: "The sound of anything coming at you – a train, say, or the future – has a higher pitch than the sound of the same thing going away." But since history, "like all falling bodies . . . constantly accelerates," he turns to his grandparents and their temporal position as they experienced it:

I would like to hear your life as *you* heard it, coming at you, instead of hearing it as I do, a sober sound of expectations reduced, desires blunted, hopes deferred or abandoned, chances lost, defeats accepted, griefs borne. I don't find your life uninteresting, as Rodman [Lyman's son] does. I would like to hear it as it sounded while it was passing. Having no future of my own, why shouldn't I look forward to yours?[3]

But it is difficult to hear the pure sound of hope coming to even his grandparents' ears, especially toward the end of the novel, once he confronts the pain of what lay ahead for them. What Lyman Ward hears in his explorations of his ancestral past out West is another Doppler effect, that of his grandparents' relation to their own past as they suffer, renounce, move on, regret: "Even while you paid attention to what you must do today and tomorrow, you heard the receding sound of what you had relinquished" (p. 25). As determined as he is in his belief that the present is misguided, Lyman Ward is beset with evidence of his grandparents' own forms of denial and the ephemeral comforts they reach for in difficult circumstances. Among them are Oliver Ward's drinking and even Susan Ward's artistic talent, which brings a soothing sense of eastern culture to the West and provides an aesthetic stay against constant change. In a letter to her girlfriend Augusta in New York, who has just moved into a new mansion built by Stanford White, Susan writes: "Before you put a fire in your new fireplace, gather up your children and have them stand in it, looking up, and then, with the light falling on them so, paint them and send them to me." Lyman asks, "Where was Grandmother living when she had that sentimental whim? In a dugout in Boise Canyon" (p. 25). Stegner's historian-narrator seems at times aware of what Cather's Jim Burden often is not: that the nostalgic perspective on past places and times is filtered through a distorting, aestheticizing lens. Stegner and Didion give meticulous attention to currents of self-deception in their characters, especially in relation to their immediate and more distant pasts. Blending genres of fiction, history, reportage, and memoir, their work reveals the constructedness of history, not only because of the aestheticizing distortions of the present but because the past, as lived, involved wishful longings for things lost, and for things hoped for that never arrived in the present.

In the literary genealogy this book traces, Joan Didion and Wallace Stegner are the literary heirs to the work of F. Scott Fitzgerald and Willa Cather, respectively. Their work comments allusively on them, quotes them, shares their thematic preoccupations about troubled marriages and what Nick Carraway calls "the story of the West, after all," and demonstrates throughout what Fitzgerald, following Cather himself, understood to be the distortions of nostalgia in retrospective narration. In making a past West the imaginary site of return for the disappointed, they are self-conscious about the potential, historiographical dead-end of this retrospect, even as they are acutely aware of its romantic pull and especially of the ethical injunction to try to know the past. The ethics of their retrospective revisionism derive from the need to find out where things went wrong, rather than from a desire to find the key to some illusory American success story of self-reliance and spiritual redemption and renewal. The western past is, in this sense, not past but ongoing: mistakes and deceptions and bad faith inform a tangled history connected to an ongoing present in which anything can happen and in which history may not, after all, be a measure for anything other than our own failures. This intimate and contentious relationship between past and present is refracted in Didion's and Stegner's work through fractured marriages and bonds of kinship. The heartache and failure of the personal, intimate life, its broken promises and betrayals of faith, serve as analogue to the historian's or writer's complicated relationship to a western past he or she can neither renounce nor redeem. Their work relinquishes any faith in individual autonomy and freedom, especially given the relational demands between the sexes and the burdens of historical knowledge.

Whereas Fitzgerald makes Gatsby's romance with Daisy a metonym for the dream of the New World and Cather self-consciously and ironically exposes just such a metonymic relation forged by her male narrators, Didion's and Stegner's work makes female subjectivity – and not simply a woman's relationship to a man – a literary site for exploring the West's significance, the unsettled desires and dissatisfactions in its history. In short, as with Cather, their women do not fulfill the role assigned them by a conventionally masculine romance. If women in the West were generally thought to be a civilizing force to male lawlessness and desire, Didion's and Stegner's women adopt that role only to call the western romance with civilization into question by following their own desires beyond the marital contract. The hope of the West, literally and figuratively, will not be reproduced as it is in Owen Wister's Western. The loss of Susan Ward's child, followed by the suicide of her extra-marital lover in *Angle of Repose*; Lily Knight McClellan's abortion of a child whose father may not be her husband in *Run River*: these pivotal moments can be easily, but reductively, read as conservative admonitions against the breaking of marriage vows. They are more complicated and ethical than that. They figure the aborted hopes of a westering nation and they rewrite the nationally allegorical figurations of the feminized western landscape, submissive before male desire and control. They signal that the West has never, in fact, been simply domesticated and civilized, as its allegorical romance would indicate, or even as Wallace Stegner in his more reactionary moments might seem to suggest. The ongoing West is in part a story of American civilization's betrayals and violence coming home to itself.

Joan Didion's *Run River* (1963) shows its literary debts to *The Great Gatsby*. Set in the Sacramento River Valley in the years before and after the Second World War, Didion's first novel is a tale of careless westerners caught up in a chain of marital betrayals, murder, suicides, and meaningless, accidental deaths. Didion brings Fitzgerald's sense of a grotesque East to California, and the golden land has rarely been rendered more bleakly. Unlike Fitzgerald's novel, Didion's equivalent of Daisy and Tom Buchanan do not escape the harm they cause others. Everett McClellan kills the dilapidated Gatsby-figure Ryder Channing, who has been sleeping with his wife Lily, and the novel ends when he turns the gun on himself, just as Fitzgerald has Gatsby's murderer George Wilson do. Whereas Fitzgerald's narrator evokes the romantic western dream that drove Gatsby, Didion's novel is possessed of no such dream; her characters are only haunted by the notion that someone supposedly once had one. Her characters do not know why they have made the choices they have made, least of all to marry the people they do. "Shortly before noon [Lily] told Everett that she would marry him . . . It seemed as inescapable as the ripening of the pears, as fated as the exile from Eden." It had been "no decision at all: only an acquiescence. Was it, after all, so inevitable?"[4] Unlike Gatsby, none of Didion's characters knows what he or she wants; the literal and figural light at the end of the dock is "burned out and not replaced" (p. 260). And unlike Nick Carraway, who in the end can retreat into his romanticized midwest, Didion's characters have nowhere to go – except for Lily and Everett McClellan's son Knight, who decides to leave, after accidentally witnessing Lily with Ryder, and goes back East to Princeton; and Everett's sister, Sarah, who marries an easterner and moves to Philadelphia. To the extent that this is also a story of the West, it is about the failure of western migration to add up to anything like progress. "What had it all been about: all the manqué promises, the failures of love and faith and honor" (p. 262) in a family "come down through twelve generations of circuit riders, county sheriffs, Indian fighters, country lawyers, Bible readers, one obscure United States Senator from a frontier state a long time ago; two hundred years of clearings in Virginia and Kentucky and Tennessee and then the break, the void into which they gave their rosewood chests, their silver brushes; the cutting clean which was to have redeemed them all" (p. 263). Didion's vision is about more than just the frontier dream's failure; it contemplates what it means, for the descendants of frontier pioneers, not to have a dream in the first place – to believe, in contrast to Turner, that at the end of the continent and at the end of frontier history, "none of it signified . . . none of it mattered" (p. 259).

One of Didion's two epigraphs to the novel is from *Peck's 1837 New Guide to the West*, a passage Turner quotes in "The Significance of the Frontier in American History": "the real Eldorado is still further on." The frontier does not redeem. The character formed on the frontier, as Turner would have it, merely disguises and postpones defects of character.

They had been a particular kind of people, their particular virtues called up by a particular situation, their particular flaws waiting there through all those years, unperceived, unsuspected, glimpsed only cloudily by one or two in each generation, by a wife whose bewildered eyes wanted to look not upon Eldorado but upon her mother's dogwood, by a blue-eyed boy who was at sixteen the best shot in the county and who when there was nothing left to shoot rode out one day and shot his brother, an accident. It had been above all a history of accidents: of moving on and of accidents. (p. 263)

Rather than suggesting the exceptional nature of the frontier experience, Didion's stress on particularity in this passage points to its non-universal meaning. As in so many allusions in her work to the myth of Eden and the Fall, a universal, mythic story of causality and evil is suggested only to be thwarted: we have fratricide, but without meaning. The boy had simply run out of targets, or enemies. Didion's fiction and essays show a preoccupation with accidents, with the possibility that even the most significant choices and desires, whether to move on or to marry, are ignorant of their causes and their effects. A belief in redemptive possibilities "still further on" blinds her characters not only to the present but to the determinations of the past. The wife who longs to look upon her mother's dogwood, to reverse time and return to a previous home east of the West, sees the flawed linearity in the westering design. As Thomas Mallon argues, in her work Didion struggles to connect the point at which her characters lost the trail of their destinies – "a spot where personal history can only fall back on itself" – with the fate of the nation, "more specifically, the history and destiny of the American West."[5] John Wayne, for example, is able to absorb, she writes, "the inarticulate longings of a nation wondering at just what pass the trail had been lost." The individual, for Didion, is not free; he or she is burdened with a sense of national loss. In her essay on John Wayne, the man who would seem to assuage those longings of a nation can only say of the one time he actually hit someone, "It wasn't a choice; it was an accident." But in a world of "paralyzing ambiguities," John Wayne, the actor, "suggested another world, one which may or may not have existed ever but in any case existed no more: a place where a man could move free, could make his own code and live by it."[6] Didion's is a complicated form of nostalgia because it puts into question the reality of the past that is longed for, even as Didion's work feeds on the ambiguities that put at bay their threat of paralysis. John Wayne becomes an image of the lost fictionality of Turner's, and the Western's, "historical" frontier, which was already lost in the first place to Turner's present.

*Run River*'s main focus is Lily Knight, whose father lost the chance to be governor of California to a populist, and who marries the son of another prominent family, Everett McClellan, the inheritor of his father's hops ranch. While Everett leaves Lily and their new child to enlist in the army during the Second World War, Lily finds herself pregnant, probably from another man, Joe Templeton. After Everett returns for his father's funeral, Lily confesses this fact to him and escapes to San Francisco to have an abortion. Lily's father has a mistress, Rita Blanchard, whom his wife is silently aware of, and he and Rita die in an accident when their car plunges into the Sacramento River. Everett's sister Martha, perhaps the book's most memorable character, falls in love with Ryder Channing, who eventually leaves her in order to marry a woman of greater social standing in the postwar California social elite. Martha is the novel's first suicide when she drowns herself in the Sacramento River after Ryder, then married, seduces her one last time. When Everett later murders Ryder Channing after Channing has seduced not only Martha but Lily and then kills himself – the framing events of the story – the detective work of the novel is to navigate, from the indirect perspective of its main characters, the series of choices that produced this violent end, and to understand it in relation to a longer frontier history.

In *Run River*, the frontier is a family saga with an ongoing legacy for the Knights and McClellans, two families who, like Didion herself, descend from white settlers of the Sacramento Valley. After the end of the war, the aerospace industry and other forms of economic capital that Turner had worried would destroy the egalitarian ethos of frontier existence displace their families' agrarian past and importance. In the families' legacy of belief in their own importance and in their aggression against minorities and the newly rich, Turner's sense of frontier democracy is already a thing of the past. Indeed, the westering impulse, as it was for Wister, is implicitly a desire to gain distance from ethnic others and cosmopolitanism. What was fought against in the war in Europe emerges in Everett McClellan's father's social views on the west coast. He believes that "Easterners fell into two camps: goddamn pansies and goddamn Jews. On the whole, both categories had to do with attitudes, not facts, and occasionally they overlapped. His daughter Sarah had for example married a goddamn pansy and gone East to live, where she picked up those goddamn Jew ideas" (p. 57). Lily's father, Walter Knight, "had never hired a Mexican foreman expecting that they would operate under the Stanford Honor Code" (p. 36). Mr. McClellan "referred to all Mexicans and to most South Americans – including the President of Brazil, who had once been entertained on the river – as goddamn wetbacks, and to all Orientals as goddamn Filipinos. There was no use telling him that somebody was Chinese, or Malayan" (p. 56). Everett thinks of eastern cities as "another world, a world teeming with immigrants and women who spent the day in art galleries." The Sacramento Valley never was an Anglo-Eden except in the mind of those who shrink the world rhetorically and hold in disdain the ethnic groups who have an equally long, if not longer, regional history. The hyperbolically loose way that her characters use these terms suggests Didion's sense of the shaky fictional grounds upon which they base their belief in their ethnic superiority. Even an ethnic familiar is made other through an especially arbitrary use of ethnic slurs. Resenting a young man who is interested in his daughter, Everett says he looks "like a little wop in that jacket he wore up here." But the boy "was six foot two, an inch taller than Everett; was almost as blond as Everett had been at his age and as Knight was now; and had worn . . . a madras jacket identical to one hanging in Knight's closet" (p. 9). Losing a sense of their privileged identity, Didion's pioneer descendants make up denigrating distinctions of appearance, between people nearly identical physically, as a reactionary form of self-aggrandizement. The families' sense of their saga is aggressively Anglo-American, and as such, is more a social history than a private family's story. Their families mark the fate of something like Owen Wister's Anglo-Saxon-American nation out West (their names are, after all, Knight and McClellan), which is well on its way to internal collapse.

The verbal aggressions against perceived ethnic others stand in telling contrast in the novel to the fact that acts of physical violence occur among ethnic familiars and family members. It thus misses the critique of *Run River* to argue that the novel aims to "consolidate the offensive against civil rights reforms and sensibilities" and that it "enacts [a] . . . white racialist social practice."[7] Didion is at pains to show the shabbiness of cognitive reasoning and the petty, provincial defensiveness that go into her characters' views of virtually the rest of the country and the world. Her ethical critique of these views is as much realist as moralist: her characters cannot accept the reality of change. Lily and Mr. McClellan, Everett thinks,

would never seem to get it through their heads that things were changing in Sacramento, that Aerojet General and Douglas Aircraft and even the State College were bringing in a whole new class of people, people who had lived back East . . . She and his father were going to be pretty surprised if and when they ever woke up to the fact that nobody in Sacramento any more had even heard of the McClellans. Or the Knights. Not that he thought they ever would wake up. They'd just go right along dedicating their grubby goddamn camellia trees in Capitol Park to the memory of their grubby goddamn pioneers. (pp. 5–6)

Moreover, the Knights' and McClellans' investment in outmoded fantasies of ethnic superiority is part of the fundamental error in the causal narrative chain of dissatisfaction and violence. Everett, for example, marries Lily because she is, from an ethnic and class standard, safe – despite his interest in other girls such as Doris Jeanne Coe, from Oklahoma, or Naomi Kahn, who is Jewish. Their group identity ultimately trumps, for Everett, their singularity: "Everett's appreciation of Naomi's singular virtues grew until he actually regretted, for something like four days after she eloped with the Young Communist from Berkeley, that he had not asked her to marry him. Nonetheless, Naomi Kahn had not been, any more than Annis McMahon or for that matter Doris Jeanne Coe had been, someone with whom he could have lived on the ranch." That role belongs to Lily, whom he has known for years; "Lily required no commitment: Lily was already there" (pp. 168–169). The parallel histories of their families give their marriage a sense of dynastic inevitability, with incestuous overtones. Indeed, Everett's sister Martha competes with Lily for his affections and claims early on to want to marry him. In this fallen Eden, few of the original settlers' descendants are willing or able to escape the familiar and familial. In effect, they want time to stand still, whereas their ancestors committed themselves to the unfamiliar and to change. While the pioneer ancestors needed to maintain bonds of kinship to survive that commitment to the unknown, the Knights and McLellans have reduced bonds of kinship to a way of maintaining their familiar status.

Jennifer Brady has read *Run River*, *Play It As It Lays*, and *A Book of Common Prayer* through Turner's frontier thesis and argues that one of Turner's observations is key to Didion's work. While Turner stressed predominantly the antisocial, individualist tendencies the frontier produced, he does note in passing in the frontier thesis that "Complex society is precipitated by the wilderness into a kind of primitive organization based on the family."[8] For Didion, Brady argues, "the lure of the frontier revolved in many ways around its promise of individual liberty and the absence of social controls; but for this ideal to be realized, for the pioneers to survive, they had to recognize and uphold the primal loyalties due to each other as blood kin."[9] But striking out for what one wants proves, in this novel, to be the kind of Turnerian individualism at odds with primal loyalties that ensure survival. From the Donner-Reed party's cannibalism to Lily's father's infidelities, preceding generations' broken promises and betrayals of those primal loyalties haunt Didion's characters. Without those loyalties and bonds of kinship, individual desire turns destructive as if through some primal curse.

The frontier myth, as Didion understands it, involves a telling contradiction. It borrows the Christian idea of redemption implicit in Manifest Destiny – the "break, the void . . . the cutting clean" from history – but assumes none of the concomitant burden of a secularized notion of original sin, from which free agency and moral responsibility derive. What Didion's pioneer descendants need to be redeemed *from* are their ancestors' betrayals of primal loyalties in their attempt, on the frontier, to cut clean from all ties. The dream of redemption of the frontier promise, in other words, is a cause of the secular fall from Eden, and not the reverse. "If paradise lies in California," writes Leonard Wilcox of the Donner-Reed party, "it was obtained by a grotesque parody of the Eucharist."[10] The Donner-Reed party's cannibalism is for Didion a parable of the flaw buried in the western dream of the past: "My own childhood was illuminated by graphic litanies of the grief awaiting those who failed in their loyalties to one another," she writes. "The Donner-Reed party, starving in the Sierra snows, all that ephemera of civilization gone save the one vestigial taboo, the provision that one should not eat his blood kin."[11]

That taboo was broken, of course, because of presumed necessity; it was not a free choice, but a forced one. Agency becomes one of the burdens assumed after the fall from paradise, and Didion's characters want to revert to an Edenic world before the necessity of choice, to a world devoid of temporal change.[12] In wartime, Everett prizes his barracks life at "Fort Bliss" because of its ordered structure. Lily nearly does not know herself without her father: "*Your father no longer tells you when to go to bed, no longer lulls you with his father's bourbon.*" Absent paternal orders, the necessity of choice is obviated by having your own drink and by following others' desires, as when Ryder Channing seduces Lily and Martha. The contours of their lives and desires are pulled as if by the currents of the (somewhat Heraclitean) Sacramento River: "*Everything changes, everything changed,*" Lily thinks; "*Nobody chooses it but nothing can halt it, once underway: you now share not only that blood but that loss*" (p. 47). That so much death occurs alongside or in the Sacramento River links the necessity of time's flowing river with mortality, as it is in the postlapsarian myth. The opening of James Joyce's *Finnegans Wake*, "riverrun, past Eve and Adam's," is inverted in Didion's title, as is the Edenic myth in the novel. The fall, born of the drive to find paradise, has robbed her characters of choice rather than giving it to them, who want to be saved not so much from mortality or sin as from the mortal necessity to choose: "*A little late for choosing, she had said to Everett, quite as if it hadn't always been. Was there ever in anyone's life span a point free in time, devoid of memory, a point when choice was any more than [the] sum of all the choices gone before? A little late for choosing:* her father had known it, even as he denied it. But deny it he had. *You say what you want and strike out for it,* he told Lily on the morning of her sixteenth birthday" (p. 33). This is the father's curse: to encourage Lily to perpetuate the frontier dream of a new beginning. Yet "she wanted now only to see her father, to go back to that country in time where no one made mistakes" (p. 95).

Didion's seemingly conservative sense of the historical past belies an underlying and almost paralyzing skepticism not only about narratives of progress and fresh starts, but about the uses of the past, even about its narratability. The West is burdened by the accumulation of teleological narratives because the West is the last resort for the accomplishment or fulfillment of their ends. California is especially burdened because it is, as she writes in *Slouching Towards Bethlehem*, where we run out of continent. Didion's West is filled with people whose story or whose world does anything but confirm the truth of narratives about first causes, ultimate ends, and grand designs, whether spiritual or national, revolutionary or socially ameliorative. *Run River* reveals an almost circular structure in its sense of history. We begin at the end and we end at the beginning, with Everett's murder of his wife's lover. (In this structure, it also borrows from *Finnegans Wake*, the last words of which, "A way a lone a last a loved a long the," syntactically precede the novel's opening, "riverrun.") In between, the novel's temporal references range from the settling of California to Lily's and Everett's familial and marital histories in an attempt to discern some historical explanation for how everything happened. Framed by a husband's acts of murder and suicide, acts that occur in rapid succession in "real" time, the novel's temporal structure, despite the title of the long intermediate section "1938–1959," is anything but linear and progressive. Its circular, regressive structure embeds between the acts of murder and suicide a history of overland journeys and settlement, marital infidelities, an abortion, and a family's decline. It broods, like Mr. McClellan, "upon causes and effects" (p. 105).

The novel's opening attends to numerical detail and problems of sequence, as if this critical moment in time – Everett's murder of Ryder – can somehow be understood or situated within an accretion of marital and familial dates and memories.

Lily heard the shot at seventeen minutes to one. She knew the time precisely because, without looking out the window into the dark where the shot reverberated, she continued fastening the clasp on the diamond wrist watch Everett had given her two years before on their seventeenth anniversary, looked at it on her wrist for a long time, and then, sitting on the edge of the bed, began winding it.
    When she could wind the watch no further she stood up. (p. 3)

There is an odd symmetry or coincidence in the fact that Lily's watch says "seventeen minutes to one" and that the watch was given to her on her seventeenth wedding anniversary by the man who has fired the shot that will end their marriage. The symmetry in number erases differences in duration. It marks how one instant of violence collapses all time frames into each other – their wedding, this shattered moment. This notion is echoed later in the novel when Lily, longing "to go back to that country in time where no one made mistakes," recalls the biblical lines, "For a thousand years in thy sight are but as yesterday when it is past, and as a watch in the night" (p. 95). Her watch, the night of the murder, becomes the sign equally of seventeen years and seventeen minutes; the past is relative the minute a violent act becomes irrevocable. This Didionesque (and Fitzgeraldian) semblance of an almost self-reflexive pattern introduces the reader to the equally self-reflexive relation of causes and effects that are the history of Lily's and Everett's marriage.

Separating and acknowledging their respective responsibilities for this violent outcome is the task of the succeeding narrative, which shifts subtly among Lily's, Everett's, Martha's, and an omniscient point of view. In the immediate aftermath of the gunshot, Lily's series of infidelities become to her "all, now, one error in taste" as she recalls after one night of infidelity how "she had begun to see it all as Everett's fault. It would not have happened had Everett been at the party instead of home brooding about his sister" (pp. 6, 7). The causes of her infidelity amount to nothing more than circumstance: "A party could begin it all again – two drinks, someone from out of town, Everett ignoring her, that was all it would take" (p. 7). Helpless before circumstances and her own seeming lack of agency, she recalls Everett suggesting that same afternoon, in frontier fashion, that they "go away": "Go away where?" she asks. He replies, "Somewhere" (p. 8). Anything recollected becomes a way to imagine a different outcome: had Everett not been brooding about his sister one night; had Everett agreed to go away with her when she took the children in the summer of 1957; had he not enlisted in the war effort; had she, especially, known why she married Everett. Later she recalls Everett asking her long before

when they would be married.

"I don't know," she said finally one morning on the river. "I mean I don't want to think about it right now."

"When do you want to think about it? Next year? The year after?"

"Everett. Stop talking that way. I'm nervous. All brides are nervous." She had read in a magazine that all brides were nervous, and had wondered whether that might not be her only problem: an apprehension which would turn out to be not unique but common to all women. (p. 64)

Marriage is figured in the future subjunctive; Lily's reluctance is put in the future context of a larger social history: the dawning awareness of women's limited options (the novel, as some have noted, appeared the same year as Betty Friedan's *The Feminine Mystique*). Years later, however, after her decision to marry Everett has come to seem inevitable, more local contexts – and the helplessness of past subjunctives – frame the question of agency. In the aftermath of the shooting she "began to wish immediately that she had never answered the telephone at all" when Ryder had called to ask her to meet him down by the dock, "began to wish that she and Everett could have stayed in bed while the sun gradually left the room . . . began to regret that they could not have lain inviolable on that walnut bed from five o'clock until the following morning" (p. 12). Like the watch that she winds until it can be wound no more, retrospection serves to immobilize and to confuse temporal categories and contexts. "The future was being made, [Everett] heard Channing say" at an earlier point chronologically and a later one narratively, "right here in California. Starting now" (p. 157). But the present already points subtly to the past in Didion's use of the past progressive tense, having framed the quotation in indirect discourse: it "*was* being made." Conjoined with the deictic terms "here" and "now" that ambiguously situate us in space and time, Didion's rendition of Channing's statement displaces the present onto an ongoing past. The use of the past progressive tense and the passive voice suggests Didion's view of the regressive nature of idealism, which subsumes, by predetermining, the agency of its adherents and deprives them of a realistic understanding of the present's open-endedness. In a state that *was* always making the future, Didion's characters are obsessed with unmaking the past that has made them. But it remains "a little late for choosing." The future cannot be "made" any more than the past can be unmade.

After the murder, Everett's sense of his own and everyone else's lack of agency is conjoined with an inability to plan the next moment.

Now that it was done, now that Channing lay dead . . . it seemed to Everett that none of them, least of all Lily, could have been involved; that all of them . . . had simply been spectators at something that happened a long time ago to several other people . . .

He had not thought of there being alternatives, solutions, next steps. Although he could not now focus upon how it happened or what would happen next, he seemed to have known all along . . . not only that it would happen but that everything he knew would be obliterated by it. (p. 19)

Didion's depiction of Everett's thoughts triangulates three forms of knowledge into an annihilating dialectic: the knowledge of his act's inevitability, the knowledge of "everything" he knew, and the knowledge that this act would obliterate all knowledge. Violence ruptures linear time, collapsing predictive, ongoing, and retrospective experience. As we saw in chapter 2, a dialectic operates in Turner's frontier thesis, which represses violence, such that a transcendent "spiritual significance" is what the figuration of the frontier's finitude enables Turner to read. For the Donner-Reed party, as for Everett, however, the violent end of experience not only forbids any higher spiritual meaning to emerge from a causal chain of events but disembodies experience by making a person other to himself and what he knows. Everett's orientation to his own acts is no different from his orientation to the Donner-Reed party: "something that happened a long time ago to several other people." The West's legacy of violence, in Didion's fiction, while it ends countless stories, is an unending story of how even the violence closest to home does not really hit home.

The Knights and McClellans are thus both made and unmade by their pioneer ancestry. Its conferral of honor upon them is simultaneously a destructive burden few of them escape. When Everett strikes out for his own form of frontier escape by serving non-combatant duty during the war, his sister Martha gives him *The McLellan Journal: An Account of An Overland Journey to California in the Year 1848.* Taking the journal East by train, Everett continues the story of the McLellans but reverses its geographical telos. Martha's gift of family pride is also a curse, invested as she is in the doom and grief that awaited women in the past like Tamsen Donner. Her "favorite game as a child had in fact been 'Donner Party,' a ritual drama in which she, as its originator, always played Tamsen Donner and was left, day after day, to perish by the side of the husband whose foolish miscalculations had brought them all to grief." Lily will re-enact this drama when she holds her dead husband in her arms at the novel's end. Martha's embrace of the martyr role makes it seem "an ineradicable mote in [her] eye that everyone from whom she was descended had, unlike Tamsen Donner, gotten through, and when Lily told her that someone in her father's family had traveled with the Donner-Reed Party as far as the Applegate Cut-off, Martha had been despondent for several days" (p. 100).[13] Circumscribed by a masculinist romance in which women suffer their men's foolishness, Martha is also an incipient feminist who, if she cannot imagine a wholly new story for women, rewrites the masculine frontier by foregrounding and imaginarily elevating the roles played by women. In a parenthetical aside, Didion writes,

(In Martha's re-enactments, the Winning of the West invariably took on this unobtrusively feminist slant; in another game, "Central Pacific," the power behind the transcontinental railroad turned out to be not Collis Potter Huntington at all, but Leland Stanford's wife Jane, and Lily grew up with the distinct impression, planted by Martha and uncorrected for years, that the *éminence grise* behind the California Republic had been Jessie Benton Frémont.) (p. 100)

Early on, Martha bucks female convention by having on her childhood bedroom walls "neither Degas ballet dancers nor scenes from *Alice in Wonderland* but a framed deed signed by John Sutter in 1847 . . . and a large lithograph of Donner Pass on which Martha had printed, in two neat columns, the names of the casualties and the survivors of the Donner-Reed crossing" (p. 100). But no kind of feminist, heroicizing revision of the masculine western past can prevent Ryder Channing from acting out the same opportunistic, masculine role he plays. Nor, without a radically rearranged social landscape, can Martha imagine for herself another role than that of female martyr. Didion's portrait of Martha is so caught between the ideals of heroic aspiration and feminist resistance and the reality of her role as martyred mistress that her eventual suicide by drowning, Ophelia-like, in the Sacramento River has the feel of a re-enactment of her own stage-play about nineteenth-century frontier women who win the West but lose their men.

Her drowning in the river signifies a claim on a particular history left out of the triumphalist reading of the frontier and reveals the costs of claiming the settled lands of the West. Passed down in Lily's family, for example, is the story of the oldest grave on her family's property, that of the first Knight to die in California, a baby. "It was a favorite story, passed on from Knight to Knight and documented periodically in the historical supplements to the *Sacramento Union*," a story of how the baby outlived the crossing but died in Sacramento the first winter, leaving the baby's twenty-year-old mother "deranged for months." She orders to be engraved on her child's tombstone in the garden the line "*By the rivers of Babylon, there we sat down*" (p. 84). The "symbolic nature" of this mother's garden was "for the Knights, this story's *raison-d'être*. 'I think nobody owns the land until their dead are in it,' Walter Knight had said to Lily," who responds, "Sometimes I think this whole valley belongs to me" (pp. 84, 85). The predictive truth in Lily's claim and in the family's myth comes at the end of the novel, when she sits down by the river next to her dead husband. Finally to own the land – legally and symbolically – is to lose the family that claims it, in the Knight family's mythology. It's a tough bargain.

The legacy of the frontier is, for Didion, a highly ambiguous one of irreconcilable causes and effects, of Edenic drives and hellish results, of perpetual erasures of the past that only produce a haunting. To explore the frontier dream's legacy is to learn at what high cost hope is purchased; it is to follow "the trail of an intention gone haywire," as she describes it in her essay "Some Dreamers of the Golden Dream."[14] Didion's detective work, it should be noted, arrives at no conventionally moralistic conclusions or verdicts. Rather, it is intensely interested in how characters read the past, and whether they read it at all. At the end of *Run River*, all of the usual questions of motive, causality, and responsibility that would otherwise arise at the end of a crime story are washed free of their significance in Everett's mind: "whatever had happened in the years between did not signify much. Channing did not signify much . . . whether Channing had tried to grab the gun to protect himself or because he thought Everett intended to shoot Lily; whether he had shot Channing because he had intended to all along or because he was angered by Channing's thinking he could hurt Lily; none of it mattered" (p. 259). To start all over again, as pioneers had intended to do, or to end it all: both intentions go haywire in so far as they negate the past.

In Didion's essay "Some Dreamers of the Golden Dream," which is about Lucille Miller's alleged murder of her husband, Lucille's guilt or innocence is not the point; a diagnosis of the country that surrounds this real-life case of *Double Indemnity* is. The State's prosecution is more limited and focused in its aims than Didion is in her essay.

It was a spotty case, and to make it work at all the State was going to have to find a motive . . . They set out . . . to determine what might move a woman who believed in all the promises of the middle class . . . who had come out of the bleak wild of prairie fundamentalism to find what she imagined to be the good life – what should drive such a woman to sit on a street called Bella Vista and look out her new picture window into the empty California sun and calculate how to burn her husband alive in a Volkswagen.[15]

Didion frames her examination of the marital murder case more broadly and environmentally. This story "begins with the country," the particular, "ominous" landscape and climate of San Bernardino County, with its harsh Santa Ana winds and the "curious and unnatural" flora, with lemon groves that are "too lush, unsettlingly glossy, the greenery of night-mare . . . a place for snakes to breed." The San Bernardino mountains loom "too high, too fast . . . right there above the lemon groves." It is a "fallen" landscape with inhabitants who aspire to too much, a natural landscape and cultural climate of extremes, the "last stop for all those who come from somewhere else."[16] Once again, it is the Fall inverted: rather than falling into responsibility and history, Didion's dreamers seek to escape them, which is the cause of their error. The closing frame of her essay involves just this relation to history: "time past is not believed to have any bearing upon time present or future, out in the golden land where every day the world is born anew." She makes this claim in rela-tion to the question of whether Arthwell Hayton, the man whom Lucille Miller purportedly killed her husband in order to wed, had ever suffered as a result of her fate: "[p]erhaps he did not." In any case, he married again, and Didion concludes her essay with the telling line about his new bride's appearance: "A coronet of seed pearls held her illusion veil."[17] The near oxymoron of "seed pearl," with its conflation of something sown and something reaped – indeed its conflation of beginnings and endings – links the country's illusions with the bridal veil, the beautiful lie of the progressive, frontier notion of new beginnings, the faith that love can spring naturally from murder or that one can ever escape the scene of the crime. In *Run River*, Didion's narrative structure brings the final murderous end not only back to the seeds of love, and to the beginning of the novel, but to a frontier past that already showed how saying what one wants and striking out for it can come to a chilling end, as it did for the Donner-Reed party, before it had even seemed to begin. For Didion, running headlong from the past is the surest way to run into it.

In Wallace Stegner's *Angle of Repose*, the same effect is true of running from the present. While Frederick Jackson Turner and Owen Wister saw a clear line between the frontier and post-frontier, or old and new, Wests, Didion and Stegner counterbalance that view by stressing the continuity of the past in the form of its determinations on the present. The historical break between the frontier and post-frontier Wests may exist only *as* a belief in such, and the consequence of that belief is often an incapacity to deal with the present or a tendency to react negatively to it. It would seem to involve a dramatic difference in one's social and political views whether one nostalgically admires an imagined older West and its values, or whether one esteems a new beginning in the present severed and freed from the past. But from another perspective, these conservative-to-reactionary and liberal-to-radical impulses are two sides of the same retrospective coin that would mark a divide in history. The utopian impulse and the reactionary sense of a fallen present draw upon the myths of Eden and a postlapsarian world. The West as a cultural idea has been made to stand, irreconcilably, for both. In the divide between these mythic trajectories lie the struggles of the ongoing western present.

At first glance, these two stances in relation to history span the generational "gulf" between Lyman Ward and his son Rodman in *Angle of Repose*. But they have long been more commonly allegorized through gender difference, by having women represent the claims of an older civilization and by having men stand for the pursuit of a new life out West, emancipated from tradition. Stegner makes this point in his essay "History, Myth, and the Western Writer": "[t]he typical western writer loves the past, despises the present, of his native origin. In a way the dichotomy between the past and the present is a product of two forces frequently encountered in both western fiction and the Western; the freedom-loving, roving man and the civilizing woman."[18] Of *Angle of Repose* in particular, Stegner has argued that it presents to some extent "an absolutely standard, almost cliché, situation: the wandering man and the nesting woman – the woman representative of stability and stasis and civilization, and the man a restless, creative creature in a wide-open environment."[19] As Melody Graulich has argued, Stegner's "interest in marriage, therefore, grows inevitably from his understanding of and in relation to a western literary tradition" that Stegner calls "inescapable."[20] The genders are figured oppositionally as competing ideologies not unlike those, such as savagery and civilization, that Turner argued the frontier synthesized.

But Lyman's grandparents only superficially represent these literary types; indeed, they rewrite them in ways that bring their past uncomfortably close to the present that Lyman despises, in which his wife Ellen has played the part of wanderer.[21] The nesting woman and the wandering man, the figures in Stegner's first novel *Big Rock Candy Mountain* (1943), are both represented and reversed in *Angle of Repose*. While it is Oliver's fitful search for financial success in boom-and-bust western towns that Susan follows, it is Susan's desires that Oliver cannot ultimately domesticate, just as Lyman cannot domesticate his wife's. While Susan Ward represents eastern civilization, Oliver Ward is in the process of "paving" (the way for) civilization with the cement he invents – a civilization that even Lyman admits is in doubt: at one point he says that "their whole civilization was wrong" (p. 385). While Lyman wanders around the West, he does so under economic constraint; in acting out her desire for her husband's best friend Frank Sargent, Susan goes against the stereotype of female constraint. Because these contraventions of gender stereotype bring the past uncomfortably close to his personal situation, and also because his polemic against the present is inherently self-contradictory, as I will explore, Lyman wants to decouple his grandparents' marriage from the history of the West that he professes. Whereas Stegner's novel braids western history and the Wards' marriage together in the novel, Lyman Ward compartmentalizes them, insisting to his son, " 'I'm not writing a book of Western history . . . I'm writing about something else. 'A marriage,' I guess . . . not the West they spend their lives in. What really interests me is how two such unlike particles clung together, and under what strains, rolling downhill into their future until they reached the angle of repose where I knew them. . . . That's where the meaning will be if I find any. . . . 'A marriage,' I say. 'A masculine and a feminine. A romantic and a realist' " (p. 211). Given that his central metaphor for the marriage is a geologic one, and given that Lyman describes his grandfather's cement – which "some think ruined" the West – as the forcing of unlike substances "into an insoluble marriage" (p. 192), it is difficult to separate the marriage from the western materials it is mixed with, particularly the historical mixing of romance and realism in western designs. As Graulich argues, "Stegner uses marriage as a realistic institutional structure through which he can examine the interplay between, the wedding of, the West's inextricably tied and competing themes . . . externalized in female and male character . . . . Unlike his creator, Lyman Ward just doesn't realize that by writing about a marriage, he *is* writing western history."[22] Regarding the environmentally destructive nature of his grandfather's invention, Lyman admits, "My feelings about this are mixed, for it would have made me uneasy to be descended from Santa Cruz cement" (p. 192). Separating out Lyman's feelings from the history he gives us is a nearly impossible task, as difficult as it would be to claim, along with Lyman, that this story of a marriage is not a story of the West. Admitting that it is both would force Lyman to see that his western present is also, as he himself is, the descendant of the past, and Lyman insists that there is no such relationship between the two Wests.

Indeed, Lyman Ward seems to be typical of the western writer Stegner describes who loves the past and despises the present. On one level, *Angle of Repose* seems to offer a similar critique of the western belief that, as Didion puts it, "time past is not believed to have any bearing upon time present or future." The novel begins with Lyman contemplating the nature of time, as he states "the place and date of a sort of beginning and a sort of return: Zodiac Cottage, Grass Valley, California, April 12, 1970" (p. 15), the home of his grandparents whose marital history, as they settled in western places, he is about to explore and write. He complains that his son Rodman, like "most of his generation, was born without the sense of history . . . The world has changed, Pop, he tells me. The past isn't going to teach us anything about what we've got ahead of us. Maybe it did once, or seemed to. It doesn't anymore" (pp. 15–16). Lyman views time somewhat evasively and self-servingly as a Heraclitean river and his sense of cumulative identity echoes Lily's sense in *Run River* that choice is always the sum of all the choices gone before:

I started to establish the present and the present moved on. What I established is already buried under layers of tape [he is speaking into a microphone]. Before I can say *I am*, I was. Heraclitus and I, prophets of flux, know that the flux is composed of parts that imitate and repeat each other. Am or was, I am cumulative, too. I am everything I ever was . . . I am much of what my parents and especially my grandparents were – inherited stature, coloring, brains, bones . . . plus transmitted prejudices, culture, scruples, likings, moralities, and moral errors that I defend as if they were personal and not familial. (p. 15)

As Lyman explores his family's history, history becomes, as it were, personal for a man who cannot help but read the past through his disdain for the present. Part of Lyman's continuous inheritance is the sense of being severed from the past – not from the historical past of his grandparents, but from the more recent and personal past of his wife and family, a severance which repeats his grandparents' history of leaving past worlds behind. Coming to terms with his present is what he escapes having to do by fleeing to his grandparents' past. By invoking the Heraclitean model of time, he keeps the troubling present just beyond his touch.

Stegner's novel is consistently reminding us of two basic propositions: there is no disembodied history and there is no narrative history without imagination. By foregrounding the limitations of Lyman's body, upon which others direct so much labor and care, *Angle of Repose* brings the reader back continuously to the limited, particularized, and physically situated nature of all historical retrospection. By drawing directly upon historical sources (namely, the letters of Mary Hallock Foote) that he then fictionalizes, and by framing the novel as the personal exploration of a historian, Stegner highlights the literary constructedness of historical understanding. The novel's second narrative – the one that, as it were, is not "intentionally" written by the narrator – becomes for the reader the object of a comparative reading; the narrative of his grandparents is a comparative history, implicitly, to Lyman's own personal story. Far from setting up a parallel allegory, the narrative structure puts the two narratives into dialogical relationship, and what emerges from this is a sense of the constantly changing nature of history itself. Historical reconstruction is a work always in progress; seamless history can only be an illusion. Like Oliver and Susan Ward's marriage, history is filled with unexpected ruptures, troughs, and meanderings.

Stegner's nearly lifelong silence about the most shocking moment in his family history speaks loudly. In 1940, seven years after he had abandoned his wife and children, Wallace's father George Stegner, in a jealous rage, killed a woman companion by shooting her in the back and then killed himself in Salt Lake City. It was possibly in reaction to this that Stegner defined his sense of marital values, but more importantly that he may have modeled Lyman's repressions. (Wallace Stegner's son Page recalled that Stegner never said "twenty-five words" about Page's grandfather.[23]) As a historian, Lyman finds things he was not looking for as a grandson, and at moments excludes them from his narrative or raises them in order to paint them in a particular light. He discovers, for example, other forms of emotional attachment in his grandmother's devotion to Augusta, whom Susan, he admits, was "in love with" (p. 32). Though Lyman admits that "the suggestion of lesbianism" is "uncomfortably explicit" in some early letters between Susan and Augusta and that we "might conclude" that Augusta "was an incipient dike," he chooses to emphasize, in Victorian fashion, his grandmother's "capacity for devotion. The first passion of her life lasted *all* her life" (p. 34). Because he is reacting against his wife's abandonment of him, the case of two women who did not seem to desire men as much as they did each other becomes a lesson in Victorian commitment rather than being valued as an illustration of non-normative desire.[24] Lyman only has a bifurcated vocabulary for this desire, which imitates his bifurcation of the past and present. The more radical implications of his grandmother's desire for Augusta, in terms of how it causes both the history Lyman is writing and indeed his own existence, falls through the breach of this disjunction: it *is* the continuity between his present and their past. In the first place, Susan's marriage to Lyman, "perhaps not even with her full consent," he admits, is a direct reaction against Augusta's marriage to Thomas once she had been forced to "[relinquish] one sort of possibility" (p. 58). In the second place, the letters between the two women constitute the chief historical record upon which Lyman can write his history that brings him closer to an understanding of his wife's own desires. As Susan "saw herself losing both lover and friend" (p. 56) to Thomas, she writes to Augusta,

I so want to put my arms around my girl of all the girls in the world and tell her that whether I move to New York or stay home, whether she sign herself "Very truly your friend" or "Your ownest of girls," I love her as wives love their husbands, as friends who have taken each other for life . . . Now please don't call yourself truly my friend again. I can stand arguments and scoldings, but – truly your friend! And then to miss you by only that widening gap of water! . . . I'm going to hang onto your skirts, young woman, genius though you may be. You can't get away from the love of your faithful SUE (pp. 57–58)

"Within two days after she heard of the engagement of Augusta and Thomas," Lyman writes, "Oliver Ward wrote that he was coming home from the West" (p. 59), and the consequent shape of Susan's life – her marriage and her move West – is the result of her narrowing options. "If the threesome was to be split by marriage (though Augusta and Thomas swore it would not be) New York might be a less happy place, and a Western adventure looked attractive. And if Augusta, despite all her vows, found herself ready to give up art for housekeeping, perhaps her defection demonstrated that after all marriage *was* woman's highest role" (pp. 62–63), Lyman imagines. He also imagines Susan confronting a stunned Augusta with news of her engagement and move West: "Augusta was incredulous, aghast, and accusatory; Susan stubborn and just a shade triumphant. You see? I am not defenseless, I am not to be left out after all . . . 'just as you have every right to fall in love and marry, so have I. One doesn't always know – does one? – when things are headed that way' " (p. 63). Such is the unconventional "cause" of Susan's marriage and western life – what Lyman imagines Augusta calls "a mistake that will ruin your career and lead you a desolate life" (p. 65) – as it is the cause of Lyman's being.

What Lyman is left with in the end is not a narrative that confirms the model of marriage he uses to justify his anger at his wife; his grand-mother's desire for another man after years of marriage brings Lyman back to his embodied self. The novel's intricate negotiations between past and present create at times a stereoscopic sense of their relationship and at other times a sense of a displaced, if not silenced, present that inconveniently intrudes upon the historian's – and hence our own – consciousness. The present, one could say, breaks into the past, influencing its narrative transitions, allegorically magnifying or shrinking particular events. But throughout it is Lyman's consciousness, with its attentions and repressions, which becomes the not very subterranean subject of a novel ostensibly about his grandparents.[25] Their past is largely animated or unnarrated according to his state of mind, particularly his intolerance of pain. At one nadir of his grandparents' marriage, Lyman writes, as partially cited in chapter 1, "Miserable, both of them, everything hopeful in them run down, everything joyous smothered under poverty and failure. My impulse, and I hereby yield to it, is to skip it all, to document not one single miserable hour until a day in November 1888" (p. 432). Because Lyman barely has the courage to explore the causes of his wife's abandonment and takes refuge in the history of his grandparents' marriage as a way of affirming the possibility of hope, there is a huge narratorial investment in what gets narrated, and what gets left out.

After the amputation of his leg – Stegner's most overdetermined metaphor in the novel of the severance between past and present – Lyman states at the beginning,

If there was no longer any sense in pretending to be interested in where I was going, I could consult where I've been. And I don't mean the Ellen business. I honestly believe this isn't that personal. The Lyman Ward who married Ellen Hammond and begot Rodman Ward and taught history and wrote certain books and monographs about the Western frontier, and suffered certain personal catastrophes and perhaps deserved them and survives them after a fashion and now sits talking to himself into a microphone – he doesn't matter that much any more. (p. 17)

But the insistence of this self-negation suggests that this history *is* "that personal," that his broken marriage, about which he progressively speaks more, is the whole animating reason for his interest in the past, and for jumping two generations to find some clothes to live in: "I'd like to live in their clothes a while, if only so I don't have to live in my own ... I want to touch once more the ground I have been maimed away from," he says (p. 17). What that ground is, what he has been maimed away from, and especially why he has been maimed, are left for the time being unanswered, as is the ultimately painful and severing question of touch for his grandmother: a touch, and what it sets in motion, nearly shatters her marriage. What touches Lyman most may be what he keeps the greatest distance from: those very people who come knocking, and especially himself. The novel's first sentence, "Now I believe they will leave me alone," evinces all of his curmudgeonly solitude and isolation yet invokes his family; his son and daughter have recently visited him. The question of Lyman's caretakers, especially his secretary Shelly Rasmussen, hovers around the novel. By the end, he is anxious that Shelly will be leaving him. Why, we are left to wonder from the start, does the historian who tells this story not "matter that much any more" if his point of view frames the significance, not to mention the narrative sequence and style, of his grandparents' lives? If this history comes to us from a "history-haunted skull" (p. 18), why does the cause of that haunting not matter? It matters decidedly.

Increasingly, the past becomes the allegory of the present. The allegory operates not only on Lyman's marriage, but, given Stegner's reading of the relationship between past and present through the relationship between the genders, the allegory operates on the whole social and national scene in the 1960s. Lyman reacts against the period's pervasive break from the past and blames it, initially, for the collapse of his marriage. In his own break from his immediate family's past, he identifies with his peripatetic grandparents:

the conditions are similar. We have been cut off, the past has ended, and the family has broken up and the present is adrift in its wheelchair. I had a wife who after twenty-five years of marriage took on the coloration of the 1960s. I have a son who, though we are affectionate with each other, is no more my true son than if he breathed through gills. That is no gap between the generations, that is a gulf... This present of 1970 is no more an extension of my grandparents' world, this West is no more a development of the West they helped build, than the sea over Santorin is an extension of that once-island of rock and olives. My wife turns out after a quarter of a century to be someone I never knew, my son starts all fresh from his own premises.

My grandparents had to live their way out of one world and into another, or into several others, making new out of old the way corals live their reef upward. I am on my grandparents' side... We live in time and through it, we build our huts in its ruins, or used to, and we cannot afford all these abandonings. (pp. 17–18)

Lyman describes models of relationship between the past and the present through natural similes: his son might as well be a fish; the present West might as well be the sea that engulfed the rock of the past; his grandparents, in contrast, lived in new worlds by adding coral to the reef of time. But the forced claims here – that he "never knew" his wife of twenty-five years, that the West he lives in is no extension of the one his grandparents helped to build – ring artificial. Moreover, this passage, which makes huge distinctions between generations and Wests, begins with a claim of similarity, as if there is, in fact, a line of influence between the past and the present. The greater contradiction in his claim is how much it resembles his son's. As Jackson K. Putnam argues, "if the past is totally unrelated to the present, then Rodman is certainly justified when he 'starts all fresh from his premises.' "[26] Starting fresh from one's own premises imitates Turner's formulation of the pioneer, Fitzgerald's rendition of Gatsby, and, indeed, the way Lyman's grandparents were forced to live, even though his grandmother sought to bring the civilized past along with them. Cut off as he is in physical, emotional, and figural ways, Lyman is stuck between a present he cannot adapt to and a past he can neither change nor let go of, by forgiving, for example, his wife for leaving him.

Who, though, is abandoning whom? And which is the greater abandonment: of the past, or of the present? The ambiguous, general nature of "these abandonings" comes to include Lyman's neglect of his wife among them, as he confesses, "I did take her for granted, I did neglect her for history," in Stegner's tellingly ambiguous phrase (p. 444). The reverse – to neglect history for her – would be to forgive, to "put the past behind him," as Lyman imagines Ellen wishes he would do (p. 443). It would also be to give her the kind of attention that might have obviated her dissatisfactions in the marriage. The reader must pose critical questions of a novel filled with narrative lacunae: Lyman's imaginative energy regarding his grandparents' lives is not matched by his ability to imagine his own wife, whose filtered point of view powerfully shapes what gets said. "Did she harbor all those years a resentment at giving up her own degree and her own career? . . . I suppose all the time the life that I thought sane and quiet and good was *too* quiet for her . . . I will never understand it. Maybe toward the end I might have noticed something if I hadn't been preoccupied" (pp. 440–441). But since she "laid no charges" against him, Lyman feels he has "to conclude that what finally led her to break away from me was my misfortunes – missing leg, rigid neck, solidifying skeleton." He concludes, "The hell with her" (p. 444). Immediately, here, he shifts back to his grandmother and the grudge she nurses against her husband for his drinking: "Grandmother, take it easy. Don't act like a stricken Victorian prude . . . Ask yourself whether his unhappy drinking has really hurt you, or your children, or him" (p. 444). He could as well ask himself about his own.

The central dilemmas of marriage for women are embedded in Lyman's and his grandparents' name "Ward." "To ward" is to be on guard, protect, defend, control; but also to nurse (including a grudge or a drink), take care of, watch after. It can also mean to keep in close custody or confinement, to imprison. The ambiguity of the term points to the ambiguous causes of the failure of Lyman's marriage. Did he not sufficiently protect or take care of her? Did she feel confined or imprisoned by the marriage in his neglect of her "for history"? Has she failed to care for him? The ambiguity of the name is played out in Lyman's confinement as an amputee: he is confined and nursed simultaneously. And from his vantage point whether as historian or as grandchild, he is powerless to protect his grandparents from the history he sees coming at them. What had been an escape becomes at times a futile attempt to ward off the future. Whether his own marital fate or theirs, what Lyman faces or escapes produces the same helpless result – the sense of betrayal, the unwillingness to forgive. Contemplating his wife leaving him, he ruminates,

Perhaps pure accident, perhaps an opportunity or willingness that both recognized at the first touch, and I absolutely unaware. There is a Japanese story called *Insects of Various Kinds* in which a spider trapped between the sliding panes of a window lies there inert, motionless, apparently lifeless, for many months, and then in spring, when a maid moves the window for a few seconds to clean it, springs once and is gone. Did Ellen Ward live that sort of trapped life? Released by the first inadvertent opportunity, was she? Seduced because she was waiting for the chance to be? (p. 507)

Lyman asks the obvious question of his grandmother's and Frank's seduction of each other that his wife's seduction by the surgeon who amputated Lyman's leg brings to the forefront of his mind: did the sexual act occur? "I know none of the intimate circumstances; I only guess backward from the consequences," he writes (p. 506), as he proceeds to narrate the imagined scene and his grandmother's feelings. The scene occurs 4 July 1890 – Stegner's allegorizing clue as to why this story of a marriage is a story of the West, after all. The date commemorates, as it did for Susan's marriage, both an end and a beginning, the beginning of the Republic and the end of the frontier. Susan, he imagines, was "utterly cut off, sunk into the West . . . adrift in the hopeless West" (p. 499). "To flee failure, abandon hopelessness, disengage herself from the stubborn inarticulate man she was married to, and the scheme *he* was married to, would have been a real temptation," he writes; "And, of course, in 1890, for Susan Burling Ward, utterly unthinkable. What went on? I don't know. I gravely doubt that they 'had sex,' in Shelly's charming phrase" (p. 508). His justification for this belief, however, betrays just the sort of patriarchal rigidity which his own wife might have wanted to flee.

"I cannot imagine such a complete breakdown in my grandmother, who believed that a woman's highest role was to be wife and mother, who conceived the female body to be a holy vessel, and its union with a man's – the single, chosen man's – woman's highest joy and fulfillment" (p. 508), he says, as if her artistic talents and central same-sex friendship amount to little. Here, the historian becomes the articulator of patriarchal values, and the history stops, even though he might have tried to imagine his own parallel history in its stead: "Yet I have seen the similar breakdown of one whose breakdown I couldn't possibly have imagined until it happened, whose temptations I was not even aware of" (p. 508). Lyman's lack of awareness about a woman's subjectivity on this question – including his own wife's – is the conditional limit of his historical knowledge. A woman's body as she experiences it is unimaginable, for him, from the way in which these conventional (patriarchal) values imagine a woman's body. "I cannot imagine it" is indistinguishable from not wanting to imagine it – from not wanting the values that might allow him to imagine it, but more implicitly from not wanting to admit his complicity in his wife's restless desire, or his grandfather's in his grandmother's.

Though Stegner described the historical trajectory of the novel's three marriages in an interview as one of "progressive decline,"[27] the novel suggests something more complicated than Stegner's admittedly ambivalent feelings about sixties' progressive causes.[28] Lyman does not explore forty years of his grandparents' marriage because those years mark a commitment only to some kind of permanent estrangement, a quite common adaptation in the nineteenth century to strict marriage laws.[29] The place at which he stops is the crisis that most tested their marriage, the shattering moment at which the marriage must either break apart or find some angle of repose – a geological term describing the angle at which sliding rocks come to rest. His grandmother, he speculates, visited Frank Sargent in order to end the affair, bringing her daughter Agnes along as a cover. While Susan is not paying attention to her, Agnes drowns in a creek. One day after the child's funeral, Frank, "blaming himself not unjustly for everything that had happened," as Lyman imagines, "blew the top of his head off" (p. 536). "I not only don't want this history to happen, I have to make it up, or part of it," Lyman prefaces his narrative of these events. "All I know is the *what*, and not all of that; the *how* and the *why* are all speculation" (p. 524).

Beyond this event, the historian cannot imagine, or chooses not to: the angle of repose is a kind of death to narrative, the beginning not so much of repose as a begrudging resistance to starting fresh, as Oliver Ward never fully forgives his wife, from whom he remains permanently estranged. Forrest Robinson has argued that "Stegner's work is nearly as replete as Willa Cather's with examples of the anguish and potential for disaster in marriage and procreation."[30] In this light, Shelly Rasmussen and her common law husband, invested in progressive causes, seem relatively happy and free of the resentments Lyman inherits from his father. If Lyman cannot answer the *how* and the *why* of the key tragic moment in his grandparents' marriage, he is certainly, at least, the embodied answer as to the *what* of its effects. His grandparents' need to send Ollie, the historian's father, away for long periods in his childhood and their prolonged estrangement from each other scarred him, and he passed those scars, it seems, on to his son, the narrator. The questions of marriage and of the present's relationship to the western past intersect through that of forgiveness, the letting go of the past through knowledge of it. The fact that Lyman cannot let go of the past qualifies Lyman's complaint that Shelly and Rodman and those of their generation do not know the past. The greatest angle of repose in the novel is thus between past and present, such that the claim of neither is ignored – this angle of repose can only happen dialogically, in the mind of the reader, since Lyman never quite bridges competing claims, but harangues Shelly for her idealistic, communitarian projects.

In between Lyman's narrative of Susan's affair with Frank and the story of its tragic consequences, Stegner inserts Lyman's thoughts about Shelly, "who will be leaving very soon, with consequences to me and to my routines" (p. 512). This chapter begins with "the sense of something about to come to an end," as Lyman then proceeds to recall "that old September feeling . . . Another fall, another turned page: there was something of jubilee in that annual autumnal beginning, as if last year's mistakes and failures had been wiped clean by summer" (p. 512). Now, however, he feels only an ending and no beginning coming near, as Shelly spends more time with Larry Rasmussen, Lyman's intellectual antagonist. Shelly shares with Lyman the manifesto that Larry has drafted for a new commune, which argues "that this society with its wars, waste, poisons, ugliness, and hatred of the natural and innocent must be abandoned or destroyed. To cop out is the first act in the cleansing of the spirit" (p. 514). Lyman proceeds to dissect the document, as he tells Shelly just how derivative this manifesto is: from Plato to Thoreau, this itch for the transcendental, for new beginnings from clean slates, is an old story. "Civilizations grow by agreements and accommodations and accretions, not repudiations," he argues. "The rebels and the revolutionaries are only eddies, they keep the stream from getting stagnant but they get swept down and absorbed, they're a side issue. Quiet desperation is another name for the human condition. If revolutionaries would learn that they can't remodel society by day after tomorrow . . . I'd have more respect for them" (p. 519).

Jackson K. Putnam has also pointed out another looming contradiction in Lyman's impassioned critique. Having claimed originally that his present is totally cut off from the past, his argument that civilizations grow by accretions, not repudiations, is antithetical to that original claim.[31] Indeed, Shelly is more aware of the connections between his grandparents' world and her own than Lyman is. In the argument between the reactionary historian and the young idealist lies the novel's historical angle of repose. Shelly asks Lyman,

Haven't you sort of copped out yourself? What's this but a rural commune, only you own it . . . Take marriage, say. Is that such a success story? Why not try a new way? Or look at your grandfather. Is this manifesto so different from the come-on he wrote for the Idaho Mining and Irrigation Company, except that he was doing it for profit? He was trying something that was pretty sure to fail, wasn't he? Maybe it wasn't even sound, maybe that sagebrush desert might better have been left in sagebrush, isn't that what you think? All that big dream of his was dubious ecology, and sort of greedy when you look at it, just another piece of American continent-busting. But you admire your grandfather more than anybody, even though the civilization he was trying to build was this cruddy one we've got. Here's a bunch of people willing to put their lives on the line to try to make a better one. Why put them down? (pp. 517–518)

As Putnam argues, Shelly here attempts the historian's project of connecting the past to the present, by seeing Larry Rasmussen as the "modern-day counterpart" to Oliver Ward.[32] I do not believe, however, as Putnam does, that Stegner shares with his character a failure to resolve the main historiographical problem in the novel – namely, to come to an understanding of how the present came about. The contradiction that Lyman seems not fully to absorb is that the United States, including the American West, has, since its inception, shown repeated attempts at new beginnings, including the story of Oliver and Susan Ward. Lyman emphasizes that these attempts to start fresh have often resulted in failure. But that Lyman cannot see how his grandparents' story is related to the culture of the sixties is his own, not the author's, blindness. Despite Stegner's reactionary moments, the novelist-historian imagines his way into a paradox about western and American experience that only a one-sided interpretation of the novel can get us out of: the very impulse to abjure the past keeps us connected to it, whether we are conscious of it or not. Indeed, it was the naivete of the sixties' generation that Stegner most criticized, not their fundamental impulses. But Lyman Ward's naivete would seem to suffer the same critique. Insisting that his story is one of marriage, and not the West, and arguing that the present West is in no way connected to the past, he remains blind, at least until the end of the novel, to those painful truths closest to him. The desire to know the past, when it derives from a desire to ignore the present, can be as limited in its historiographical potential as the desire to neglect history.

At the end of the novel, Lyman questions whether he is "man enough to be a bigger man than my grandfather" (p. 569). Like Wister's *The Virginian*, the novel questions masculinity, at the end, but unlike Wister's novel, it is female autonomy, and not anxiety about the heterosexual imperative, that puts this question in motion. It is the question of women's subjectivity, and not the celebrated masculine individual, that sets the terms and limits for historical reckoning and understanding. Lyman's misogyny marks the limits of his search: "if there is one thing above all others that I despise, it is fingers, especially female fingers, messing around in my guts. My guts, like Victorian marriage, are private" (p. 438). Yet he is messing around in his grandparents' Victorian marriage by revealing its most painful moment. In relegating sex to the realm of privacy, Lyman would seek to hold off questions about his sexual body. His body's sense of emasculation and betrayal animates this writing of history, and this novel. Just so, his grandmother's reaction to same-sex desire and heartache motivated her to marry. In the end, Lyman's dream reveals just how vulnerable he is to touch, especially to the touch of history. "By touch we are betrayed and betray others," he states toward the end (p. 506). Having begun by claiming, "I want to touch once more the ground I have been maimed away from" (p. 17), Lyman's desire for the past is simultaneously a means of bringing him in touch with the pain of the present; the past offers no escape. At the moment that he narrates Frank's fingers closing around his grandmother's foot, he is brought back to his wife's betrayal of him: "It was probably touch . . . that betrayed Ellen Ward . . . And maybe pure accident, maybe she didn't know she had been waiting. Or had that all been going on behind my back for a long time?" (pp. 506–507). Lyman is stuck at a crossroads in that he cannot begin to forgive his wife unless he knows the cause of her betrayal, but he is unwilling to see her, and to hear her out, because he cannot forgive – and, indeed, because he does not want to know his failings. His emasculated body marks the unreconciled divide between multiple pasts – personal, generational, national – and an indeterminate future.

The marital issue is thus paradigmatic of the historiographical problem the novel poses: how to approach the middle ground not only between the claims of men and women but between the past and the future, and more broadly between literature and history. Four years before the publication of *Angle of Repose*, in his essay on "History, Myth, and the Western Writer," Stegner admits to his own form of western nostalgia, but insists that "you don't choose between the past and the present; you try to find the connections, you try to make the one serve the other . . . I do not think we can forget the one or turn away from the other."[33] *Angle of Repose* returns that task to the reader, who must negotiate between the historical dialogue and between the contemporary fractures the novel represents. As Forrest Robinson argues, "the desired balance is never easily or fully or permanently achieved. Such is the leading moral to be drawn from *Angle of Repose*."[34] I am not sure what kind of moral this is, except that it returns us to the problem of an ending, the problem Stegner resolves for himself in *Angle of Repose* by not resolving it. Whether Lyman will be "a bigger man," or what that might mean to his wife if he were, is left unanswered. What makes the formula Western a deeply conservative genre is in part its sense of an ending: it resolves the contradictions it creates through a happy ending – a marriage, or a rescue from dilemma or captivity. It is "escapist" most broadly in its relation to historical dynamics. Stegner's conservatism is of a different order entirely, since it is suspicious of all forms of resolution, whether Larry Rasmussen's manifesto ("NOW THEREFORE") or Lyman's resolve not to forgive ("To hell with her"). Stegner resolves, instead, to remain open to possibility, including that of failure or self-critique, but also the possibility, however remote, that the middle ground between history and fiction is a ground we can actually stand on. Concluding his important essay on western literature and the New Western History with a discussion of Stegner, Robinson argues that this middle ground is achievable by "avoiding the pitfalls of nostalgia and cynicism along the way."[35] To the extent that western literature has often been rooted in what Stegner calls the "historical, the rural, the heroic[,] it does not take account of time and change. That means that it has no future either, except to come closer and closer to the stereotypes of the mythic."[36] In the years since Stegner's diagnosis, western literature has taken time into account. The result has been a remarkable

reshaping of western literary genres and sensibilities. If Stegner provides – for Forrest Robinson's essay as for this chapter – a sense of an
ending, it is because his work and the ongoing response to it demonstrate how, despite the respective allure of both nostalgia and presentism, the past is an argument with our present that continues to make
ourselves strange and, as a result, to make others more familiar in their
own terms.

# Afterword

One subject of this study, the imbrication of literary and historical forms of knowledge, raises these questions: what do western literary critics want from western historians and their writing of history, and what do historians want from literature and literary theory? Put another way: what do these two disciplines imagine the other lacks? I pose these questions as matters of desire because the disciplines of literary and historical study have often envied and emulated each other, competed with and cross-dressed as the other. At times they have conjugated, at others divorced; at still others lived in unholy contention: as R. Gordon Kelly once put it, "the marriage between literary criticism and history seems not to have been made in heaven."[1] Marjorie Garber has written about "discipline envy," that form of interdisciplinary desire in which disciplines mark their distinctions from each other while containing the disciplined other within themselves.[2] The dialogue between disciplines is not simply one between self and other but within the self-as-other, an internalized dialogue within each about what it is not and hence what it imagines itself to be. Not surprisingly, a discipline often does not recognize itself in what other disciplines imagine about or desire from its methods and its (unstable) objects, such as "fiction" and "historical truth."

I want briefly to look at some of those imaginations and desires on the part of western literary critics and historians, particularly as scholars engage the implications of postmodernist theory for what they do. Postmodernism is not a term central to this book – a term that can sometimes cloud more than it clarifies things – but to the extent that the term describes a tendency more than a period, my book has shared some of its views on narrative and authority and on the relationship between reality and representation. My aim here is not to provide a way out of the various impasses that postmodernist and poststructuralist theories seem to pose in their assertions of the potentially infinite distance between representations and reality, but to point out some important questions

224

they raise about what narrative is and does. Finally, I want to ask what light those questions can shed both on the social and thematic interests of this book in marriage, violence, and the nation, and on some aspects of the present historical moment.

In the 1996 documentary series *The West*,[3] creative writers such as Terry Tempest Williams and N. Scott Momaday appeared with western historians Patricia Limerick and Richard White, among others. The presence of historical and creative authorities in the nationally televised documentary was telling, as if historians become storytellers, and storytellers historians, in the televisual public market of western significance. While Limerick has claimed that the public is paying absolutely no attention to debates among western historians about the "frontier," the same can be said more accurately about those missing from the documentary: literary and cultural critics. The way in which historians can play both academic and public roles speaks to the ongoing and greater authority that "the historical" has when it comes to broad discussions about the West, matched only by the authority of the "mythic" West in much popular culture. Yet these two poles of cultural authority are interdependent: if historians imagine their job is to "correct" the myth, for example, to speak truth to its cultural power, then historians ineluctably and continuously reassert the myth's power in their construction and rehearsal of it, as they presume a straightforward "story" against which they pose their more complicated and accurate version of the past. Yet much of the New Western History's present need for self-revision, as Limerick demonstrates in her essay "Turnerians All," derives from misreading some past historiography and literature as constituting a more monolithically dominant or ideological set of beliefs than they possess.

Such are the arguments that western literary critics make in the collection *The New Western History: The Territory Ahead.* Canonical fiction, including canonical popular Westerns, they assert, demonstrates a much more ideologically complicated and conflicted set of beliefs than many western historians imagine. Indeed, as the present study has also argued, they contain seeds of revision that predate western historians' own. In her essay in the collection, Krista Comer argues that "nearly all major literary Westerns by men written between about 1910 and the late 1950s are heavily ironic in their representations of the West, Western masculinity, and Western race relations."[4] Stephen Tatum argues that the New Western historians (predominantly Limerick and Donald Worster) have reductively figured "popular" forms of culture as producers of false consciousness and of dishonest denial about the realities of western experience. But in many such popular forms of culture that get lumped together and demonized in historians' minds, Tatum argues, "critical thinking about ideals [and] drives ... can and does occur" even in "the most seemingly retrograde" texts.[5] The New Western historians figure their version of the popular, however, as a kind of "twilight zone" (Limerick's phrase for "myth and symbol") against which their work fosters the daylight of historical truth that banishes, with its "frank, hard look" (Worster's phrase), the deceptions of the popular. Despite the New Western historians' tragic and ironic narratives of the western past, their narratives about themselves in such instances figure them as Gast figured the spirit of "American Progress" in his famous lithograph: they are, as Tatum writes, a "deliverer" figure "who doesn't blink in the hard light of day ... and whose perspective redeems the community."[6] The volume's editor, Forrest Robinson, argues in his prize-winning essay, which I discussed in the previous chapter, that historians fail to take into account the postmodernist awareness of the discursive, constructed nature of all representation, including the historiographical. By disregarding those postmodernist lessons, he argues, the New Western History is able to maintain the unstable distinction between the mythic and historical West. Additionally, the New Western historians distort the meaning of Turner's work and neglect previous readings of Turner as more pessimistic than they imagine him to be: they "are not, after all so new, and ... their claims to originality rest on a partial, blandly monochromatic reading" of the historian.[7] Robinson makes quick work of other historians who conflate literature with myth and who deny postmodernist lessons – that, he argues, Stegner's *Angle of Repose* seems presciently to anticipate – about the literary constructedness of history.

What do these literary critics (and I do not exempt myself from their desires) want from historians? A confession of bad faith in their claims to originality, it seems, and a recognition of the historical value of literature for their own revisionist enterprise. Literary critics want historians to want what they do. As the collection's title itself suggests, there is a kind of envy at work over the New Western History's authority and influence: *we* will show the historians the new territory ahead of them; literature *is* that new territory – albeit one that sells better dressed up as *The New Western History*. We (literary critics) will correct historians' false consciousness, just as historians think they are correcting the public's false consciousness about "the mythic." The structure of Gast's image comes to mind yet again: the territory ahead must be cleared of obfuscation and confusion, of the darkness of self-deception. The difference for literary critics, of course, lies in the fact that most do not presume to have access to some "real" West so much as to a better way of reading the West in all of its textual manifestations. In short, literary critics feel they are more attuned to the notion that "the Real" is forever mediated by representations that have no actual "original," to the notion that all "facts" come clothed in discourse. For all of their ironic stances toward the "old" western history, New Western historians suffer from an irony deficiency that literary critics, it would seem, do not.

What, then, do western historians want from literature and literary critics, when not using them as a foil for their more "accurate" scholarship? Among the more attuned to the value of literary models for historical understanding is William Cronon, who wrote another prize-winning essay in which he immersed himself in literary theory – and then partially dried himself off. Cronon recognizes the "dangerous" double-edged sword of narrative – that its selectivity both voices and silences, includes and excludes; that it naturalizes cultural constructions; that it gives causality to contingency; that it refers more to human discourse than external "reality," for example. Because he discusses environmental narratives, he is particularly intent to show how narratives are anything but "natural," and that "If we fail to reflect on the plots and scenes and tropes that undergird our histories, we run the risk of missing the human artifice that lies at the heart of even the most 'natural' of narratives."[8] This is a sentiment with which most literary critics would agree, though possibly with a bit of bemusement that Cronon should have to convince others that the artificial "heart" of narrative is not "natural." But what Cronon goes on to say in this essay about the value of narrative is revealing about the impasses between historians and literary critics: each wants in the other what the other does not want – or find – in itself. What Cronon, in the end, wants from narrative is a moral or values that are a guide to living; and he wants to be "moved."[9] Cronon views narratives as "intrinsically teleological forms, in which an event is explained by the prior events or causes that lead up to it." Because we care about the consequences of actions, he writes, "narratives – unlike most natural processes – have beginnings, middles, and ends," the differences among which give "us our chance to extract a moral from the rhetorical landscape."[10]

If historians would seem to literary critics to have an irony deficiency, then literary critics, in their self-consciousness about representation, would seem to historians to have an emotion deficiency, if not a deluding denial of the very existence of reality and a morally confused "relativism" that is paralyzing and politically ineffectual. (Historians are not alone, of course, in this recurring complaint: Andrew Sullivan used the attacks of 11 September to indict what he rather bizarrely called "the illogic and nihilism of the powerful postmodern left.")[11] Cronon's assessment of the historian's task as storyteller would seem to imitate Lyman Ward's attempt to find the meaning of a past that brings him to his own present by writing the story of his grandparents' marriage. But what is "the" moral of *Angle of Repose*, or even of the nineteenth-century "historical" narrative within the novel? If one argues that it is the need to forgive – a not unsupportable "moral" – we have already left the complexity of the text behind. And complexity, it seems to Cronon, is what we sometimes need to avoid in order not to leave history behind: "The uneasiness that many historians feel in confronting the postmodernist challenge (that the past is "infinitely malleable" in the face of our ability to tell stories about it) comes down to this basic concern, which potentially seems to shake the very foundations of our enterprise. If our choice of narratives reflects only our power to impose our preferred version of reality on a past that cannot resist us, then what is left of history?" Thus, "less may be more: A simple story well told may reveal far more about a past world than a complicated text that never finds its own center."[12]

But then, a literary critic might ask, what is left of literature? *Angle of Repose* also demonstrates what Cronon wants to resist: a text struggling to find its own center that *cannot* do so in the uneasy dialogue between past and present. It can only instead find an angle at which unequal lines, such as past and present, come to rest in a manner that threatens a paralyzing stasis but also leaves the future an open question. No conclusion, no easy moral, no simple story at all. And yet, what we have is a deeply dialogic understanding of the unfinished business of the past within the literary imagination. No clear beginning, no final end; instead, as in Didion's *Run River*, we have a beginning that is a kind of ending, and an ending that returns to a beginning: we are left with Lyman's question about himself in a moment of subjective doubt. When read for its complexity, literature does not provide a moral or a guide, and that may be the only ethical lesson it teaches: it returns the reader to the ambiguity of herself and her present, which is always demanding an interpretation that is never simple.

Like many historians willing at least to follow their trail, Cronon is "only willing to follow the postmodernists so far . . . if we wish to deny that all narratives do an equally good job of representing the past."[13]

The problem with this resistance is twofold: for one, he has not followed them quite far enough insofar as he makes the common relativist claim leveled against postmodernists. Most postmodernist theory claims instead that our narratives are always *our* narratives, not the past's – it does not assert that all narratives do equally good jobs of representing it, but quite different ones with different sets of values and desires (including desires for a "moral"). Most basically, postmodernism refutes the possibility of *objective truth* when it comes to facts, values, and narratives. Secondly, he conflates postmodernism with deconstruction when he complains that there is "something profoundly unsatisfying and ultimately self-deluding about an endless postmodernist deconstruction of texts that fails to ground itself in history, in community, in politics." Yet deconstruction aims to thwart self-delusion, the kind that would pretend to universalize narratives – to read "reality" through master narratives and to make the world conform to the word – and also the kind of delusion that would pretend that, as Cronon claims, postmodernism "threatens to lose track" of why we *care* about the subject of a narrative.[14]

What the invocation of "caring" seems to elide or ignore are two interrelated matters of subjectivity and authority (whether legal, religious, national, etc.), both of which shape what narratives mean in necessarily different contexts for different readers. Literary theory aims not to get people to stop caring about the subject of a narrative but to think about the narrative and political uses to which affect is put, especially insofar as one person's or group's values can mean another's demise. It is not as long a leap as it might at first seem, from nineteenth-century master narratives to a postmodernist sensibility in a western context: what narratives of American conquest, for example, mean to Native Americans, for whom the distance between American words and acts is indeed infinite, has produced a literary legacy of a particular kind of deconstruction and postmodernist irony, all in the name of native subjectivity and cultural authority – and Indians did not need European theory to show them the way. Postmodernism aims not to eradicate subjectivity but to decouple it from (especially hegemonic) authority, including the kind of authority that would ground the meaning and value of literary and historical narratives.

This notion of "grounding" literature in history is twin to the notion of grounding history in narrative theory, and it characterizes critical movements of the last few decades in everything from the New Historicism to Hayden White's discussions of historiography. According to Dominick LaCapra, this shared grounding remains traditional in the strongest sense in that it maintains the borders or distinctions between history and literature, each of which serves as a kind of hermeneutic authority for or check against the other. How, then, do we resolve this dilemma between the claims of representation and the claims of "reality" without seeming to reduce all reality to "text" and without abandoning those things Cronon justifiably values: the past, community, politics? LaCapra proposes a more intensive self-reflection on the dialogic interrelatedness of these conventional categories that mutually determine history and literature. Such mutual influence, I would argue, is already apparent in the intensively dialogic structure of *Angle of Repose*, a novel written by a historian and told by a fictional historian who draws upon "actual" sources Stegner fictionalizes, a novel that renders the present as a dialogue with the past and the past as its own internalized dialogue with its past and imagined future. The historian cannot escape his own contemporary interests, LaCapra asserts – as did Turner – and by bringing them to the forefront, we can reflect on the past in a self-critical manner.[15]

This is not to argue for presentism, which treats the past as either usable or of no interest at all if it cannot confirm some aspect of the present's vantage point. Much western history and literary criticism proceed from this assumption that what is valuable in the past will confirm present values. The challenge of dialogism is the willingness to incorporate what one was not looking for, to recognize the otherness within the self rather than trying to locate the self in the other; or to recognize the past in the present rather than the reverse. There is immense value in listening for what we do not fully understand – the strangeness, foreignness of the past, including the ways in which the past was a stranger to its own self-conceptions. What literature has to offer anyone who reads it closely is the demanding, unavoidable ambiguity and estranging effect of literary expression itself.[16] The way in which highly figural language and literary narratives stand between at least two meanings, always renegotiating the literary distance between the figural and the real, is not so much an analogue to the distance between literature and history, as its hermeneutic bridge. Reading and interpretation challenge one not to choose between reality and representation (or present and past), but to learn how to inhabit the ground between them, which is always the only ground we have.

The use of western historians as "straw men" for what makes western literary study worthwhile is counterproductive, ultimately, and it repeats the historians' use of their own straw men: it keeps us within our anxious boundaries that would demarcate what we do. (It can also seem to ignore the debt literary critics owe to historians for re-invigorating the field of western studies, as Krista Comer observes they have done.) And it can divert us from paying closer attention to our own critical contradictions. What we (literary critics) theorize and what we do sometimes puts us in the position of acting in bad faith – believing, on one hand, in the importance of revising the canon (because representations and people have a relationship), and on the other, chiding historians for believing unproblematically that their narratives render the reality of historical experience; or, teaching our students to read ethically, "as if" narratives speak for others, while at the same time arguing that literary discourse refers only to itself and that we should approach all stories with an equal eye, an obligation that Forrest Robinson claims postmodernism places upon us.

Yet we do not approach all stories with an equal eye, precisely because our eyes are always interested, as my own have been in reading marriage and nation through each other in the name of revisionist western historical significance. My aim in this book has been in part to see marriage with estranged eyes: neither as the culmination of the love plot, nor as the normative structure it has often been, but as the unexpected means by which we are able to imagine western significance against the significance that nationalist ideology would assign it. Literary western marriages are not, in fact, unions, either of two represented subjects, or, allegorically speaking, of the personal and the national. Instead, as the dialogic nature of language and of the relation between self and other would suggest, they are riddled with internalized difference, in a manner that a national ideology would not recognize. They never "reproduce" a national mission even when they are assigned the figural burden of such. Literary marriages are, to varying degrees of success, representations of competing subjectivities, desires, and narratives that often clash and generate scenes of violence. Those narratives – about the role of women, about national progress, about freedom and consent – both produce desires often incommensurate with reality and battle with desires that are often incompatible with narrative regulation. Rather than serving to regenerate, as Richard Slotkin argues about the symbolic work of frontier violence, the representations of intra-ethnic violence in these texts are often the degenerative sign of a failed project of national union and identity, a project that irreconcilably believed violent conquest was necessary for freedom. Like the actual violence of 11 September, the represented violence in fictions of western marriages is bound up, in significant part, with the collision of often Manichean narratives (of "civilization" and "evil," for example), the very kind poststructuralist theory wants us to care about deconstructing. While conservative commentators claim that the destruction of 11 September shows up the "nihilism" of postmodernism (because, in contrast, the disaster was so traumatically "real"), such nihilistic violence demonstrates just the postmodernist point about how narrative constructs rather than merely reflects reality: the terrorists shrouded themselves in a fairly unambiguous narrative. The kind of relativism that would refuse to subscribe to mono-narratives, that refuses to choose sides absolutely between subjective positions, whether in a marriage or an international crisis, is not moral nihilism: it often aids survival, and certainly the survival of any intimate relationship.

Postmodernism aims to substitute a relation to pleasure for the subject's relation to legal or religious authority, given the insistent, embodied resistance that pleasure has to regulation. Such pleasure is the very thing that recent battles against (and even those for) same-sex marriage aim to regulate, by codifying in law a "definition" of marriage abstracted from any subjectivity, gay or straight, in the name of nation and civilization and some fairly gross oversimplifications of the centuries-old history of marital practices, especially during debates over the 1996 Defense of Marriage Act, which had broad bipartisan support.[17] (Ironically but not surprisingly, the rhetoric against Mormon polygamy in the nineteenth century is one the Mormon Church now joins Congress and others in using against sexual nonconformists.) The narrative constructedness of such legalized fictions, no less than the narrative constructedness of political violence, demonstrates a postmodernist truism: that reality is narratively malleable.[18] In light of that fact, we have choices and commitments to make, self-conscious of the narratives we use to make them. The present historical moment demands not the abandonment of postmodernist play and deconstructionist critique, but their vigorous reassertion with the goal of de-naturalizing narratives that regulate and do violence to human subjectivities and bodies. For indeed, subjectivity – one's own and others' – is on the line when we read and write, no less than when we act in the world. Literature's challenge to the imagination (to imagine others, especially) is one of its enduring values: this claim, which sounds almost reactionary after revolutions in literary theory, has nevertheless not lost its potentially revolutionary edge in a nation in which many Americans have still barely begun to absorb historical loss and the meaning of their own violent past, and in which façades of national unity are still so easily purchased, in 1991 as in 2001, at the cost of thousands of unimagined lives.

It is an important moment in western studies: rarely has there been such extensive and self-reflective debate about not just the western past but about what western myth, history, and literary representation are, what they mean, and what their relations can be to each other. Though both literary and historical western studies have belatedly been catching up with literary theory, it may be that the West, which has seen the clash of so many stories, may yet prove to be an important domain for a return to literary complexity and for understanding how and why narrative continues to matter.

# Notes

INTRODUCTION

1 Though he too easily aligns imagination and myth – and leaves out literature – the historian Richard White has argued that "The mythic West imagined by Americans has shaped the West of history just as the West of history has helped create the West Americans have imagined. The two cannot be neatly severed," *"It's Your Misfortune and None of My Own": A History of the American West* (Norman: University of Oklahoma Press, 1991), p. 616. Patricia Limerick has also written about how "the Real West" and "the imagined West" have ended up "tied together, virtually Siamese twins sharing the same circulatory system," but reasserts the validity of such distinctions, however difficult it is to disentangle them. *The Real West*, commentary by Patricia Nelson Limerick; introduction by Andrew E. Masich (Denver: Civic Center Cultural Complex, 1996), p. 13.

2 A notable exception in the field of western historiography is Kerwin Lee Klein's *Frontiers of Historical Imagination: Narrating the European Conquest of Native America, 1890–1990* (Berkeley: University of California Press, 1997).

3 Nathaniel Lewis, "Unsettling the Literary West: Authenticity, Authorship, and Western American Literature." Unpublished ms.

4 Michael Kowalewski, *Deadly Musings: Violence and Verbal Form in American Fiction* (Princeton: Princeton University Press, 1993), p. 18.

5 Wallace Stegner, *The Sound of Mountain Water* (Lincoln: University of Nebraska Press, 1985; orig. pub. 1969), p. 20.

6 Nancy Cott, *Public Vows: A History of Marriage and the Nation* (Cambridge, Mass.: Harvard University Press, 2000), pp. 10; 17–18; 23; 25; 4.

7 Glenda Riley, *Building and Breaking Families in the American West* (Albuquerque: University of New Mexico Press, 1996), p. 79.

8 For studies of marriage, adultery, and the novel in the Anglo-American traditions, see Joseph Allen Boone, *Tradition Counter Tradition: Love and the Form of Fiction* (Chicago: University of Chicago Press, 1987); Allen F. Stein, *After the Vows Were Spoken: Marriage in American Literary Realism* (Columbus: Ohio University Press, 1984); and Tony Tanner, *Adultery and the Novel: Contract and Transgression* (Baltimore: Johns Hopkins University Press, 1979).

234

9 Doris Sommer, *Foundational Fictions: The National Romances of Latin America* (Berkeley: University of California Press, 1991). Southern American literature has configured a different set of familial models for understanding the relationship between past and present, and between region and nation. For a comparative study of post-slavery genealogies in the Americas, see George B. Handley, *Postslavery Literatures of the Americas: Family Portraits in Black and White* (Charlottesville: University Press of Virginia, 2000). For a study of the effects of slavery and miscegenation on both literal and figurative patriarchal forms of American citizenship, see Russ Castronovo, *Fathering the Nation: American Genealogies of Slavery and Freedom* (Berkeley: University of California Press, 1995).

## I WESTERN UNIONS

1 Joan Didion, *Slouching Towards Bethlehem* (New York: Farrar, Straus, & Giroux, 1968), pp. 71–72.
2 *Rereading Frederick Jackson Turner: "The Significance of the Frontier in American History" and Other Essays*, with commentary by John Mack Faragher (New York: Henry Holt and Co., 1994), p. 53.
3 Kathleen Neils Conzen, "A Saga of Families" in Clyde A. Milner II, Carol A. O'Connor, and Martha Sandweiss, eds., *The Oxford History of the American West* (New York: Oxford University Press, 1994), pp. 322; 321.
4 Quoted in Milner, *et al.*, eds., *Oxford History*, p. 319.
5 Quoted in Milner, *et al.*, eds., *Oxford History*, p. 322.
6 Milner, *et al.*, eds., *Oxford History*, p. 323.
7 Glenda Riley, *Building and Breaking Families in the American West* (Albuquerque: University of New Mexico Press, 1996), p. 72.
8 Amy Kaplan, "Manifest Domesticity," *American Literature* 70 (September 1998), 581–606.
9 Christine Bold, *Selling the Wild West: Popular Western Fiction, 1860 to 1960* (Bloomington: Indiana University Press, 1987); Lee Clark Mitchell, *Westerns: Making the Man in Fiction and Film* (Chicago: University of Chicago Press, 1996); Richard Slotkin, *Gunfighter Nation: The Myth of the Frontier in Twentieth-Century America* (New York: Atheneum, 1992). Other recent studies of the Western include Jane Tompkins, *West of Everything: The Inner Life of Westerns* (New York: Oxford University Press, 1992); Forrest G. Robinson, *Having It Both Ways: Self-Subversion in Western Popular Classics* (Albuquerque: University of New Mexico Press, 1993); and Robert Murray Davis, *Playing Cowboys: Low Culture and High Art in the Western* (Norman: University of Oklahoma Press, 1991). For two earlier, influential studies, see John G. Cawelti's *The Six-Gun Mystique* (Bowling Green, Ohio: Bowling Green University Popular Press, 1971) and *Adventure, Mystery, and Romance: Formula Stories as Popular Art and Popular Culture* (Chicago: University of Chicago Press, 1976), pp. 192–259.

10 Krista Comer, *Landscapes of the New West: Gender and Geography in Contemporary Women's Writing* (Chapel Hill: University of North Carolina Press, 1999); Susan J. Rosowski, *Birthing a Nation: Gender, Creativity, and the West in American Literature* (Lincoln: University of Nebraska Press, 1999).

11 Leslie Fiedler, *The Return of the Vanishing American* (New York: Stein and Day, 1968), p. 24.

12 Tompkins argues that Westerns are bent on destroying female authority and everything women represent, especially domesticity and religion.

13 For a study of nineteenth-century America's need to create a national identity explicitly against the status and rights of Native Americans, see Susan Scheckel, *The Insistence of the Indian: Race and Nationalism in Nineteenth-Century American Culture* (Princeton: University of Princeton Press, 1998). For a study of the impact of Native presence in the formation of American literature, see Joshua David Bellin, *The Demon of the Continent: Indians and the Shaping of American Literature* (Philadelphia: University of Pennsylvania Press, 2001).

14 Girard also refers to this as the "sacrificial crisis," René Girard, *Violence and the Sacred*, trans. Patrick Gregory (Baltimore: Johns Hopkins University Press, 1977; orig. pub. 1972), p. 49.

15 *The Works of Mark Twain*, vol. II, edited by Harriet Elinor Smith and Edgar Marquess Branch (Berkeley: University of California Press, 1993), pp. 392–394.

16 Quoted in Darwin Payne, *Owen Wister: Chronicler of the West, Gentleman of the East* (Dallas: Southern Methodist University Press, 1985), p. 89.

17 Kaplan, "Manifest Domesticity," p. 582.

18 Girard, *Violence and the Sacred*, p. 49.

19 This is the kind of argument President Grant made in 1869 in his first message to Congress: "A system which looks to the extinction of a race is too horrible for a nation to adopt without. . . engendering in the citizen a disregard for human life and rights of others [that is] dangerous to society," quoted in Alan Trachtenberg, *The Incorporation of America: Culture and Society in the Gilded Age* (New York: Hill and Wang, 1982), p. 28.

20 Nancy F. Cott, *Public Vows: A History of Marriage and the Nation* (Cambridge, Mass.: Harvard University Press, 2000), p. 3.

21 Tony Tanner, *Adultery and the Novel: Contract and Transgression* (Baltimore: Johns Hopkins University Press, 1979), p. 15.

22 See especially Annette Kolodny, *The Lay of the Land: Metaphor as Experience and History in American Life and Letters* (Chapel Hill: University of North Carolina Press, 1975).

23 Mitchell, *Westerns*, p. 96.

24 Michael Kowalewski, *Deadly Musings: Violence and Verbal Form in American Fiction* (Princeton: Princeton University Press, 1993), p. 18.

25 Willa Cather, *A Lost Lady*, edited by Charles W. Mignon and Frederick M. Link (Lincoln: University of Nebraska Press, 1997), p. 22.

26 Emerson Hough, *The Passing of the Frontier: A Chronicle of the Old West*, vol. 26 in the Chronicle of America Series, edited by Allan Johnson (New Haven: Yale University Press, 1921), p. 2.

27 James R. Grossman, ed. *The Frontier in American Culture: Essays by Richard White and Patricia Nelson Limerick* (Berkeley: University of California Press, 1994), p. 94.

28 Hough, *Passing*, pp. 2–3, 173.

29 Thomas Jefferson, *Letters*, edited by Merrill D. Peterson (Library of America, 1984), p. 1097. Letter to James Monroe, 24 November 1801.

30 Quoted in John Mack Faragher's, "Afterword," to *Rereading Frederick Jackson Turner: "The Significance of the Frontier in American History" and Other Essays* (New York: Henry Holt and Co., 1994), p. 230.

31 Anders Stephanson, *Manifest Destiny: American Expansion and the Empire of Right* (New York: Hill and Wang, 1995), p. 5, emphasis in original.

32 Quoted in Jan Willem Schulte Nordholt, *The Myth of the West: America as the Last Empire*; trans. Herbert H. Rowen (Grand Rapids: William B. Eerdmans Publishing Company, 1995), p. 9. Nordholt's study is a comprehensive source for the long history of the heliotropic myth. See also Loren Baritz, "The Idea of the West," *American Historical Review* 66 (April 1961), 618–640.

33 Quoted in Stephanson, *Manifest Destiny*, p. 19.

34 Trachtenberg, *Incorporation*, pp. 26–27.

35 *Crofutt's New Overland Tourist and Pacific Coast Guide* (Chicago: Overland Publishing Company, 1878), p. 300, emphases in original.

36 Cott, *Public Vows*, p. 27.

37 Willa Cather, *The Professor's House* (London: Virago, 1986; orig. pub. 1925), pp. 201–202.

38 Doris Sommer, *Foundational Fictions: The National Romances of Latin America* (Berkeley: University of California Press, 1991), p. 41. See her discussion, "Love and Country: An Allegorical Speculation," pp. 30–51.

39 Stephen Aron, "Lessons in Conquest: Toward a Greater Western History," *Pacific Historical Review* 63 (May 1994), 131. Defending the use of the term frontier *as* a legacy of conquest, Aron argues in favor of the concept's usefulness against anti-frontier historians such as Patricia Limerick, even though his model also refutes Turner's progressivist reading of western expansion.

40 Donald Worster, "New West, True West: Interpreting the Region's History," *Western Historical Quarterly* 18: 2 (April 1987), 143–144.

41 See Walter Nugent, "Where is the American West? Report on a Survey" in Walter Nugent and Martin Ridge, eds., *The American West: The Reader* (Bloomington: Indiana University Press, 1999), pp. 11–23.

42 Kerwin Lee Klein, *Frontiers of Historical Imagination: Narrating the European Conquest of America* (Berkeley: University of California Press, 1997), p. 3.

43 Owen Wister, *The Virginian* (New York: Macmillan Company, 1955), p. ix.

44 Cather, *A Lost Lady*, pp. 31, 75.

45 See especially *The Content of the Form: Narrative Discourse and Historical Representation* (Baltimore: Johns Hopkins University Press, 1987).

2 TURNER'S RHETORICAL FRONTIER

1 See William Cronon, "Revisiting the Vanishing Frontier: The Legacy of Frederick Jackson Turner," *Western Historical Quarterly* 17: 2 (April 1987), 157–176; Donald Worster, "New West, True West: Interpreting the Region's History," *Western Historical Quarterly* 17: 2 (April 1987), 141–156; and John Mack Faragher's Afterword to *Rereading Frederick Jackson Turner: "The Significance of the Frontier in American History" and Other Essays* (New York: Henry Holt and Co., 1994), pp. 225–241. For the most comprehensive discussion of shifting patterns in western American historiography, including responses to Turner, see Kerwin Lee Klein, *Frontiers of Historical Imagination: Narrating the European Conquest of Native America, 1890–1990* (Berkeley: University of California Press, 1997). Other sources for Turner's influence on subsequent historians and historiographical debates include Richard Hofstadter, *The Progressive Historians: Turner, Beard, Parrington* (Chicago: University of Chicago Press, 1979); Wilbur Jacobs, *On Turner's Trail: 100 Years of Writing Western History* (Lawrence: University Press of Kansas, 1994); Patricia Limerick, "Turnerians All: The Dream of a Helpful History in an Intelligible World," *American Historical Review* 100 (1995), 697–716; Martin Ridge, "The Life of an Idea: The Significance of Frederick Jackson Turner's Frontier Thesis," *Montana: The Magazine of Western History* 41 (Winter 1991), 2–13; Clyde A. Milner II, ed., *A New Significance: Re-Envisioning the History of the American West* (New York: Oxford University Press, 1996); Gerald Nash, *Creating the West: Historical Interpretations 1890–1990* (Albuquerque: University of New Mexico Press, 1991); and Patricia Limerick, Clyde Milner II, and Charles Rankin, eds., *Trails Toward a New Western History* (Lawrence: University Press of Kansas, 1991).
2 Cronon, "Revisiting the Vanishing Frontier," p. 159.
3 "The Significance of the Frontier in American History," *Rereading Turner*, p. 18, emphasis in original. Further citations from Turner's essays in this collection will be cited parenthetically in the text.
4 Patricia Limerick, *Something in the Soil: Legacies and Reckonings in the New West* (New York: W.W. Norton & Co., 2000), p. 164. This article first appeared in *American Historical Review*, cited above.
5 Limerick, *Something in the Soil*, p. 151 (emphasis in original).
6 Limerick, *Something in the Soil*, p. 150.
7 Limerick, *Something in the Soil*, p. 143.
8 Cronon, "Revisiting the Vanishing Frontier," p. 160.
9 Cronon, "Revisiting the Vanishing Frontier," p. 158.
10 Worster, "New West, True West," p. 144.
11 Cronon, "Revisiting the Vanishing Frontier," p. 160; Ronald Carpenter, *The Eloquence of Frederick Jackson Turner* (San Marino: Huntington Library, 1983), p. 3.
12 James R. Grossman, ed., *The Frontier in American Culture: Essays by Richard White and Patricia Nelson Limerick* (Berkeley: University of California Press, 1994), pp. 67–95.

13 Henry Nash Smith observes, "sometimes, especially when the conception of nature as the source of occult powers is most vividly present, Turner's metaphors threaten to become themselves a means of cognition and to supplant discursive reasoning," *Virgin Land: The American West as Symbol and Myth* (Cambridge, Mass.: Harvard University Press, 1950), p. 254. Although others have pointed out or analyzed Turner's rhetoric, Smith's brief analysis demonstrates how Turner's language often constitutes his ideas. Ronald Carpenter, in contrast, argues that "never" in Turner's historical writing did he "Subordinate content to form, substance to style" (*Eloquence*, p. 95). Yet the very distinction between content and form is antithetical to Turner's Romanticist inheritance; his style is of his message's essence.

14 Henry E. Huntington Library, Turner Papers, box 59. Turner saved the publisher's 1920 and 1921 book lists that gave prominent attention to his volume, listed between Einstein's *Relativity: The Special and General Theory* and Henri Bergson's *Mind-Energy*. The collection won profits for the publisher. Allan G. Bogue, *Frederick Jackson Turner: Strange Roads Going Down* (Norman: University of Oklahoma Press, 1998), p. 440. The Huntington Turner collection will hereafter be cited as HEH TU.

15 Carpenter, *Eloquence*, p. 21.

16 Carpenter, *Eloquence*, p. 21.

17 Philip Fisher, *Still the New World: American Literature in a Culture of Creative Destruction* (Cambridge, Mass.: Harvard University Press, 1999), p. 6.

18 David Noble has called the frontier thesis a Jeremiad and Turner a Jeremiah. *Historians Against History: The Frontier Thesis and the National Covenant in American Historical Writing Since 1830* (Minneapolis: University of Minnesota Press, 1965), pp. 3–4.

19 HEH TU vol. III (1); HEH TU box 31A. Turner to Arthur Meier Schlesinger, 18 April 1922.

20 Allan Bogue argues that Turner's orations "in some degree forecast [his] professional style as a historian." See his biography *Frederick Jackson Turner*, p. 25.

21 Carpenter, *Eloquence*, p. 117.

22 Carpenter, *Eloquence*, p. 117.

23 Carpenter, *Eloquence*, p. 119.

24 Carpenter, *Eloquence*, p. 120.

25 Carpenter, *Eloquence*, p. 123.

26 Carpenter, *Eloquence*, p. 95.

27 William Cronon, "Turner's First Stand: The Significance of Significance in American History," in Gerald D. Nash and Richard W. Etulain, eds., *The Twentieth Century West: Historical Interpretations* (Albuquerque: University of New Mexico Press, 1989), pp. 73–101.

28 Brooks Atkinson, ed., *The Selected Writings of Ralph Waldo Emerson* (New York: Random House, 1940), p. 346 (emphases in original).

29 Grossman, ed., *Frontier*, p. 90.

30 Joel Fineman, "The Structure of Allegorical Desire," in Stephen Greenblatt, ed., *Allegory and Representation* (Baltimore: Johns Hopkins University Press, 1981), p. 45.
31 Ray Allen Billington, *The Frontier Thesis: Valid Interpretation of American History?* (New York: Holt, Rinehart, Winston, 1966), p. 29.
32 Renato Rosaldo, *Culture and Truth: The Remaking of Social Analysis* (Boston: Beacon Press, 1989), pp. 69, 70.
33 Rosaldo, *Culture and Truth*, p. 70.
34 Fineman, "Structure," p. 28.
35 See Dayton Duncan, *Miles from Nowhere: Tales from America's Contemporary Frontier* (New York: Viking, 1993), pp. 6–7. Duncan cites a 1990 census study that claims thirteen percent of the contiguous United States has fewer than two people per square mile – the definition of the frontier Turner adopted from the census in 1890.
36 Limerick, *Something in the Soil*, p. 158.
37 Carpenter, *Eloquence*, pp. 48–49 (emphases in original).
38 Emerson, *Selected Writings*, p. 264.
39 Paul de Man, *Blindness and Insight: Essays in the Rhetoric of Contemporary Criticism* (London: Methuen, 1983), p. 188.
40 Quoted in De Man, *Blindness*, pp. 188–189.
41 Billington, *The Frontier Thesis*, p. 30.
42 Grossman, ed., *Frontier*, p. 94.
43 Klein, *Frontiers of Historical Imagination*, p. 12.
44 Hayden White, *Metahistory: The Historical Imagination in Nineteenth-Century Europe* (Baltimore: Johns Hopkins University Press, 1973). See especially his introduction, pp. 1–42.
45 Myra Jehlen, "Literary History and Historical Literature." Paper presented before the Modern Language Association in San Diego, December 1994.
46 See Annette Kolodny, "Letting Go Our Grand Obsessions: Notes Toward a New Literary History of the American Frontiers," *American Literature* 64: 1 (March 1992), 1–18.
47 Frederick Jackson Turner, "The West – 1876 and 1926," in *The Significance of Sections in American History* (Gloucester, Mass.: Peter Smith, 1959; orig. pub. 1932), p. 236.
48 Limerick, *Something in the Soil*, p. 149.
49 *Rereading Turner*, p. 19.
50 Limerick, *Something in the Soil*, pp. 149–150.

3 MARRYING FOR RACE AND NATION: WISTER'S OMNISCIENCE AND OMISSIONS

1 Theodore Roosevelt, "Race Decadence," in *The Works of Theodore Roosevelt*, vol. XIV (New York: Scribner's Sons, 1924), pp. 159; 161.
2 Quoted in Darwin Payne, *Owen Wister: Chronicler of the West, Gentleman of the East* (Dallas: Southern Methodist University Press, 1985), p. 201.

3 Owen Wister to Sarah Butler Wister, 5 August 1902. Quoted in Payne, *Owen Wister*, p. 204.

4 See Lee Mitchell's argument that the novel is a reaction against the politics of suffragism in "the Equality State," as Wyoming was called for being first to give women the vote. *Westerns: Making the Man in Fiction and Film* (Chicago: University of Chicago Press, 1996), pp. 113–116.

5 Richard Slotkin, *Gunfighter Nation: The Myth of the Frontier in Twentieth-Century America* (New York: Atheneum, 1992), pp. 177; 178.

6 Owen Wister, *The Virginian: A Horseman of the Plains* (New York: Macmillan Company, 1955; orig. pub. 1902), p. 125. Subsequent references from this edition of the novel will be cited in the text.

7 Malcolm Bell, Jr., *Major Butler's Legacy: Five Generations of a Slaveholding Family* (Athens: University of Georgia Press, 1987), p. 471. For a discussion of Wister's neurasthenia and the "West cure" that family friend Dr. Weir Mitchell prescribed for him, see Barbara Will, "The Nervous Origins of the Western," *American Literature* 70: 2 (June 1998), 293–316.

8 Quoted in Payne, *Owen Wister*, p. 227.

9 Christine Bold, "How the Western Ends: Fenimore Cooper to Frederick Remington," in *Western American Literature* 17: 2 (Summer 1982), 123. Bold argues that the ending to *The Virginian* does not, however, successfully fulfill the imperatives of the sentimental reconciliation.

10 "The importance of all other subjects depends absolutely upon treating this subject as of far more importance," Roosevelt wrote about reproduction in marriage. *The Works of Theodore Roosevelt*, vol. XIV, p. 158.

11 *The Works of Theodore Roosevelt*, vol. XIV, pp. 151, 160.

12 What drove both Wister and Frederick Remington, Christine Bold argues, "was a desire to create, in stylized fiction, an alternative to the pattern of Western history. They struggled to present the Western archetypes in ways which would protect their own versions of the West from the changes happening on the real frontier," *Selling the Wild West: Popular Western Fiction, 1860 to 1960* (Bloomington: Indiana University Press, 1987), p. xv.

13 Darwin Payne notes Wister's difficulty with the incompatibility of narrative styles, but adds that Wister chose to let them remain (*Owen Wister*, p. 193). Lee Mitchell argues that Wister's "very lack of success in integrating stories and points of view only contributed to the novel's appeal" by encouraging "a series of imitations that strained to clarify Wister's materials but ended reinforcing generic tendencies that allowed mutually contradictory possibilities to coexist" (*Westerns*, p. 97). Lee Mitchell is the only critic to have addressed the novel's structural incoherence. He does so in order to make sense of "the strange oscillation in our view of the Virginian as at once decidedly verbal and yet somehow inarticulate." Chiefly contributing to this effect is "the overinvested narrative perspective . . . " (*Westerns*, p. 101).

14 Payne, *Owen Wister*, 209.

15 Jane Tompkins, *West of Everything: The Inner Life of Westerns* (New York: Oxford University Press, 1992), p. 147.

16 Wister quoted this letter in full in his memoir *Roosevelt: The Story of a Friendship* (New York: Macmillan Company, 1930), pp. 248–256.

17 See Malcolm Bell, Jr.'s study of the Butler family, *Major Butler's Legacy*. Wister's great-great-grandfather on his mother's side was the slaveholder Pierce Butler of South Carolina, delegate to the US Constitutional Convention, who introduced the motion that became the fugitive slave clause in the Constitution. His grandson, Pierce Butler, was notorious for having squandered his inherited fortune and for having to sell 450 slaves as a result in order to keep his plantation. In an undated manuscript, Wister wrote, "I was brought up to revere my Grandfather . . . Only since I have been past middle life have I gradually made out that on the whole he couldn't have been a good person . . . Butler was cold. Never forgave" (quoted in *Major Butler's Legacy*, p. 476).

18 Forrest G. Robinson makes this point, since "it is part and parcel of the cowboy's culture to be suspicious of marriage. He regards matrimony as all that is artificial, constraining, corrupting and hypocritical in civilization," *Having It Both Ways: Self-Subversion in Western Popular Classics* (Albuquerque: University of New Mexico Press, 1993), p. 41.

19 Quoted in Payne, *Owen Wister*, p. 201.

20 Letter from Owen Wister to Sarah Butler Wister, 5 July 1902. Fanny Kemble Wister, *Owen Wister Out West: His Journals and Letters* (Chicago: University of Chicago Press, 1958), p. 18.

21 Tompkins, *West of Everything*, p. 155. Robinson also gives attention to this passage in *Having It Both Ways*, p. 42.

22 Given the Virginian's future as corporate manager, Alan Trachtenberg reads the novel as the cultural equivalent of an economically incorporated America. Richard Slotkin also reads the Virginian as embodying the privileged classes' rights of aggression against the laboring classes. Alan Trachtenberg, *The Incorporation of America: Culture and Society in the Gilded Age* (New York: Hill and Wang, 1982), p. 24; Slotkin, *Gunfighter Nation*, pp. 173–4.

23 Robert Murray Davis, ed., *Owen Wister's West: Selected Articles* (Albuquerque: University of New Mexico Press, 1987), p. 107.

24 See especially William R. Taylor, *Cavalier and Yankee: The Old South and American National Character* (New York: Oxford University Press, 1993; orig. pub. 1961).

25 Slotkin, *Gunfighter Nation*, p. 176.

26 Robinson, *Having It Both Ways*, p. 45.

27 Robinson, *Having It Both Ways*, p. 45.

28 Slotkin, *Gunfighter Nation*, p. 176.

29 Describing the narrative as "curiously uneventful," Mitchell points out that "the Western's most distinctive stock features are never actually shown: the Indian attack, roundup, and lynching each forms instead a narrative lacuna, alluded to proleptically and after the fact but never represented directly." The novel thus "raised expectations for a genre it did not actually quite

define, prompting readers to exceed the text in their own reconstructions" (*Westerns*, p. 96).

30 "Literature, Gender, and the New Western History," in Forrest G. Robinson, ed., *The New Western History: The Territory Ahead* (Tucson: University of Arizona Press, 1997), p. 112. For an analysis of how this imperative was consolidated – at just the historical moment *The Virginian* appeared – see Eve Kosofsky Sedgwick, *Epistemology of the Closet* (Berkeley: University of California Press, 1990), pp. 1–63.

31 Tompkins, *West of Everything*, p. 151.

32 See Blake Allmendinger, *Ten Most Wanted: The New Western Literature* (New York: Routledge Press, 1998), p. 158.

33 Payne, *Owen Wister*, pp. 104, 116.

34 "Hank's Woman," *Harper's Weekly* (27 August 1892), 821.

35 Payne, *Owen Wister*, pp. 127–128, 133, 134.

36 Payne, *Owen Wister*, pp. 197, 203, 196.

37 Payne, *Owen Wister*, pp. 299, 328–9.

38 Payne, *Owen Wister*, pp. 297–298.

39 *Owen Wister's West*, p. 144.

40 Letter from Owen Wister to Mr. Hancock, 2 September 1933, quoted in N. Orwin Rush, *Fifty Years of The Virginian, 1902–1952* (Laramie: University of Wyoming Library Association, 1952), pp. 2–3.

41 *Owen Wister's West*, p. 115.

42 *Owen Wister's West*, p. 115.

43 Payne, *Owen Wister*, p. 78.

44 Payne, *Owen Wister*, p. 162.

45 Mitchell, *Westerns*, p. 102.

46 *The West of Owen Wister: Selected Short Stories* (Lincoln: University of Nebraska Press, 1972), p. 6. Further citations from the 1900 version of "Hank's Woman" will be made parenthetically in the text.

47 "Hank's Woman," *Harper's Weekly*, 822.

### 4 POLYGAMY AND EMPIRE: GREY'S DISTINCTIONS

1 "The ruthlessness of Mormonism in that period of Western development is laid bare with great accuracy," wrote one reviewer of the novel in 1912, quoted in Carlton Jackson, *Zane Grey: A Biography* (Boston: Twayne, 1989; orig. pub. 1973), p. 41. While Carlton Jackson argues that in his "treatment of changing Mormonism, Grey put the stamp of historical research on his novels" and "contributed to an understanding of that period in American history" (p. 21), Jane Tompkins' reading of the novel scarcely mentions the Mormon distinction, *West of Everything: The Inner Life of Westerns* (New York: Oxford University Press, 1992), pp. 157–177. Forrest G. Robinson gives it some attention but argues that Grey "shrank from a full, conscious engagement with the contemporary social issues that caught his attention," *Having It Both Ways: Self-Subversion in Western Popular Classics* (Albuquerque: University

of New Mexico Press, 1993), pp. 3–11; 10. Richard Slotkin also mentions the Mormon element, *Gunfighter Nation: The Myth of the Frontier in Twentieth-Century America* (New York: Atheneum, 1992), pp. 211–217, but argues that "the characters and conflicts of the novel are not attempts at representing distinctive frontier types or situations but a distillation and abstraction of literary conventions" (p. 215). Some critics see the Mormon threat as an analogical vehicle for the voicing of other cultural anxieties and concerns: in an extended discussion of Grey's novel, Lee Clark Mitchell argues in part that Grey "replaces the panderers of the white slavery tracts with equally ruthless Mormons," *Westerns: Making the Man in Fiction and Film* (Chicago: University of Chicago Press, 1996), p. 144, while Stephen Tatum, in "The Problem of the 'Popular' in the New Western History," reads the Mormon "invisible hand" motif in the context of "then-contemporary concerns over the corporate form of ownership evolving in the era's finance capitalism based on industrial technology." Grey's characterization of the soulless Mormon patriarchy, Tatum asserts, "recapitulates the critique of modern corporate ownership" in American culture at the turn of the century, which saw it as "invisible" and "soulless," Forrest G. Robinson, ed., *The New Western History: The Territory Ahead* (Tucson: University of Arizona Press, 1997), p. 177. For a discussion of Grey's Mormon novels, see also Gary Topping, "Zane Grey in Zion: An Examination of His Supposed Anti-Mormonism" in *Brigham Young University Studies* 18: 4 (Summer 1978), 483–490.

2 For an account of Grey's travels among Mormons beginning in 1907, his friendship with Jim Emmett and his experiences with Buffalo Jones, their effect on his Mormon novels, and his sympathy particularly for Mormon women, see Stephen J. May, *Zane Grey: Romancing the West* (Athens: Ohio University Press, 1997), pp. 46–65; Frank Gruber, *Zane Grey: A Biography* (New York: Signet Books, 1971), pp. 68–77; and Graham St. John Stott, "Zane Grey and James Simpson Emmett," in *Brigham Young University Studies* 18: 4 (Summer 1978), 491–503.

3 Terryl L. Givens, *The Viper on the Hearth: Mormons, Myths, and the Construction of Heresy* (New York: Oxford University Press, 1997), pp. 151, 152.

4 See Noel Ignatiev, *How the Irish Became White* (New York: Routledge, 1995); and David R. Roediger, *The Wages of Whiteness: Race and the Making of the American Working Class* (London: Verso, 1991).

5 Zane Grey, *Riders of the Purple Sage* (Middlesex: Penguin, 1990; orig. pub. 1912), p. 131. Subsequent citations from this edition of the novel will be given parenthetically in the text.

6 Blake Allmendinger explores through nineteenth-century anti-polygamy fiction how "the nation's dominant culture equated the two groups of outcasts . . . refashioning early captivity narratives in order to demonize religious and racial minorities." The event that most fueled the sense that Mormons and Indians were hostile co-conspirators was the Mountain Meadows Massacre, in which Mormons dressed as Indians, and possibly Indians also, attacked

and killed 137 immigrants from Arkansas in what is now southern Utah in 1857. *Ten Most Wanted: The New Western Literature* (New York: Routledge, 1998), p. 60.

7 Mitchell, *Westerns*, p. 134.

8 Quoted in Gary L. Bunker and Davis Bitton, *The Mormon Graphic Image, 1834–1914* (Salt Lake City: University of Utah Press, 1983), p. 46.

9 Thomas Alexander, *Mormonism in Transition: A History of the Latter-Day Saints, 1890–1930* (Urbana: University of Illinois Press, 1986), p. 4; B. Carmon Hardy, *Solemn Covenant: The Mormon Polygamous Passage* (Urbana: University of Illinois Press, 1992), p. 49; Givens, *Viper*, p. 39.

10 Quoted in Wayne Stout, *History of Utah*, volume 1: *1870–1896* (published by the author, Salt Lake City, 1967), p. 25.

11 S. A. Kenner, *Utah As It Is, With a Comprehensive Statement of Utah As It Was* (Salt Lake City: Deseret News, 1904), p. 76.

12 Alexander, *Mormonism in Transition*, p. 19.

13 Julius C. Burrows, "Another Constitutional Amendment Necessary," *The Independent* 62 (9 May 1907), 1074–1078; Harvey J. O'Higgins, "A Reply to Colonel Roosevelt Regarding the New Polygamy in Utah," *Collier's* 67 (10 June 1911), 35–37; Burton J. Hendrick, "The Mormon Revival of Polygamy," *McClure's Magazine* 36 (January 1911), 345–361 (February 1911), 458–464; Alfred Henry Lewis, "The Viper on the Hearth," *Cosmopolitan* 50 (March 1911): 439–450, "The Trail of the Viper," *Cosmopolitan* 50 (April 1911), 693–703, and "The Viper's Trail of Gold," *Cosmopolitan* 50 (May 1911), 823–833. Alfred Henry Lewis had also written an introduction to John Doyle Lee, *The Mormon Menace, being the confession of John Doyle Lee, Danite, an official assassin of the Mormon Church under the late Brigham Young* (New York: Home Protection Publishing Co., 1905).

14 Isaac Russell, "Mr. Roosevelt to the Mormons: A Letter with an Explanatory Note," *Collier's* 47 (15 April 1911), 28.

15 Maude Radford Warren, "A Woman Pioneer: The Country of the Dry Farms," *Saturday Evening Post* (27 May 1911), 28–29.

16 Zane Grey to David Dexter Rust, 4 December 1910; 2 and 15 January and 15 February 1911, box 4, folder 7, David Dexter Rust Collection, Church Archives, Historical Department of the Church of Jesus Christ of Latter-Day Saints. Some of the most scathing articles, such as Alfred Henry Lewis' series (see n. 13 above), had yet to appear when Grey wrote these letters. Quoted in Topping, "Zane Grey in Zion," p. 485.

17 Quoted in Jackson, *Zane Grey*, p. 41.

18 Reversing the common claim that polygamy ran entirely counter to Christianity, Twain argued, with reference to Mormon women's home-liness, that "The man that marries one of them has done an act of Christian charity which entitles him to the kindly applause of mankind, not their harsh censure – and the man that marries sixty of them has done a deed of open-handed generosity so sublime that the nations should stand uncovered

in his presence and worship in silence," *The Works of Mark Twain*, vol. II,
ed. Harriet Elinor Smith and Edgar Marquess Branch (Berkeley: University
of California Press, 1993), pp. 97–98.

19 Louis Kern, *An Ordered Love: Sex Roles and Sexuality in Victorian Utopias – the
Shakers, the Mormons, and the Oneida Community* (Chapel Hill: University of
North Carolina Press, 1981), p. 203; Givens, *Viper*, p. 144.

20 Richard Allen Nelson, "From Antagonism to Acceptance: Mormons and
the Silver Screen," *Dialogue: A Journal of Mormon Thought* 10 (Spring 1977),
59–69. "Sealing" is the Mormon term for the marriage ordinance.

21 Grey, *The Rainbow Trail* (Roslyn, NY, 1943; orig. pub. 1915), p. 117. Subsequent citations from this edition of the novel will be given parenthetically
in the text.

22 Michael J. Colacurcio, *The Province of Piety: Moral History in Hawthorne's Early
Tales* (Cambridge, Mass.: Harvard University Press, 1984), p. 133; Mitchell,
*Westerns*, p. 148.

23 Kenner, *Utah As It Is*, p. 77.

24 Quoted in Hardy, *Solemn Covenant*, p. 285.

25 Givens, *Viper*, p. 18.

26 Hardy, *Solemn Covenant*, pp. 289; 40; 39; 41; 43; 296.

27 Hardy, *Solemn Covenant*, pp. 39–41.

28 Bunker and Bitton, *Mormon Graphic Image*, pp. 86; 59.

29 Winthrop D. Jordan, *White Man's Burden: Historical Origins of Racism in the
United States* (New York, 1974), p. 25.

30 Bunker and Bitton, *Mormon Graphic Image*, pp. 87; 89.

31 C. F. Budd, "Mormon Elder-berry – Out with His Six-Year Olds, Who
Take after Their Mothers." *Life* 43 (28 April 1904), 404.

32 Stephen J. May, *Maverick Heart: The Further Adventures of Zane Grey* (Athens:
Ohio University Press, 2000), pp. 78, 79.

33 John Cawelti, *Adventure, Mystery, and Romance: Formula Stories as Art and Popular
Culture* (Chicago: University of Chicago Press, 1976), p. 236. See also William
Bloodworth, "Zane Grey's Western Eroticism," *South Dakota Review* 23
(1985), 1–14; and John D. Nesbitt, "Uncertain Sex in the Sagebrush," *South
Dakota Review* 23 (1985), 15–27.

34 Alexander, *Mormonism in Transition*, p. 245.

35 Bunker and Bitton, *Mormon Graphic Image*, p. 89.

36 Jan Shipps, *Mormonism: The Story of a New Religious Tradition* (Urbana:
University of Illinois Press, 1985).

37 Nancy Bentley, "Marriage as Treason: Polygamy, Nation, and the Novel,"
in Donald Pease and Robyn Wiegman, eds., *The Futures of American Studies*
(Durham: Duke University Press, forthcoming).

38 Tompkins, *West of Everything*, p. 32; Robinson, *Having It Both Ways*, p. 5.

39 Bunker and Bitton, *Mormon Graphic Image*, p. 59.

40 Bunker and Bitton, *Mormon Graphic Image*, pp. 21; 23.

41 Mitchell, *Westerns*, pp. 136; 135; 134; 148.

42 Kenner, *Utah As It Is*, p. 77.

43 Mitchell, *Westerns*, p. 135.

44 In 1907, for example, the Mormon leadership published an "Address to the World" which functioned both to reassure the country of the church's motives and to criticize federal actions in the past: "We do not believe it just to mingle religious influence with civil government, whereby one religious society is fostered and another proscribed in its spiritual privileges, and the individual rights of its members, as citizens, denied . . . The Church of Jesus Christ of Latter-Day Saints holds to the doctrine of the separation of church and state; the non-interference of church authority in political matters," B. H. Roberts, *In Defense of the Faith and the Saints* (Salt Lake City: Deseret News, 1907), p. 156.

45 Renato Rosaldo, *Culture and Truth: The Remaking of Social Analysis* (Boston: Beacon Press, 1989), p. 69.

46 Givens, *Viper* p. 16. Givens cites Leo Tolstoy's reputed opinion that Mormonism was the quintessentially American religion, an opinion shared by Harold Bloom in his *The American Religion: The Emergence of a Post-Christian Nation* (New York: Simon & Schuster, 1992).

47 Hardy, *Solemn Covenant*, p. 58.

48 Hardy, *Solemn Covenant*, p. 49.

## 5 UNWEDDED WEST: CATHER'S DIVIDES

1 Quoted in L. Brent Bohlke, ed., *Willa Cather in Person: Interviews, Speeches, and Letters* (Lincoln: University of Nebraska Press, 1986), pp. 71–72.

2 For a representative overview of the history of Cather criticism that takes particular, biting aim at the last twenty years of it, see Joan Acocella, *Willa Cather and the Politics of Criticism* (Lincoln: University of Nebraska Press, 2000).

3 Sharon O'Brien observes that in her 1890s journalism Cather had savagely attacked women writers like Ouida and Marie Corelli "because their breathless, uncontrolled, extravagant prose resembled her own overly emotional and undisciplined writing," Sharon O'Brien, *Willa Cather: The Emerging Voice* (New York: Oxford University Press, 1987), p. 425.

4 Willa Cather, *Stories, Poems, and Other Writings* (New York: Library of America, Viking Press, 1992), p. 26. Further citations from this story will be given parenthetically in the text.

5 David Laird, "Willa Cather's Women: Gender, Place, and Narrativity in *O Pioneers!* and *My Ántonia*," *Great Plains Quarterly* 12 (Fall 1992), 243.

6 To what extent Cather read Wister and Roosevelt and what she thought of them is cloudy. Cather met Theodore Roosevelt in 1917 at the semicentennial commencement of the University of Nebraska at Lincoln, where they both received honorary doctorates. (Letter to Ferris Greenslet, 25 June 1917, Houghton Library; bms Am 1925 (341): 53.) Cather and Roosevelt shared not only a fascination with the West, but also a distaste for muckrakers: Roosevelt publicly attacked the kind of muckraking journalism for which McClure's magazine was famous in 1906, after he was re-elected

President and when Cather was working there. McClure's was therefore in some ways an alien environment for her. Cather valued the West, as did Roosevelt and Wister, as a place free of urban political cant. She "couldn't talk comfortably, she said, with people who were obsessed with the destruction of social evils," Hermione Lee, *Willa Cather: Double Lives* (New York: Vintage, 1991), p. 65. For Roosevelt's 1906 attack, see E. K. Brown, *Willa Cather: A Critical Biography* (New York: Alfred A. Knopf, 1953), p. 130.

7 G. Edward White, *The Eastern Establishment and the Western Experience: The West of Frederic Remington, Theodore Roosevelt, and Owen Wister* (New Haven: Yale University Press, 1968), p. 65. See "The East and Adolescence," pp. 52–74 of this important study, for a lengthier description of Wister's and Roosevelt's motives in going West. For an account of Roosevelt's and Wister's western experiences and their relation to ideas about masculinity, see the final chapter, entitled "Smile When You Carry a Big Stick," of Kim Townsend, *Manhood at Harvard: William James and Others* (New York: W. W. Norton & Co., 1996), pp. 256–286. For an exploration of how Roosevelt's sense of violent masculinity informed his views on the nation, see Gail Bederman, *Manliness & Civilization: A Cultural History of Gender and Race in the United States, 1800–1917* (Chicago: University of Chicago Press, 1995), pp. 170–215.

8 Susan Rosowski, *Birthing a Nation: Gender, Creativity, and the West in American Literature* (Lincoln: University of Nebraska Press, 1999), p. 69. See also pp. 58–78 for her discussion of how Cather's early western stories chart an awakening of female desire in an otherwise male-dominated literary landscape.

9 Letters of 16 July 1913 and 7 March 1925 in *"Dear Lady": The Letters of Frederick Jackson Turner and Alice Forbes Perkins Hooper, 1910–1932*, edited by R. A. Billington (San Marino: Huntington Library, 1970), pp. 149, 365.

10 While Cather wrote of *McTeague* that "a new and a great book has been written," three months later (in July 1899), she wrote of *The Awakening* that "next time I hope that Miss Chopin will devote that flexible, iridescent style of hers to a better cause," *Stories, Poems, and Other Writings*, pp. 911; 912.

11 O'Brien, *Willa Cather*, p. 403.

12 O'Brien, *Willa Cather*, p. 403.

13 O'Brien, *Willa Cather*, p. 7.

14 Elizabeth Shepley Sergeant, *Willa Cather: A Memoir* (Athens, Ohio: Ohio University Press, 1992; orig. pub. 1953), p. 95.

15 Sergeant, *A Memoir*, p. 92.

16 Sergeant, *A Memoir*, pp. 90–91.

17 O'Brien, *Willa Cather*, p. 144. For another description of these letters and this experience, see James Woodress, *Willa Cather: A Literary Life* (Lincoln: University of Nebruska Press, 1987), pp. 6–8. This important trip is the subject of Woodress' prologue to his biography.

18 O'Brien, *Willa Cather*, p. 404.

19 Sergeant, *A Memoir*, pp. 90; 91–2.

20  *Stories, Poems, and Other Writings*, pp. 902; 903.

21  *Stories, Poems, and Other Writings*, p. 963.

22  *Stories, Poems, and Other Writings*, pp. 889; 890.

23  *O Pioneers!*, edited by Susan J. Rosowski and Charles Mignon (Lincoln: University of Nebraska Press, 1992), pp. 12; 13. Further citations from this edition of the novel will be made parenthetically in the text.

24  Woodress, *Willa Cather*, p. 182.

25  David Laird argues that "Cather was at pains to show that . . . [w]hile the frontier may initially liberate, it soon sees the reenactment of those various constraints and limitations that characterize the social landscape of more settled, more traditional societies." "Cather's Women," p. 246.

26  In contrast to my interpretation, David Daiches argues that "to some degree" Alexandra's "growth, development, and final adjustment," like Ántonia's, "is a vast symbolic progress, interesting less for what it is than for what it can be made to mean." Daiches argues (as does Wallace Stegner) that by the end of the book Alexandra is "a kind of Earth Goddess symbolic of what the pioneers had achieved," but this meaning's "epic quality . . . makes one resent the intrusion of incidents drawn to a smaller scale," David Daiches, *Willa Cather: A Critical Introduction* (Ithaca: Cornell University Press, 1951), p. 44.

27  Laird, "Cather's Women," p. 246.

28  Letter from Ferris Greenslet to Willa Cather, 3 October, 1944, Houghton Library, bMS Am 1925 (341): 417.

29  Guy Reynolds, *Willa Cather in Context: Progress, Race, and Empire* (New York: St. Martin's Press, 1996), pp. 83; 84. See Werner Sollors, *Beyond Ethnicity: Consent and Descent in American Culture* (New York: Oxford University Press, 1986).

30  Reynolds, *Cather in Context*, pp. 96; 97.

31  James E. Miller, Jr., "*My Ántonia* and the American Dream" in Harold Bloom, ed., *Willa Cather's My Ántonia* (New York: Chelsea House, 1987), p. 106.

32  Miller, "*My Ántonia*," p. 102.

33  Blanche Gelfant, "The Forgotten Reaping-Hook: Sex in *My Ántonia*," in Bloom, ed., *Cather's My Antonia*, p. 81.

34  Reynolds, *Cather in Context*, p. 84.

35  Rosowski, *Birthing a Nation*, pp. 79–92.

36  Letters to Ferris Greenslet, February 1918, Houghton Library; bMS Am 1925 (341): 74; and 9 July 1918, Houghton Library; bMS Am 1925 (341): 79.

37  *My Ántonia*, edited by Charles Mignon (Lincoln: University of Nebraska Press, 1994), p. x. Further citations from this scholarly edition will be made parenthetically in the text.

38  *Stories, Poems, and Other Writings*, p. 903.

39  James Clifford, "On Ethnographic Allegory" in James Clifford and George Marcus, eds., *Writing Culture: The Poetics and Politics of Ethnography* (Berkeley: University of California Press, 1986), pp. 98–121.

40 John Murphy does discuss briefly in his study of the novel the "appropriately racist and sentimental passage" as suggesting "the lack of objectivity built into Jim's narrative," *My Ántonia: The Road Home* (Boston: G. K. Hall & Co., 1989), p. 75. Others discuss Cather's biographical source, but not Jim's characterizations. One critic reads the passage as a Dionysian "rhapsody to man's instinctive urge for pleasure," Evelyn Helmick, "The Mysteries of Ántonia," *Midwest Quarterly* 17 (1976), 174. Some critics, reading the scene as about music, not race, compare d'Arnault to Orpheus.

41 Letters to Ferris Greenslet, 2 July 1918, Houghton Library, bms Am 1925 (341): 78; 12 May 1915, Houghton Library, bms Am 1925 (341): 14.

42 Otakar Odlozilík, formerly of Czecholovakia and later professor of history at Columbia University, indicated in a letter dated 4 November 1960 that "It is true that in Czech... the ending in that name would not be *a* but *e*, that is Antonie," Mildred R. Bennett, "How Willa Cather Chose Her Names," *Names* 10 (March 1962), 35.

43 Rosowski, *Birthing a Nation*, p. 92.

44 Rosowski, *Birthing a Nation*, p. 82.

45 *A Lost Lady*, edited by Charles Mignon and Frank Link (Lincoln: University of Nebraska Press, 1977), p. 53. Further citations of this edition of the novel will be given parenthetically in the text.

46 The only two surviving pages of the first draft of *The Great Gatsby* were sent to Cather by Fitzgerald, who wrote to Cather that he was concerned his description of Daisy was too close to her description of Marian Forrester. See Matthew J. Bruccoli, "'An Instance of Apparent Plagiarism': F. Scott Fitzgerald, Willa Cather, and the First *Gatsby* Manuscript," *Princeton University Library Chronicle* 39 (Spring 1978), 171–178.

47 Lee, *Double Lives*, p. 200.

48 Lee, *Double Lives*, p. 193.

49 A. S. Byatt has made this observation. "Introduction," *A Lost Lady* (London: Virago, 1980), p. xii.

50 Lee, *Double Lives*, p. 205.

51 Lee, *Double Lives*, p. 207.

52 Lee, *Double Lives*, p. 10.

6 ACCIDENT AND DESTINY: FITZGERALD'S FANTASTIC GEOGRAPHY

1 F. Scott Fitzgerald, *The Great Gatsby*, ed. Matthew J. Bruccoli (Cambridge: Cambridge University Press, 1991), p. 140. Further citations from this edition of the novel will be given parenthetically in the text. Borrowing this phrase for the title of her study, Louise H. Westling reads in the extended passage a "subtle rhetoric of blame"; the feminized landscape as purposeful seductress. *The Green Breast of the New World: Landscape, Gender, and American Fiction* (Athens: University of Georgia Press, 1996), p. 4.

2 Walter Benn Michaels, *Our America: Nativism, Modernism, and Pluralism* (Durham: Duke University Press, 1995), p. 25.

3 *Rereading Frederick Jackson Turner: "The Significance of the Frontier in American History" and Other Essays*, with commentary by John Mack Faragher (New York: Henry Holt and Co., 1994), p. 93. The quotation is from "Contributions of the West," first published in 1903.

4 It was Edmund Wilson, not Fitzgerald, who selected the title *The Last Tycoon* for the unfinished novel. Matthew Bruccoli's 1993 edition carries the title in the author's working notes because "Fitzgerald was in fact writing a western – a novel about the last American frontier," editor's introduction, *The Love of the Last Tycoon: A Western*, ed. Matthew Bruccoli (Cambridge: Cambridge University Press, 1993), p. xvii.

5 *Rereading Turner*, p. 95.

6 Richard Lehan, *The Great Gatsby: The Limits of Wonder* (Boston: Twayne Publishers, 1990), p. 47. See pp. 42–51 for Lehan's discussion of the novel's frontier context.

7 "The Significance of the Frontier in American History," *Rereading Turner*, p. 47.

8 Michaels, *Our America*, p. 26.

9 For a history of the design, see *The History of the Seal of the United States* (Washington, DC: Department of State, 1909). Although the front of the seal had already appeared on printed money before the twentieth century, the obverse side did not appear until 1935.

10 See John Seelye, "Beyond the Shining Mountains: The Lewis and Clark Expedition as Enlightenment Epic," *Virginia Quarterly Review* 63 (1987), 36–53.

11 Bernard DeVoto, ed., *The Journals of Lewis and Clark* (Boston: Houghton Mifflin Co., 1953), p. xvii. In his 1904–1905 edition of the journals, Reuben Thwaites amended Lewis' reference to "that illustrious personage Thomas Jefferson" by adding "the author of our enterprise" (28 July 1905).

12 David Trask has argued, "Dr. T. J. Eckleburg is none other than a devitalized Thomas Jefferson, the pre-eminent purveyor of the agrarian myth," "A Note on Fitzgerald's *The Great Gatsby*," *University Review* (formerly *University of Kansas City Review*) 33 (Spring 1967), 200. See also Leo Marx, *The Machine in the Garden: Technology and the Pastoral Ideal in America* (Oxford: Oxford University Press, 1964), pp. 354–365.

13 John M. Kenny, Jr., "The Great Gatsby," *Commonweal* 2 (3 June 1925), 110.

14 F. Scott Fitzgerald to Maxwell Perkins, July 1922. *Correspondence of F. Scott Fitzgerald*, ed. Matthew J. Bruccoli and Margaret M. Duggan (New York: Random House, 1980), p. 112.

15 Slavoj Žižek, *The Sublime Object of Ideology* (London: Verso, 1989), p. 95. Further citations from this book will be made parenthetically in the text.

16 *Rereading Turner*, p. 32.

17 Friedrich Nietzsche, *The Gay Science* (1882), trans. Walter Kaufmann (New York: Random House, 1974), p. 173.

18 Matthew J. Bruccoli, ed., *The Notebooks of F. Scott Fitzgerald* (New York: Harcourt Brace Jovanovich, 1972), p. 160.

19 *Rereading Turner*, p. 93.
20 *Rereading Turner*, p. 67.
21 Quoted in Ross Posnock, "'A New World, Material Without Being Real':
   Fitzgerald's Critique of Capitalism in *The Great Gatsby*" in Scott Donaldson,
   ed., *Critical Essays on F. Scott Fitzgerald's The Great Gatsby* (Boston: G. K. Hall
   & Co., 1984), p. 204.
22 Posnock, "A New World," p. 203.
23 *The Love of the Last Tycoon: A Western*, ed. Matthew J. Bruccoli (New York:
   Simon & Schuster, 1994), p. 20. Further citations from this edition will be
   made parenthetically in the text. See John Callahan, *The Illusions of a Nation:
   Myth and History in the Novels of F. Scott Fitzgerald* (Urbana: University of Illinois
   Press, 1972), pp. 200–207.
24 Joan Didion, *Slouching Towards Bethlehem* (1968; New York: Farrar, Straus and
   Giroux, 1995), p. 213. Further citations are made parenthetically in text.


7 PROMISES AND BETRAYALS: JOAN DIDION AND WALLACE STEGNER

 1 Joan Didion, "When Did the Music Come This Way? Children, Dear, Was
   It Yesterday?" *Denver Quarterly*, 1: 4 (1967), 62.
 2 Joan Didion, *Slouching Towards Bethlehem* (New York: Farrar, Straus and
   Giroux, 1990; orig. pub. 1968), pp. 120, 96, 98. Emphases original.
 3 Wallace Stegner, *Angle of Repose* (New York: Penguin, 1992; orig. pub. 1971),
   p. 25. Further citations from this edition of the novel will be made parenthetically in the text.
 4 Joan Didion, *Run River* (New York: Vintage Books, 1991; orig. pub. 1963),
   p. 63. Further citations from this edition of the novel will be made parenthetically in the text.
 5 Thomas Mallon, "The Limits of History in the Novels of Joan Didion," in
   Ellen Friedman, ed., *Joan Didion: Essays and Conversations* (Princeton: Ontario
   Review Press, 1984), p. 64. (Orig. pub. in *Critique: Studies in Modern Fiction*,
   21:3 (1980), 43–52.)
 6 Didion, *Slouching Towards Bethlehem*, pp. 31; 36; 30–31.
 7 Krista Comer, *Landscapes of the New West: Gender and Geography in Contemporary
   Women's Writing* (Chapel Hill: University of North Carolina Press, 1999),
   p. 74.
 8 *Rereading Frederick Jackson Turner: "The Significance of the Frontier in American
   History" and Other Essays*, with commentary by John Mack Faragher
   (New York: Henry Holt and Co., 1994), p. 53.
 9 Jennifer Brady, "Points West, Then and Now: The Fiction of Joan Didion,"
   in Friedman, ed., *Joan Didion: Essays and Conversations*, pp. 44–45. (Orig. pub.
   in *Contemporary Literature*, 20:4 (1979), 452–470.)
10 Leonard Wilcox, "Narrative Technique and the Theme of Historical
   Continuity in the Novels of Joan Didion," in Friedman, ed., *Joan Didion:
   Essays and Conversations*, p. 70.
11 Didion, "On Morality," in *Slouching Towards Bethlehem*, p. 158.

12 Katherine Usher Henderson has discussed this aspect of the Edenic myth in Didion's novel in *Joan Didion* (New York: Frederick Ungar Publishing Co., 1981), pp. 50–51.

13 In this wry passage, Didion may be poking fun at her passion for bleak narratives, since her own ancestors did indeed break away from the Donner-Reed party before the catastrophe. While Didion may have preferred the image of disaster rather than of escape in her own family history, her very existence is owed to her ancestors' escape.

14 Didion, *Slouching Towards Bethlehem*, p. 5.

15 Didion, *Slouching Towards Bethlehem*, p. 15.

16 Didion, *Slouching Towards Bethlehem*, pp. 3; 5; 6; 4. In a later essay, "James Pike, American," Didion identifies Nick Carraway's notion of the "common deficiency" he shares with his fellow "westerners" with Pike's "moral frontiersmanship," his desire to "forget it and start over" through his repeated divorces. *The White Album* (New York: Farrar, Straus and Giroux, 1979), pp. 56, 57.

17 Didion, *Slouching Towards Bethlehem*, p. 28.

18 Wallace Stegner, *The Sound of Mountain Water* (Lincoln: University of Nebraska Press, 1985; orig. pub. 1969), p. 195.

19 Wallace Stegner and Richard Etulain, *Conversations With Wallace Stegner on Western History and Literature* (Salt Lake City: University of Utah Press, 1983; rev. edn. 1990), p. 172.

20 Melody Graulich, "The Guides to Conduct that a Tradition Offers: Wallace Stegner's *Angle of Repose*," *South Dakota Review* 23: 4 (Winter 1985), 87; "It is inescapable . . . .Male freedom and aspiration versus female domesticity, wilderness versus civilization, violence and danger versus the safe and the tamed," Stegner, *The Sound of Mountain Water*, p. 195.

21 Graulich also makes this point: the "easy dichotomizing" of the Wards according to the western myth "reduces the complexity of the characters of both Susan Ward, who emerges from Lyman's narrative as certainly a restless and creative creature, and Oliver Ward, who is reliable and consistent and dedicated to civilization," "The Guides to Conduct," p. 94.

22 Graulich, "The Guides to Conduct," pp. 87–88.

23 Quoted in Mark Hunter, "In the Company of Wallace Stegner," *San Francisco Magazine* 23 (July 1981), 38–43. Also cited in Richard Etulain, "Wallace Stegner, Western Humanist," in Charles E. Rankin, ed., *Wallace Stegner: Man and Writer* (Albuquerque: University of New Mexico Press, 1996), p. 56.

24 Carol Smith-Rosenberg has demonstrated the predominant importance of same-sex friendship for women in "The Female World of Love and Ritual: Relations Between Women in Nineteenth-Century America," *SIGNS* 1 (1975), 1–30.

25 Two critics who do not read Lyman as an unreliable narrator are Audrey Peterson, "Narrative Voice in Wallace Stegner's *Angle of Repose*" and Kerry Ahearn, "*The Big Rock Candy Mountain* and *Angle of Repose*: Trial and Culmination" in Anthony Arthur, ed., *Critical Essays on Wallace Stegner*

(Boston: G. K. Hall & Co., 1982), pp. 176–183; 109–123. Two critics who do read Lyman as unreliable are Graulich, "The Guides to Conduct" and Forrest Robinson, "Clio Bereft of Calliope: Literature and the New Western History," in Forrest G. Robinson, ed., *The New Western History: The Territory Ahead* (Tucson: University of Arizona Press, 1997), pp. 90–93. Graulich wonders why any writer would call an entirely trustworthy narrator Lyman, and although Stegner denied intending that meaning, I wonder the same thing.

26 Jackson K. Putnam, "Wallace Stegner and Western History: Some Historiographical Problems in *Angle of Repose*," *Vis à Vis: An Interdisciplinary Journal* 3: 2 (September 1975), 54.

27 Stegner and Etulain, *Conversations*, p. 94.

28 Stegner complained that although he liked their emotions and "was on the same side with them on a good many issues," young radicals of the 1960s "*didn't* have any sense of history" and "had no notion that anybody had had those ideas before them," *Conversations*, pp. 96, 95.

29 In this regard, see Hendrik Hartog's *Man and Wife in America: A History* (Cambridge, Mass.: Harvard University Press, 2000).

30 Forrest G. Robinson, "Wallace Stegner's Family Saga: From *The Big Rock Candy Mountain* to *Recapitulation*," *Western American Literature* 17: 2 (Summer 1982), 104.

31 Putnam, "Wallace Stegner and Western History," p. 56.

32 Putnam, "Wallace Stegner and Western History," p. 57.

33 Stegner, *The Sound of Mountain Water*, pp. 200–201.

34 Robinson, "Clio Bereft," p. 91.

35 Robinson, "Clio Bereft," p. 91.

36 Stegner, *The Sound of Mountain Water*, p. 199.

## AFTERWORD

1 R. Gordon Kelly, "Literature and the Historian," Lucy Maddox, ed., *Locating American Studies: The Evolution of a Discipline* (Baltimore: Johns Hopkins University Press, 1999), p. 92. This article, which marked an important moment in the interdisciplinary development of American studies beyond its founding disciplines of literature and history, originally appeared in *American Quarterly* 26: 2 (May 1974).

2 Marjorie Garber, *Academic Instincts* (Princeton: Princeton University Press, 2001).

3 Originally aired on the Public Broadcast Service, fall of 1996, in nine episodes. A documentary produced by Stephen Ives, Jody Abramson and Michael Kantor. Executive Producer Ken Burns. Written by Geoffrey C. Ward and Dayton Duncan.

4 Forrest G. Robinson, ed., *The New Western History: The Territory Ahead* (Tucson: University of Arizona Press, 1997), p. 110.

5 Robinson, ed., *New Western History*, p. 164.

6 Robinson, ed., *New Western History*, p. 161.

7 Robinson, ed., *New Western History*, p. 65.

8 William Cronon, "A Place for Stories: Nature, History, and Narrative," *The Journal of American History* 78: 4 (March 1992), 1367. A particularly influential study of the literary nature of "natural" narratives is Gillian Beer's *Darwin's Plots: Evolutionary Narrative in Darwin, George Eliot, and Nineteenth-Century Fiction* (London: Routledge & Kegan Paul, 1983).

9 Cronon, "A Place for Stories," p. 1374.

10 Cronon, "A Place for Stories," p. 1370.

11 Andrew Sullivan, "The Agony of the Left," *Wall Street Journal*, 4 October 2001, p. A22.

12 Cronon, "A Place for Stories," pp. 1370–1371.

13 Cronon, "A Place for Stories," p. 1372.

14 Cronon, "A Place for Stories," p. 1374.

15 See especially Dominick LaCapra's *Rethinking Intellectual History: Texts, Contexts, Language* (Ithaca: Cornell University Press, 1983); and *History and Criticism* (Ithaca: Cornell University Press, 1985).

16 Carlo Ginzburg works out the epistemological implications of the literary notion of estrangement for the writing of history in his essay "Making Things Strange: The Prehistory of a Literary Device" in *Representations* 56 (Fall 1996), 8–28.

17 Michael Warner offers a queer critique of same-sex marriage in his *The Trouble with Normal: Sex, Politics, and the Ethics of Queer Life* (Cambridge, Mass.: Harvard University Press, 1999), pp. 81–148.

18 In the same article in which she describes the "twilight zone" of myth and symbol, Patricia Limerick encourages the study of western laws and treaties as a form of literature that shaped western experience. "Making the Most of Words: Verbal Activity and Western America," in William Cronon, George Miles, and Jay Gitlin, eds., *Under an Open Sky: Rethinking America's Western Past* (New York: Norton, 1992), pp. 180–182.

# Index